VOLUME

6

MORTGAGE LENDING

Loan Officer Training

ISBN-13: 978-1-933039-62-6

Library of Congress -in-Publication Data
March 1998
Mortgage Lending – Loan Officer Basic Training

10 9 8 7 6 5 4 3 2 1

The enclosed material is designed for educational purposes only. Each State may have different certification and specific guidelines. Please refer to your State for additional and future information. The information contained herein is considered correct at the time of creation but laws and regulations are updated frequently and the reader assumes the responsibility for confirming current regulations and applicable data. The publisher and author make no warranty as to the success of the individuals using the training material contained herein. The publisher and author make no warranty as to any action taken by any individual completing this program. The reader is responsible for the appropriate use of the materials and information provided. This publication is designed to provide accurate and authoritative information concerning the subject matter. All material is sold with the understanding that neither the author nor the publisher guarantees the actions of any individual making use of the inclusions. Neither the author nor the publisher is rendering a legal opinion, accounting recommendation or other professional service. If legal advice or other expert assistance is desired, the services of a legal professional or other individual should be sought. The applicable federally released forms, disclosures and notices are generated from public domain. Copyright law does apply to all intellectual materials and all rights under said law are reserved b y the copyright owner.

Coursework is available at special quantity discounts to use as premiums and sales promotions within corporate or private training programs. To obtain information or inquire about availability please write to Director, PO Box 1, Hollidaysburg, PA 16648.

NOTICE

MORTGAGE LENDING

Loan Officer Training

I
Introduction

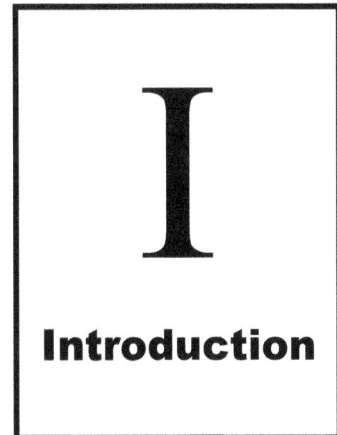

Benefits of a Mortgage Career

Congratulations on your decision to enter the mortgage-lending arena. Mortgage lending is one of the most secure, respected, and exciting career opportunities available. Each day will bring you challenges that you will overcome, the excitement of helping to create a loan program that meets the needs of both the borrower and the lender, and the satisfaction of helping each borrower achieve their dreams of homeownership. Home Mortgage Lending is an excellent career opportunity that provides stability, advancement, and a sense of satisfaction to each loan officer who obtains the knowledge and skills necessary to excel within the profession.

The training contained in the course provides specific information concerning the loan process and the part you and others play in that process. The information we offer in this program provides you with the foundation that you need to become a well rounded mortgage professional. The top of your field, you will specialize in the overall picture. You will develop the perfect mix of knowledge and skills, add to it the creativity required when overcoming the specific issues that occur during the loan process, and begin on the path that will lead you to the top of your profession.

Mortgage lending provides you with the career option that will make you one of the most highly respected professionals within your community.

The skills that you will attain over the coming weeks will make you a commodity that is in high demand in the market.

As a properly trained loan officer, you will have the freedom to create your own mini-business within the security of the larger framework of the bank or brokerage for which you choose to work.

A mortgage lender creates a mini-business within the framework of the finance arena. Each time you create the perfect loan package for a borrower, oversee a perfect loan process and ensure a smooth closing meeting, you grow your business. The borrowers you work with today will be the referral sources upon which you will build your business. Regardless of where you go within the industry, your exceptional customer service will ensure that your borrowers will go with you.

➢ As a mortgage lender who conducts their business based upon a solid foundation of knowledge and core best practices, you will gain the ability to choose the environment in which you wish to work.

  You may choose to conduct your business

    From your home

    In an office

    Within a bank

  The skills you are obtaining are so prized within the mortgage industry that you will gain the ability to obtain any position you set your sights on.

➢ You will receive an income that relates directly to how hard (or smart) you work.

  The pay structure within the mortgage industry is based primarily upon the number of loans closed and the value, including face amount, interest, and points of each loan. This structure enables you to expand your income to heights that are unattainable in other, similar career options!

➢ A loan officer's business is built around a core customer base of satisfied borrowers.

  Each time you create the perfect loan package for a borrower, oversee a perfect loan process and ensure a smooth closing meeting, you grow your business. The borrowers you work with today will be the referral sources upon which you will build your business. Regardless of where you go within the industry, your exceptional customer service will ensure that your borrowers will go with you.

➢ You will obtain the freedom available only through being the in charge of your career.

Mortgage Lending – Loan Officer Training

A loan officer is one of the few individuals who have the ability to blend the respect of being a business professional with the security of working under the umbrella of a corporate environment and the flexibility of being in charge of their own business!

➢ You will have the opportunity to use your creativity and ingenuity to become the best in your chosen profession.

Loan guidelines are in place for each lending source that you will work with during your career.

Each borrower will have specific issues and situations within their lives that must be correlated to the correct loan program.

Through the application of creative thinking and a comprehensive understanding of the lending arena, you can blend the lender guidelines with the borrower situation to create the perfect loan package for every application!

Research has shown that the most important attribute of a successful loan officer is the drive to succeed within their chosen profession. The drive to succeed surpasses educational degrees, experience and personal attributes. Purchasing this program shows that you have the initial drive needed to begin on the path toward career stability and success and the ability attain top-producer status.

This program will assist you in gaining the base foundation you need to begin building your new career.

Mortgage Lending is perhaps one of the most satisfying career options available. You will perform the service of allowing people to fulfill their dreams of homeownership. The industry is fast-paced, exciting and offers a stable opportunity to anyone willing to put forth the effort necessary to succeed. Each file you receive will contain a myriad of variations that will ensure every workday provides you with the challenge to perform at your best.

The coursework builds the foundation that you will need in the coming days, months, and years. Each segment of the program builds upon the previous to ensure that you gain the knowledge base that will allow you to enter your new profession with confidence and competence. The program format allows you to gain each component essential to your success in an organized and efficient manner. Each section contains a self-test whose correct completion enables you to feel confident that you are gaining the knowledge, tools, and skills you need to succeed. Upon successful completion of the coursework and an understanding of each review section, you will find that you are have a higher industry skill level then 90% of your competing loan officers.

CHAPTER 1

Gaining a comprehensive understanding of the lending arena and the processes that occur between the application by a borrower and the purchase of packaged closed loans on the secondary market is the first step you must take on the path to career success.

The mortgage market is divided into two classifications.

- The primary mortgage market

- The secondary mortgage market

The primary mortgage market is the area where lenders work directly with borrowers to originate, document and close loans. Examples of entities within the primary mortgage market are

- Mortgage Brokerage Office
- Savings Banks
- Commercial Banks
- Mutual Savings Bank
- Credit Union

These lending institutions work directly with borrowers who need funding to purchase real estate.

The employees who work within the mortgage department at these locations are known as loan processors, loan originators, mortgage brokers and loan officers.

COMMON TITLES

A **Loan Originator** is someone who spends a great part of the workday on the streets soliciting borrower referrals from affinity groups. They bring these borrower referrals back to their office, structure the loan package that meets the borrowers needs, and document a package that will enable the lending institution to fund a solid loan. The act of being an originator means that your primary focus is to originate loans.

A **Loan Officer** is someone who spends a great deal of his or her time in the office, interviewing potential borrowers and structuring the available loan products to meet the needs and specific situation of the borrower. The primary goal of the loan officer is to ensure that each loan closed provides all of the parties involved with the best possible loan package.

A **Mortgage Broker** is someone who uses their vast knowledge of the mortgage industry to bring potential borrower packages to the right lending institution and obtain the loan program that meets the needs of both the borrower and lender. The broker acts as a liaison bringing the potential borrowers together with the right lender and loan program to ensure that the borrower achieves their dreams of homeownership.

A **Loan Processor** assists the borrower in obtaining all of the documents and services that are required to complete the loan process and purchase transaction. The essential element of the loan-processing career is to act as a liaison between the borrower and all other individuals whose assistance is required to achieve a closed loan. The loan processor's primary focus during the loan process is to ensure all tasks are completed in a timely manner and that all items incorporated into the closing package are correct and free of errors.

Each of these individuals will work directly with the borrower to accomplish the tasks that lead to a home loan funding.

- Complete the mortgage loan application or 1003.

- Obtain loan stipulations or documentation required by the stipulations list or sales agreement.

- Order affiliate services such as Title Searches and Appraisals.

- Generate the borrower's good faith estimate.

- Provide all required disclosures and notifications to the borrower.

- Structure the mortgage loan funding and borrower down payment to meet the parameters of the loan approval.

- Arrange and oversee the borrowers closing on the property.

Many borrowers assume that the bank where they make the loan application funds the mortgage loans through available cash resulting from the deposits of the individuals who conduct their banking activity at that bank. In some cases, this is exactly where the funds required to provide a mortgage loan originate. However, these depository funds are often inadequate to meet the borrowing needs of all of the individuals who obtain loan proceeds from the local institution.

SECONDARY MORTGAGE MARKET

Lenders within the primary mortgage market will underwrite and fund mortgage loans that the borrower applies for with the cash that they have on hand. Once the lender has a group of funded loan packages, they will combine the many funded loan packages into one large package and offer it for sale to the secondary mortgage market.

The secondary mortgage market includes entities such as

- Insurance Companies

- Primary Lenders with excess deposits

- Pension Funds

- Individual Investors

The secondary mortgage market purchases funded and closed loans from the direct lender in the primary mortgage market.

- This purchase of the closed loans enables the banks and institutions within the primary market to fund more loans than would be possible if they had to fund and service all of the debt load within their portfolio themselves.

- This funding enables the entities on the secondary market to obtain the return on their investment generated through the interest and penalty figures applied to the borrowed funds.

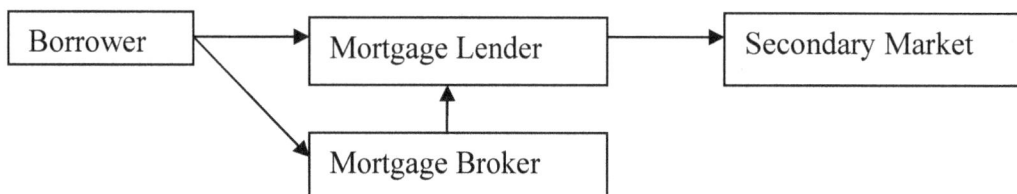

Figure 1:1 Mortgage Market Structure

How it works:

1.   The borrower makes a mortgage application with mortgage loan officer or mortgage loan processor who works in a Mortgage Bank that funds its own loans or in a Mortgage Brokerage that works with multiple funding sources.

2.   The mortgage lender provides the borrower with the funds to purchase the home.

3.   The mortgage bank or loan funding institution completes this process as many times as possible with the funds that they have available.

4.   The mortgage bank or loan funding institution then packages the loan with other loans that have been funded with their capital.

   ▪   If the overall loan package is large enough (worth enough money), the funding institution offers that package for sale to investors within the secondary mortgage market.

   ▪   If the mortgage-funding source does not have enough loan products to package into large enough groups to meet the needs of the secondary mortgage market, they will package them into a smaller grouping and offer the package to another lending institution or a smaller investing group.

   This smaller group of investors forms what is termed an investing pool. An investing pool can include anyone who is seeking a low risk, long-term investment and has the capital available to purchase the packaged loan products.

   This investing pool will then collect the interest on the loans that they have purchased and achieve the return on their capital investment that meets their needs.

   ▪   If the loans are packaged and sold to another lending institution, that institution will package the purchased loans with their own funded loan packages and create an overall offering large enough to be offered to the secondary mortgage market.

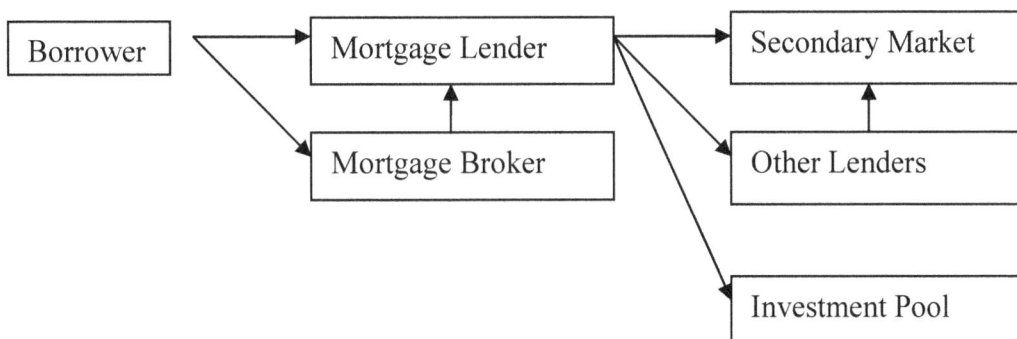

As a loan officer, you will play a critical part in the success of all of these entities. The fundamental beginning that enables all of the described processes to function will rest on the work you will complete in assisting borrowers in fulfilling all of the stipulations required to obtain loan approval and close the loan package. You will complete these tasks for either a mortgage bank or a mortgage brokerage.

BANKING VS BROKERING

The first decision you will make as a loan officer is whether you will choose to create your business within the structure of a traditional banking institution or within a mortgage brokerage. Included within this decision is whether you will base your office out of a home office or within the conventional environment of the mortgage bank or brokerage.

Working in a Bank

A bank is a lending institution that typically underwrites, processes, and funds mortgage loans with their own money. The benefits of working with a traditional banking environment are obvious.

- Traditional banking institutions are typically located within the community that they serve. Working within a recognized community institution will provide you with name recognition that gives your borrowers an immediate sense of reliability.

- Traditional lenders often retain their own team of loan underwriters, processors, closers, and post-closers that will enable you to create a "team" atmosphere that may assist in smoother loan processes and closings.

- The loans that you originate and process will be funded by the bank for which you work. This in-house funding typically creates a smoother loan process in that the underwriters will usually not change the loan terms, stipulations, or requirements after you have obtained an initial approval of the application.

Working for a bank also has its downside.

- A bank will have a limited number of products available and these will have very specific guidelines.

  The limited program availability from a bank means, if your borrower does not fit within those guidelines, they will be declined.

  Since you will only have access to the products or loan types offered by the bank for which you work, a borrower who is declined for your loan products will need to "shop" other lenders to obtain their mortgage loan.

- Banks are more likely to have only "A" paper product available. This limited product availability limits your borrowers to those who have "A" credit. Most banks do have additional programs for those B/C borrowers who fall just below the A Paper criteria but the programs are typically not as competitive as the products your Brokering competition can locate.

  This lack of product availability will place limitations on how large your personal business is able to grow because you will only be able to work with those borrowers in your region who meet the specified guidelines of your bank. The remaining borrowers will work with another loan officer.

Working in a Brokerage

A Mortgage Broker acts as a liaison between the borrower seeking mortgage funds and multiple funding sources. The mortgage brokerage will typically not fund any loans but will fulfills the task of shopping for the perfect loan to meet each borrowers specific situation and mortgage needs.

- A Broker typically works with multiple lenders enabling them to offer a variety of loan programs. You will find most Brokerages have contracted to write loans for between 40 and 200 different lenders. This variety allows you to shop many programs making it relatively easy to find an approval program for more of the loan applications that you originate.

- As a loan officer with a mortgage brokerage, you will have the ability to obtain competing approvals for the funding of each loan application that you process. Rather than one cut and dried approval that may kill your deal at the time of loan application, you should be able to find options that allow you to customize the loan program to suit your borrower's needs.

Example:	Lender 1 approves the borrower's application with a low interest rate but requires that the borrower place a large amount of money down as a contingency of the approval.
Issue:	Your borrowers are cash poor but are willing to make a higher monthly payment.
Solution:	You locate another lender within your contracts that is willing to fund the loan at a slightly higher interest rate in exchange for the borrower's ability to place less money down.

Working at a mortgage brokerage also has some inherent disadvantages that you would need to overcome.

- You are not on the same "team" as your underwriters, closers and post-closers but you will find that if you build respectful rapport with these individuals your goals are the same – closed loans.

- Mortgage Brokerage offices are typically not as recognizable within the community. Banking institutions offer many services to their customers beyond the mortgage loan service enabling the loan officer within the bank to originate more borrowers from the customer base of the bank. A mortgage brokerage typically offers only loan services. This will limit the name recognition of the company within the community and the available customer pool will be related only to the mortgage processes rather than a diverse group of customer offerings.

Regardless of the employment method you choose, there are as many ways to put a loan package together as there are borrowers in your town. It will be up to you to combine your knowledge of the industry and the products available to you with the essential drive and creativity that led you to the lending arena.

Working from Home

Many banks and brokerages are now hiring loan officers as full W-2 employees and enabling them to base their business out of their own home. These loan officers originate, process, and document loan packages in the same manner as the more conventional specialists working out of an office.

Some banks and brokerages will hire a loan officer who will e-commute and blend the two location options to customize their business around their lifestyle. A loan officer working in this manner will spend a portion of their time in the office and the remainder of their time working from home.

- Through e-commuting or setting your office up entirely out of your home, you will be able to customize your career around your lifestyle and family to create the career option that will enable you to excel within the industry.

- You will be able to use the resources of the bank or brokerage for which you work during your in-office time but service your customers from your home office enabling you to build a customer base that depends entirely on you. If you transfer positions or companies, you will retain the customer base you have built providing you with a solid foundation upon which to build your career.

- You are considered an employee with all of the benefits of W-2 employment while you retain the freedom and independence of being your own boss.

There are varieties of positions available within the Mortgage Lending arena to suit your personal goals, needs and personalized career path. You will customize your career path around your situation, desired level of managerial input, and the freedom you need to build your career successfully.

Upon completion of this coursework, you will be better trained than 90% of the loan officers currently employed within the mortgage industry. You will be an asset in the industry with the ability to build your career to suit your needs and desired level of success.

CHAPTER

2

ETHICS AND DISCLOSURES

The Federal Government and most State Governments have established laws and acts that you will use to create the policies and procedures with which you handle each potential borrower and business contact.

These laws are in place to protect the interest of the public and to make the obtainment of housing and home mortgage funds a fair practice for all applicants. You must incorporate the required practices into your daily task list to ensure you disclose all of the required information to your borrowers.

Another facet of your job is borrower education. As a professionally trained home-mortgage loan officer, you must act in an ethically sound way and educate the borrower to assist them in gaining the knowledge that they need to protect themselves in the future.

Many States are in the process of or have completed the implementation of required licensure training for home-mortgage loan officers. One goal of this educational training is to ensure that you have the necessary knowledge base to protect your borrowers, inform the consumers, and behave in an ethical manner that complies with all federal and state statues and laws.

During this section, we will address specific guidelines of behavior and disclosure that are in place and strive to make you as well educated concerning these laws as possible.

Learning the materials included will assist not only your borrower but also your overall career success. Adherence to the guidelines and laws we will review will prove your dedication to professionalism and raise your customer service beyond that of much of your competition.

You are entering a professional career much like that of a physician or attorney and you must ensure that your behavior and actions are above reproach.

Home Mortgage Disclosure Act

The Home Mortgage Disclosure Act (H. M. D. A.) was enacted by Congress in 1975 and implemented by the Federal Reserve Boards Regulation C. This act requires lending institutions to report public loan data.

This data is used to aid in determining whether financial institutions are serving the housing needs of their communities. It is used to assist public officials in distributing public-sector investments and to attract private investment to areas where it is needed. It is used in identifying possible discriminatory lending patterns.

This regulation applies to certain financial institutions, including banks, savings associations, credit unions, and other mortgage lending institutions. Using the loan data submitted by these financial institutions, the Federal Financial Institutions Examination Council creates aggregate and disclosure reports for each metropolitan area.

Information that is included in the report should be gathered at the time the 1008 and 1003 are completed. Much of the information required for reports is incorporated into the 1003 application. The obtainment of this data should be a regulated portion of your application interview. Obtaining the correct data at the time of application ensures concise reporting is maintained.

The H. M. D. A. REPORT will contain identifying details relating to the specific loan package being reported.

SAMPLE HMDA REPORT

Applicant(s) Name_____
Loan Officer Name: _____ Lender Name: _____
Property Address: _____
Date of Application: _____

LOAN TYPE:
__1. Conventional
__2. FHA
__3. VA
__4. Other

PROPERTY TYPE:
__1. Single Family
__2. Manufactured Housing
__3. Multifamily

LOAN PURPOSE:
__1. Home Purchase
__2. Home Improvement
__3. Cash-out Refinance
__4. Rate/Term Refinance

OCCUPANCY:
__1. Owner Occupied
__2. Non-Owner Occupied

2:1 Sample Form – HMDA – HUD Release

ACTION TAKEN:
__1. Loan originated
__2. Application approved but not accepted
__3. Application denied
__4. Counter-offer denied
__5. Application withdrawn by applicant

APPLICATION TYPE:
__1. By Mail
__2. By Phone
__3. Face-to-Face
__4. Internet

REASONS FOR DENIAL:
__1. Excessive Debt to income ratio
__2. Insufficient Employment history
__3. Credit history
__4. Collateral
__5. Insufficient cash available
__6. Other _____

2:1 Sample Form – HMDA – HUD Release Continued

HMDA REPORT EXPLANATION

Date of Application

The date the application was received or the date shown on the application form will be the date you use for reporting. The date that is entered on the form will dictate the timeline for all reporting matters and actions taken relating to the loan file.

Loan Type

Indicates whether the loan granted, applied for, or purchased was non-conventional, conventional, government-guaranteed, or government-insured.

If the loan falls in an unconventional or special category, you will select the option "Other" and enter a descriptive heading for the type of loan.

Property Type

The specific type of property being financed must be included within the wording of the report. The choices for property type are

Single Family
Manufactured Housing
Multifamily

Loan Purpose

Each applicant will be making the loan application for a specific purpose. The planned use of the loan funds affects the handling of the loan process. You will include the purpose details with in the report.

Home Purchase
Home Improvement
Cash-out Refinance.

Rate and Term Refinance

You should select multifamily dwelling regardless of the loan type for dwellings that are five-or-more families.

Occupancy

The type of occupancy relating to the property will also dictate many of the application, processing, and funding related actions. The property will be either

Owner Occupied
Non-Owner Occupied

Action Taken Type

The action taken type field defines the disposition of the loan application.

Loan originated
Application approved but not accepted
Application denied
Counter-offer denied
Application withdrawn by applicant

Action Taken Date

If the application results in a closed loan, you will enter the settlement or closing date of the loan.

If the application does not result in an origination, you will enter the date when the action to cancel the loan application was taken or when the notice of denial was sent to the applicant.

If the application was expressly withdrawn by the applicant, you will enter either the date shown on the applicant's withdrawal letter, or the date you received the letter or notice.

For loans that an institution purchased, the date of the purchase is entered.

Application Type

The type of application or method of making the application dictates the timelines for the remittal of certain disclosures. You will define the method that the borrower used to make the loan application within the report.

By Mail
By Phone
Face-to-Face
Over the Internet

Reasons For Denial

If the loan application was denied, you must define the reasons for the denial. Common reasons are listed as options and include

Excessive debt to income ratio
Insufficient employment history
Credit history
Collateral
Insufficient cash available

If the application was denied for another reason, you will enter a description of that reason in the area labeled other.

Applicant Race

The government will monitor the handling of files as they relate to each segment of society. This monitoring is conducted to ensure that fair lending opportunities are being provided to all individuals. One monitoring segment relates to the race or national origin of the applicant.

This is reported for originated loans and for loan applications that do not result in an origination.

Applicant Sex

A secondary monitoring classification is the gender of the applicant

This is reported for originated loans and for loan applications that do not result in an origination

Census Tract/BNA

A Census Tract identifies a statistical subdivision of a county.

Census Tract numbers ranges from 0001.00 to 9499.99. The number assigned to an area is unique within a county.

A Block Numbering Area (BNA) identifies a subdivision of a county. The BNA is formed for the purpose of grouping and numbering blocks in non-metropolitan counties where local census committees have not established census tracts.

BNA numbers range from 9501.00 to 9989.99 and are unique within a county.

Census Tracts and BNAs are mutually exclusive. Thus, these statistical areas do not overlap. There is a census tract or BNA number for every area of the United States.

County Code	A three-digit Federal Information Processing Standards code is assigned to each geographical area. This code identifies the county where the property is located.
Dwelling	Dwelling means any residential structure whether or not it is attached to real property. The term dwelling includes condominiums, cooperative units and mobile or manufactured homes.
	It refers to single family and multifamily structures.
	Recreational vehicles such as boats or campers are not dwellings under HMDA.
Loan Application Number	Each loan will be assigned a unique identifier of up to 25 characters.
	It is recommended that institutions do not use applicant's names or social security numbers as part of the loan application number. This helps to ensure the privacy of the borrower.

Fair Housing

Fair housing laws are in place to prevent discrimination against any borrower in the sale, rental, financing, or other housing related transaction. The law prohibits the discrimination against any borrower based upon race, color, national origin, religion, sex, familial status, and handicap. A recent executive order also states that practices must eliminate, to the extent possible, barriers arising from a limited proficiency in English in the use or participation in any federally conducted program.

The Federal Fair Housing Act prohibits the use of discriminatory advertising that state a preference for a particular type of person. You may not advertise in a manner meant to attract or deter a potential borrower based on race, color, religion, sex, handicap, familial status, or national origin. HUD released a clarification of acceptable words and phrases that you can use when generating advertisements. You must use caution when composing your advertising so as not to include any item that is discriminatory in nature. More information regarding acceptable advertising is included in the Advanced Mortgage Marketing Course or you can obtain details relating to appropriate advertising practices directly from HUD.

The nature of advertising allows you a broad spectrum in which to operate. It is important to remember that discrimination in real estate practice is illegal. Providing you are not targeting particular strata of society for either positive or negative effect, staying within the guidelines is relatively easy.

Federal Agencies evaluate their policies and programs on a regular basis to determine any modifications that must be made relating to a protected class under the fair housing laws.

Along with the Fair Housing Act, the Equal Credit Opportunity Acts establishes guidelines and regulations regarding potential discrimination against borrowers. The following sections further describe practices that should and should not be employed in relationship to your borrowers. Following the explanatory sections are sample disclosures you must provide to each applicant.

Equal Credit Opportunity Act/Fair Housing Act

The Equal Credit Opportunity and the Fair Housing Acts ensure that all consumers are given the same opportunity to obtain credit.

What this does not mean is that an applicant who does not meet guidelines will obtain credit.

What this does mean is that all credit applicants must receive a level consideration regardless of outside factors or personal considerations.

Pre-qualification services must be provided to all borrowers equally. It is illegal to include discriminatory factors as criteria for the determination on a loan package.

The Equal Credit Opportunity Act and Fair Housing Act identify a number of factors that are illegal to use in evaluating an applicants qualifications.

> Race, Color, Religion, Sex, National Origin, Marital Status, Age (provided the applicant is capable of entering a legally binding contract), Source of Income, Handicap and Familial Status

A lender may decline an oral or written application as long as the decline is based upon legitimate underwriting standards applied to all loan packages and not based upon one of the prohibited items.

A loan officer must understand the difference between an "inquiry" and an "application". Many requirements apply only to applications. The regulations describe a loan application as *"An oral or written request for an extension of credit that is made in accordance with the procedures established by a creditor for the credit type listed"*.

Procedures established refer to the actual practices followed by a creditor for making credit decisions as well as its stated application procedures.

It is important to establish your particular employer's standards as they relate to the application or inquiry distinction. The quick list of required disclosures included in the appendix segment of your workbook combines the disclosure requirements at application into one checklist chart. You should refer often to this chart to ensure you are providing the required documents to all borrowers at the correct time and in the correct manner.

The Equal Credit Opportunity Act protects against other items beyond credit discrimination. It has provisions in place regarding predatory lending tactics and abusive activities with in the lending arena.

Creditors must provide applicants with notices of the actions taken on their credit application. These notices include approvals, counteroffers, and credit denial.

- Approval notices provide the applicant with specific information regarding the loan program for which they have been approved.

- A counteroffer is an approval notice that contains different terms than those that the applicant originally requested. A counteroffer notice provides vital information to the applicant in the event the loan terms are changed between the date of application and the date of closing.

Changes between the application and closing can occur for a variety of reasons.

Example: A borrower makes application with one property in mind.

The offer for that property is not accepted.

The borrower chooses a different property with slightly different contract terms.

Action: You will alter the loan offering to conform to the new property contract.

Changes to the loan between application and closing may also occur for less respectable reasons.

Example: A lender may alter the terms of the loan to incorporate additional fees into the principal borrowed.

Example: A lender offering a second mortgage may alter the terms of the loan to incorporate a refinance of the first mortgage and therefore improve their lien position and increase the loan amount funded.

These tactics, among others, fall within the term predatory lending. These tactics are unlawful under federal lending acts.

The full disclosure of any action taken on a credit application will ensure that your practices remain impeccable.

FINANCIAL DISCRIMINATION ACT
FAIR LENIDNG NOTICE

It is illegal to discriminate based on

1.   Trends, characteristics, or conditions in a neighborhood unless the financial institution is able to demonstrate that such consideration is required to ensure safety

2.   Race, color, religion, sex, marital status, familial status, national origin, ancestry, or handicap

It is illegal to consider the racial, ethnic, religious, or national origin composition of a neighborhood or geographic area surrounding a housing accommodation or whether such composition is undergoing change.

These provisions govern financial assistance for the purpose of purchase, construction, rehabilitation, or refinancing of one to four unit residences occupied by the owner.

If you have any questions about your rights, or if you wish to file a complaint you may contact:

I/we acknowledge that we received a copy of this notice:

_____   _____
Borrower Signature   Date

_____   _____
Co-Borrower Signature   Date

2:2 Sample Form – Financial Discrimination Act Fair Lending Notice – HUD Release

---

Federal Equal Credit Opportunity Act Notice

The Federal Equal Credit Opportunity Act prohibits creditors from discriminating against credit applicants on the basis of color, religion, national origin, sex, marital status, age (provided the applicant has the capacity to enter into a binding contract), because all of part of the applicant's income is derived from public assistance programs, or because the applicant has in good faith exercised any right under the Consumer Protection Act

Lending institutions are prohibited from bringing up certain specific subjects that lend themselves to discrimination. These subjects are as follows:

Whether or not an applicant has or will have children.

Whether or not there exist childcare problems.

Whether or not there will be interruptions of income due to childbirth.

Whether or not an applicant is receiving alimony, child support, or separate maintenance   unless this income is voluntarily disclosed as a source of additional income to be considered as part of the credit application

Whether an applicant is widowed, divorced, or single

Whether or not an applicant's telephone number is publicly listed

Lending institutions must take and report actions taken on your applications within a reasonable time. If the application is denied, the reason for the denial must be provided if requested.

2:3 Sample Form – Federal Equal Credit Opportunity Act Notice – HUD Release

---

Credit Information Disclosure Authorization

I / We _____ Borrower Name _____ , _____ Co-Borrower Name _____ hereby authorize you to release to _Mortgage Company Name_ information for verification purposes.

This information may include:

Employment information including past and present employers
Banking and Savings Account Records
Mortgage Loan Rating Information
Rental History Information
A consumer credit report from a credit-reporting agency

This information is for the confidential use in processing an application for a real estate loan

A copy of this authorization and applicable signature(s) may be deemed the equivalent of the original.

2:4 Sample Form – Credit Information Disclosure Authorization – HUD Release

Whenever information is gathered about an individual including credit reports, employment history, financial institution data, and tax return information; a release for such information gathering must be completed by the borrower.

During the transaction, the loan processor, loan officer, underwriter, or other individuals involved in completing the loan process will obtain information from multiple sources that enable them to assess the creditworthiness of the borrower and their ability to repay the debt.

All borrowers must sign a credit and information release authorization before you begin the process of collecting the applicable data. You will incorporate a copy of this authorization into any documentation request that you make during the loan process. It is critical that you ensure you obtain the applicable signatures on this form since obtaining credit data, including the credit report, without the applicable authorization violates the rights of the borrower.

In addition to the credit release authorization, you must provide the borrower with information indicating how their credit worthiness was determined. This disclosure notice explains

- The scores received from the bureaus.

- The factors contributing to the scores

- The fact that the bureaus do not make a credit determination but rather report the inclusions of the credit profile

Contact information and directions to inquire into the credit profile will often be incorporated into the disclosure.

Real Estate Settlement Procedures Act (RESPA)

The Real Estate Settlement Procedures Act is enforced by HUD and deals with closing costs and settlement procedures. The purpose of the act is to regulate the processes of closing practices across the United States. The Real Estate Settlement Procedures Act prohibits specific practices in relationship to the transfer of property involving a first mortgage loan on a one to four unit dwellings.

The purposes of RESPA are to:

- Help consumers in shopping for settlement services.

- Eliminate referral fees that increase the costs of certain settlement services.

The act requires that borrowers receive disclosures at various times during the mortgage application and home purchase processes.

The act prohibits a person from giving or accepting any thing of value for referrals of settlement service business.

The act prohibits a person from giving or accepting any part of a charge for services that are not performed.

The act prohibits home sellers from requiring homebuyers to purchase title insurance from a particular company.

The act restricts the amount of property tax and insurance payments that may be paid in advance at or prior to the closing of a home loan.

> The amount of property tax or insurance payments that may be paid in advance by a borrower is limited to the owner's share of the taxes and insurance that is due at the time of settlement plus $1/6^{th}$ of the amount that will become due for these items within the 12-month period following settlement.

The Federal Government as well as most State Governing bodies has established laws and acts that you will use to create the policies and procedures with which you handle each potential closing and business contact.

These laws are in place to protect the interest of the public and to make the obtainment of housing and home mortgage funds a fair practice for all applicants. You must incorporate the required practices into your daily task list to ensure that you handle each closing task in compliance with the requirements.

You are entering a professional career much like that of a physician or attorney and you must ensure that your behavior and actions are above reproach.

Required Disclosures at Application

At the time of application, mortgage brokers or lenders must give the borrowers

- An Information Booklet containing consumer information regarding various real estate settlement services.

- A Good Faith Estimate of settlement costs. This lists the charges the buyer is likely to pay at settlement. This is only an estimate and the actual charges may differ.

- If a lender requires the borrower to use a particular settlement provider, then the lender must disclose this requirement on the good faith estimate.

- A Mortgage Servicing Disclosure Statement that defines for the borrower whether the lender intends to service the loan or transfer it to another lender.

The lender gives these disclosures to the borrower at the time of a face to face application or mails it to them within three business days of receiving a mail, internet, or telephone loan application.

If the lender turns down the loan within three days, then the Real Estate Settlement Procedures Act does not require the lender to provide these documents.

When is an Application an Application?

ECOA and RESPA disclosures must be provided the borrower within a specified amount of time following an application. This brings up the question of when an application is an application. The date determination for the completion of an application will vary depending on the method used by the borrower when making the application.

➤ At the time of a face-to-face interview, customers must sign the 1003 application. The date and time of this signature is considered the date of the application.

You will check face-to-face interview in the box labeled "to be completed by interviewer" on page 3 of the 1003.

➤ The application is considered complete at the time the branch or loan officer receives the application by mail, special delivery, or through another remote means.

You will check "by mail" in the box labeled "to be completed by interviewer" on page 3 of the 1003.

You will enter the date the application was received in the office.

➤ If the information was obtained over the telephone, and you enter the data into the 1003 on behalf of the borrower, you will Check "by telephone" in the box labeled "to be completed by interviewer" on page 3 of the 1003.

You will then send the completed 1003 to the applicant for signature.

You should send copies of the GFE, TIL, and HUD Guide and Compliance books along with the blank application form. The date of the application will be the date the completed 1003 and signed disclosures are received in the office.

* It should be noted that if a potential borrower wishes to apply "by mail" they must be sent a BLANK 1003 application.

*   Mail applications would normally be in the applicants own handwriting. Loan applications completed by an individual from your office are never considered a mail application. Information taken from a customer over the telephone would constitute a "telephone application".

HMDA forms are completed, in part, from Section X of the 1003 labeled "Information for Government Monitoring Purposes". This data must be completed for all applications even if the application is not a face-to-face interview.

Applicants do not have to provide answers to these questions. If an applicant does not wish to provide government-monitoring information, they should check "I do not wish to provide this information" on the application.

The completion date of the 1003 will set the time for the remittal of other disclosures.

➤ The Good Faith Estimate and the Truth-In-Lending Statement should be provided to the borrower at the time of face-to-face meeting if the application is a face-to-face application.

If the application is completed by mail, the good faith estimate and truth in lending statement should be sent within three business days of receipt of the mail application.

If the application is a telephone application, the good faith estimate and truth in lending statement should be sent within three business days of the completion of the telephone application.

➤ The charm or Consumer Handbook on Adjustable Rate Mortgages must be provided to all ARM applicants at the time of face-to-face interview, must be mailed to all ARM applicants within three business days of receipt of mail application or completion of the telephone interview.

➤ The Affiliated Business Arrangement notice, the Appraisal Notice, the Servicing Disclosure, the rate float or lock option form, and a copy of the HUD Guide and Compliance booklet must be given to the applicant at time of a face-to-face interview or mailed within three business days of the date of receipt of a mail application or completion of a telephone application.

Applicants must sign and date an Acknowledgement illustrating the receipt of these disclosures. You should retain a copy of each acknowledged disclosure in the loan file.

If the application is a mail or telephone application, you should mail a copy of all of the applicable disclosures to the applicant with either a blank application or a copy of the telephone completed application. You should include a letter instructing the applicant to return a signed and dated copy of each Acknowledgement document.

Disclosures

	face-to-face	Mail	Telephone
ECOA: When is an ap an ap?	At the time of face-to-face interview when the 1003 is completed Customers must sign the 1003 application. Check face-to-face interview in the box labeled "to be completed by interviewer" on page 3 of the 1003.	At the time, the branch or loan officer received the application. Check "by mail" in the box labeled "to be completed by interviewer" on page 3 of the 1003. Enter the date the application was received.	At the time, information for the 1003 was obtained over the telephone. Check "by telephone" in the box labeled "to be completed by interviewer" on page 3 of the 1003. Send the 1003 to the applicant for signature, along with copies of the GFE, TIL, and HUD Guide/ Compliance booklets.
		NOTE: Customers wanting to apply "by mail" must be sent a BLANK 1003 application. Mail applications would therefore normally be in the applicant's own handwriting.	Loan applications completed by the Loan Officers are never considered a mail application. Information taken from a customer over the telephone would constitute a "telephone application".
HMDA: Section X "Information for Government Monitoring Purposes"	Must be completed for all applications even an applicant is not present at the time the application is completed. Applicants do not have to provide information: they should check "I do not wish to provide this information" in the applicable section of the 1003. The Loan Officer may make a "best guess" regarding this information based on visual observation or surname. The LO should note on page 3 that information was "BVO" (based on visual observation).	Section X does not have to be completed by the applicant when they complete a mail application. It is not necessary to ask applicants for this information if the application is returned to the office with these areas blank. The Loan Officer will mark "I do not wish to provide this information" on the 1003 if the applicant did not do so. No further information is necessary.	Section X does not have to be completed by the applicant when they complete a telephone application. If the applicant does not wish to provide this information, the Loan Officer will mark "I do not wish to provide this information" on the 1003. No further information is necessary.
RESPA/TIL: Good Faith Estimate (GFE) & Truth-In-Lending Statement (TIL)	At the time of face-to-face meeting or sent within three business days of application date if prepared by the branch.	Mail within three business days of receipt of their mail application	Mail within three business days of the completion of a telephone application
CHARM: Consumer Handbook on Adjustable Rate Mortgage	Must be provided to all ARM applicants at the time of face-to-face interview	Must be mailed to all ARM applicants within three business days of receipt of mail application	Must be mailed to all ARM applicants within three business days of the completion of a telephone application
RESPA Affiliated Business Arrangement ECOA Appraisal Notice RESPA Servicing Disclosure FLOAT/LOCK FORM	Provide copy to applicants at the time of the face-to-face appearance. Applicants must sign and date an Acknowledgement illustrating that they received the applicable disclosures. You should retain copy in the loan file.	Mail to applicants with the blank application. You should include instructions to the applicant to return the signed and dated the Acknowledgement documents. Retain copy of the signed and dated Acknowledgement in loan file.	Mail to applicants along with the completed 1003, GFE, and TIL. You should include instructions to the applicant to return the signed and dated Acknowledgement documents. Retain copy of the signed and dated Acknowledgement in loan file.

2:5 Disclosure Reference Chart

THE GOOD FAITH ESTIMATE

It is essential that you understand the components of a Good Faith Estimate and gain the knowledge necessary to generate the estimate. The inclusions on the good faith estimate serve many functions during the loan process from assisting in the creation of the HUD 1 Settlement Statement to setting borrower expectations with regard to the costs that they will incur during the obtainment of their mortgage loan. Setting the expectations of costs at the proper level is one of the most important acts that you can perform. This single act is essential to ensuring smooth closings and good relationships – with your borrowers, with the real estate offices, with the closing agents, and with your closing team!

Many of the costs involved in closing a loan including appraisal fees, pest inspections, and title costs are standard in the industry or in the region where you conduct your business.

Your funding source will require you to charge other costs that are specific to the funding source and may vary among different lenders. You will want to refer to your underwriting guidelines to determine what fees a particular lender requires.

Other costs in the good faith estimate are part of your offices payment structure. These costs should remain similar for all borrowers. It is inappropriate to charge one borrower a $500.00 application fee and another borrower a $50.00 application fee.

In general, the structure and inclusions of the good faith estimate will depend on the type of loan you are processing, the funding source of the loan, and the transaction details negotiated within the sales agreement and dictated by the lending approval.

Lender:			Sales Price:		
Address:			Base Loan Amount:		
			Total Loan Amount:		
Applicant(s):			Interest Rate:		
			Type of Loan:		
Property Address:			Preparation Date:		
			Loan Number		

The information provided below reflects estimates of the charges which you are likely to incur at the settlement of your loan. The fees listed are estimates – actual charges may be more or less. Your transaction may not involve a fee for every item listed.
THE NUMBERS LISTED BESIDE THE ESTIMATES GENERALLY CORRESPOND TO THE NUMBERED LINES CONTAINED THE HUD-1 OR HUD-1A SETTLEMENT STATEMENT WHICH YOU WILL BE RECEIVEING AT THE SETTLEMENT. THE HUD-1 OR HUD-1A SETTLEMENT STATEMENT WILL SHOW YOU THE ACTUAL COST FOR ITEMS PAID AT SETTLEMENT.

800	**ITEMS PAYABLE IN CONNECTION WITH LOAN;**		**1100**	**TITLE CHARGES**	
801	Origination Fee @ % + $	$_____	1101	Closing or Escrow Fee	$_____
802	Discount Fee @ %+$	$_____	1102	Abstract or Title Search	$_____
803	Appraisal Fee	$_____	1103	Title Examination	$_____
804	Credit Report	$_____	1105	Document Preparation Fee	$_____
805	Lender's Inspection Fee	$_____	1106	Notary Fee	$_____
806	Mortgage Insurance Application Fee	$_____	1107	Attorney's Fee	$_____
807	Assumption Fee	$_____	1108	Title Insurance	$_____
808	Mortgage Broker Fee	$_____			$_____
810	Tax Related Service Fee	$_____			$_____
811	Application Fee	$_____			$_____
812	Commitment Fee	$_____			$_____
813	Lender's Rate Lock-In Fee	$_____			$_____
814	Processing Fee	$_____			$_____
815	Underwriting Fee	$_____			$_____
816	Wire Transfer Fee	$_____			$_____

900	**ITEMS TO BE PAI DIN ADVANCE**	;	**1200**	**GOVERNMENT RECORDING AND TRANSFER CHARGES**	
901	Interest for 1 days @ $13.78 day	$_____	1201	Recording Fee	$_____
902	Mortgage Insurance Premium	$_____	1202	City/County Tax/Stamps	$_____
903	Hazard Insurance Premium	$_____	1203	State Tax/Stamps	$_____
904	County Property Taxes	$_____	1205	Intangible Tax	$_____
905	Flood Insurance	$_____			$_____
		$_____			$_____

1000	**RESERVES DEPOSITED WITH LENDER**		**1300**	**ADDITIONAL SETTLEMENT CHARGES**	
1001	Hazard Ins 3 Mo @ $ 35 Per Mo	$_____	1201	Survey	$_____
1002	Mortgage Ins. Mo@$ Per Mo	$_____	1202	Pest Inspection	$_____
1004	Tax & Assmt. 7 Mo@$110 Per Mo	$_____	1203		$_____
1006	Flood Insurance	$_____	1205		$_____
		$_____		TOTAL ESTIMATED SETTLMENT CHARGES $_____	
S/B designates these costs to be paid by Seller / Broker			A designates those costs effecting APR		

TOTAL ESTIMATED MONTHLY PAYMENT			**TOTAL ESTIMATED FUNDS TO CLOSE**	
Principal & Interest	$_____			
Real Estate Taxes	$_____	Down Payment	$_____	
Hazard Insurance	$_____	Estimated Closing Costs (not financed)	$_____	
Flood Insurance	$_____	Estimated Prepaid Items/Reserves	$_____	
Mortgage Insurance	$_____	Total Paid Items (subtract)	$_____	
Other	$_____	Other	$_____	
TOTAL MONTHLY PAYMENT	$_____	CASH FROM BORROWER	$_____	

2:6 Sample Form – Good Faith Estimate – HUD Release

The first section of the good faith estimate will define items that are payable in connection with the obtainment of the loan. The inclusions of each good faith estimate will vary slightly because the items charged to the borrower will be dependent on the structure of the loan being provided.

Always remember that alternative fees or 'junk fees' should remain similar for all borrowers regardless of their specific loan product or situation.

800 ITEMS PAYABLE IN CONNECTION WITH LOAN;		
801 Origination Fee @	% + $	$_____
802 Discount Fee @	% + $	$_____
803 Appraisal Fee		$_____
804 Credit Report		$_____
805 Lender's Inspection Fee		$_____
806 Mortgage Insurance Application Fee		$_____
807 Assumption Fee		$_____
808 Mortgage Broker Fee		$_____
810 Tax Related Service Fee		$_____
811 Application Fee		$_____
812 Commitment Fee		$_____
813 Lender's Rate Lock-In Fee		$_____
814 Processing Fee		$_____
815 Underwriting Fee		$_____
816 Wire Transfer Fee		$_____

2:7 Sample Form Extraction – Good Faith Estimate – HUD Release

800.   ITEMS PAYABLE IN CONNECTION WITH THE LOAN

801.   Origination Fee   The Origination Fee is usually known as a loan origination fee but is sometimes called a "point" or "points".

The origination fee covers the lenders administrative costs in processing the loan.

Often this fee is expressed as a percentage of the loan.

Generally, the buyer pays these fees. If the buyer and the seller negotiate a different method of payment, it will be defined within the sales agreement.

These points are charged on behalf of you or your branch. When working for a bank or a broker you have a negotiated commission schedule for all fees and points charged on the loan. You will also have a maximum limit to the points that you are allowed to charge.

You may charge points in two ways.

The first method of charging points is to wrap the points into the interest rate that you offer to the borrower. This will be discussed further in "pricing the loan".

The second method of charging points is as an up-front fee during the closing. Any up-front points will be reflected on the good faith estimate. If you do not include these fees within the good faith estimate, you will not be able to collect up-front fees on the loan.

A point is 1% of the loan amount.

802   Discount Fee

A discount fee is also called a loan discount point. A loan discount is a one-time charge imposed by the lender or broker to lower the   rate at which the lender or broker would otherwise offer the loan.

This fee may vary.

In effect, the borrower is paying up front to reduce the overall monthly debt related to the loan. You may use the application of a discount fee to reduce the interest rate on a loan if the monthly payment exceeds the D. T. I. Ratio and the necessary funds are available to pay the discount fee.

This is also an excellent tool for your borrowers if the sellers have agreed to pay a set closing cost amount and the funds have not been utilized elsewhere.

These fees are paid to the lender.

803   Appraisal Fee

The Appraisal Fee covers the cost of the Appraisal.

The amount the appraisal fee is set by the appraisal company.

- The appraisal fee is often paid in advance.

You will note this payment as paid in the details of transaction summary.

- The appraisal fee may be charged at the settlement.

These funds are paid to the Appraisal Company.

804	Credit Report	Any costs associated with the completion of the Credit Report will be disclosed on the good faith estimate.
		Many lenders or brokers require the credit report charges be paid on all closed loans.
		This amount is paid as a reimbursement to the lender.
		The cost of the credit report is set regionally or by branch location. You should check with your branch manager for the amount.
		At times, a lender may require the credit report fee be paid at the application meeting. In these cases, you will note the payment in the details of transaction summary as a fee paid in advance.
805	Lender's Inspection	If the lender requires an inspection of the property for Underwriting purposes or another reason, the costs are the responsibility of the borrower.
806	Mortgage Insurance Application Fee	If Mortgage Insurance is necessary for the loan; any associated Application Fee should be included in the good faith estimate. This fee covers the processing of an application for mortgage insurance.
807	Assumption Fee	If a loan is being assumed from the seller of the property, the lender assigning the loan to the new borrower may charge an Assumption Fee.
		This fee is charged when a buyer "assumes" or takes over the duty to pay the seller's existing mortgage loan
808	Mortgage Broker Fee	Some states or specific funding lenders require that all fees charged by the Broker be differentiated on the good faith estimate. Mortgage Broker Fees are categorized with in this section of the good faith estimate.
		This separate disclosure helps to differentiate for the borrower the costs they are paying to the lending entity and the costs that they are paying for the Brokerage services.
810.	Tax Service Fee	Some lenders will use a service to verify the tax payment status of the property. Other lenders will rely on the settlement and closing company to perform this verification activity.
		If a separate tax service entity is used to obtain the tax payment amounts and payment status, they will charge a fee for completing this action. The amount of the fee will vary by Service Company.
811	Application Fee	Some lenders or mortgage brokerage offices charge an up-front application fee.

This amount may include the credit report charges, appraisal fee, or additional costs as determined by the branch location.

- Often these charges are credited toward the closing in the event the loan is completed.

- These payments are typically kept to offset any costs incurred by the branch in the event the loan does not close.

The decision to charge an application fee is determined by a particular branch location or lender. You will want to verify whether your office charges an application fee, the amount of the fee, and how the fee will be allocated at loan closing.

You will want to be sure to note this payment in the details of transaction section of the 1003.

812 Commitment Fee

If your offices or the funding lender requires that the borrower pay a Commitment Fee, you must enter the amount into the good faith estimate. This is often termed a "junk fee".

This is a fee charged by the lender in addition to points.

These fees are sometimes split per the negotiated commission schedule with the loan processor or loan officer.

813 Lender's Lock Rate Fee

Some lenders will charge a specific fee for the task of locking the interest rate. This fee could be a service charge or may be a fee associated with the obtainment of a specific rate.

This fee is different from the discount points paid to buy down the interest rate.

814 Processing Fee

If your offices or the funding lender requires that the borrower pay a Processing Fee, you must enter the amount into the good faith estimate. This is often termed a "junk fee".

This is a fee charged by the lender in addition to points.

These fees are sometimes split per the negotiated commission schedule with the loan processor.

815 Underwriting Fee

If your office or the funding lender requires that the borrower pay an Underwriting Fee, you must enter the amount into the good faith estimate. This is often termed a "junk fee".

This is a fee charged by the lender in addition to points.

These fees are sometimes split per the negotiated commission schedule with the loan underwriter, loan officer, or loan processor but are more frequently credited entirely to the lender.

816   Wire Transfer Fee   Some lenders may charge a Wire Transfer Fee to cover the costs of wiring the required funds to close the loan.

This fee is a "buyer non-allowable fee" under some program guidelines. If a wire transfer fee is being charged on behalf of the branch or lender, you should incorporate the cost of this fee into the good faith estimate.

900	ITEMS TO BE PAI DIN ADVANCE	
901	Interest for days @ $ /day	$_____
902	Mortgage Insurance Premium	$_____
903	Hazard Insurance Premium	$_____
904	County Property Taxes	$_____
905	Flood Insurance	$_____

2:8 Sample Form Extraction – Good Faith Estimate – HUD Release

900   ITEMS REQUIRED BY THE LENDER TO BE PAID IN ADVANCE

Some fees related to the closing are recurring fees. These fees relate to costs associated with the carrying of the loan. The lender may require that the borrower pre-pay a specific quantity of these recurring fees as a condition of the loan closing. Some of these items would be accrued interest, mortgage insurance premiums, and homeowner's hazard insurance.

901   Interest   Lenders often require borrowers to pay the interest that accrues from the date of settlement or closing to the date that they will make the first monthly payment

This interest is prorated daily and based on the new loans interest rate.

902   Mortgage Insurance
      Premium   If mortgage insurance is a requirement of the loan being obtained, an up-front Premium may be charged. This premium may also be financed into the loan amount.

If the borrower pays the insured loan off within the first seven years, they may be entitled to a prorated refund of the fee.

You will include any up front premium in the good faith estimate and on the 1003.

903   Hazard Insurance
      Premium   Hazard insurance protects the borrower and the lender against loss due to

fire, windstorm, and other hazards.

Lenders often require that the borrower to bring a paid-up first year's hazard insurance policy to the settlement or to pay for the first year's premium at settlement.

The premium amount should be included on the good faith estimate as a cost to close the loan. If the borrower pays this premium before closing, you will enter the amount of the payment into the pre-paid items on the 1003.

904   City Property Taxes

The city where the property is located may charge property taxes on real estate. The costs will be prorated between the buyer and the seller based on the closing date of the property and the negotiations included on the sales agreement. You will enter the borrower's estimated share of these costs into the good faith estimate.

905   Flood Insurance

If the lender requires flood insurance as a condition of the loan, it is usually listed within the segment of the good faith estimate relating to items to be paid in advance. Many lenders will require that the borrower bring a fully paid policy illustrating coverage for the first year of homeownership as a condition of loan closing.

1004   County Property Tax

The County will assess property taxes on real estate.

The amount of property taxes collected will vary depending on the date of closing, billing cycle of the taxes, and negotiations between the borrower and the seller.

The lender may require that the borrower escrow property taxes. Escrowing taxes means that the borrower pays a portion of the expected tax billing to the lender each month. The lender or servicer then holds these payments until the tax billing becomes due. The lender or servicer then uses the funds paid by the borrower to pay the tax bills related to the property.

1100 TITLE CHARGES	
1101 Closing or Escrow Fee	$_____
1102 Abstract or Title Search	$_____
1103 Title Examination	$_____
1105 Document Preparation Fee	$_____
1106 Notary Fee	$_____
1107 Attorney's Fee	$_____
1108 Title Insurance	$_____

2:9 Sample Form Extraction – Good Faith Estimate – HUD Release

1000   TITLE CHARGES

Any costs or charges associated with securing a clear title to the property and closing of the loan will be incorporated into the good faith estimate. Although these are not lender fees, lenders must provide a quote of the estimated costs of these items and services. These quotes may vary significantly. Title charges may cover a variety of services performed by title companies and others.

1101	Closing/Escrow Fee	A Closing or Escrow Fee is paid to the settlement agent escrow holder. Responsibility for the payment of this fee should be negotiated between the seller and the buyer and will appear on the sales agreement provided to you by either the real estate agent or the borrower.
1102	Abstract/Title Search	Any fees required for the completion of the Abstract or Title Search on the property will be charged by the Title Company to the borrower.
		The payment of these fees may be negotiated as part of the sales agreement between the borrower and the seller.
		You can contact the closing company handling the settlement to obtain a figure for this field.
1105	Document Preparation Fee	Any cost charged by the title company for the service of preparing all of the closing documents not provided by the funding company will be entered into the good faith estimate under Document Preparation Fee.
		Lender or Funding Company charges for document preparation costs will be included within a different section of the good faith estimate.
1106	Notary Fee	The charge incurred for the notary who verifies the signatures of all parties on the documents during the closing should be included within the good faith estimate.
		You can contact the closing company handling the settlement to obtain a figure for this field.
1107	Attorney's Fee	In the event that the services of an attorney are required during any portion of the loan application, processing, or closing activity, the costs charged by the attorney for these services should be entered into the good faith estimate.
		The attorney will provide you with an estimate of his or her charges for the requested services.

1200 GOVERNMENT RECORDING AND TRANSFER CHARGES	
1201 Recording Fee	$_____
1202 City/County Tax/Stamps	$_____
1203 State Tax/Stamps	$_____
1205 Intangible Tax	$_____

2:10 Sample Form Extraction – Good Faith Estimate – HUD Release

1200   GOVERNMENT RECORDING AND TRANSFER

Fees charged at the courthouse where the mortgage documents are filed will be allocated in association with the loan. The borrower typically pays these costs, but you should refer to the sales agreement to ensure that no other negotiations relating to the payment of these fees has been made. These fees are payable to the government.

1201   Recording fee   A recording fee is the amount charged for the recording of each item that must be filed within the public records system.

These items are filed for the protection of both the borrower and the lender.

Recording costs vary depending on the region where the recording will occur. You will want to verify the costs with your Title Company, courthouse, or branch manager.

1202   City/County Tax Stamps City and County Taxes and Stamps are the taxes assessed when real property is transferred within a city and county.

Different areas have different tax costs. You will want to verify this figure with your Title Company, courthouse, or branch manager.

1203   State Tax Stamps   State Tax Stamps are the state required taxes involved with the transfer of the property.

Different states have different tax costs and you will want to verify this figure with your Title Company, courthouse, or branch manager.

1300   ADDITIONAL SETTLEMENT CHARGES:

Any additional charges incurred during the loan processes that have not been addressed previously will be explained and entered within the final area of the good faith estimate

1301   Survey   Many lenders accept a survey affidavit from the Title Company as verification of the property location and boundary lines.

If a survey must be performed for the property to clear underwriting, these charges are negotiated as paid by the buyer or the seller of the property and the figure is paid to the Survey Company at settlement.

| 1302 | Pest Inspections | Pest Inspections are required by some loan programs and are requested in some cases by the buyer |

The payment for these fees is negotiated on the Real Estate Sales Agreement.

These payments are paid to the inspection provider based on a billing presented at the closing table.

| 1303 | Flood Certification | A Flood Certification or verification that the property is not in a flood plain may be requested by underwriting. |

If the flood certification is completed through a service retained by underwriting, the costs of the certification are paid to the lender at the time of closing and the lender pays the certification service.

If another certification service is used to verify the flood status of the property, the name of the service will be entered into the good faith estimate and the charges imposed by the service included.

Payment to the service provider may be made during the loan process or as part of the settlement process. You should enter the applicable details into the good faith estimate.

| 1304 | Courier Fees | Courier Fees may be charged by either the funding company or closing company for the transfer of documents via courier. |

You will want to check with your closing provider and your branch manager to determine if this fee is commonly charged.

Mortgage Lending – Loan Officer Training

Lender:	Sales Price:
Address:	Base Loan Amount:
	Total Loan Amount:
Applicant(s):	Interest Rate:
	Type of Loan:
Property Address:	Preparation Date:
	Loan Number

The information provided below reflects estimates of the charges which you are likely to incur at the settlement of your loan. The fees listed are estimates – actual charges may be more or less. Your transaction may not involve a fee for every item listed.
THE NUMBERS LISTED BESIDE THE ESTIMATES GENERALLY CORRESPOND TO THE NUMBERED LINES CONTAINED THE HUD-1 OR HUD-1A SETTLEMENT STATEMENT WHICH YOU WILL BE RECEIVEING AT THE SETTLEMENT. THE HUD-1 OR HUD-1A SETTLEMENT STATEMENT WILL SHOW YOU THE ACTUAL COST FOR ITEMS PAID AT SETTLEMENT.

800	ITEMS PAYABLE IN CONNECTION WITH LOAN;		1100	TITLE CHARGES	
801	Origination Fee @ % + $	$2550.00	1101	Closing or Escrow Fee	$ 295.00
802	Discount Fee @ %+$	$	1102	Abstract or Title Search	$
803	Appraisal Fee	$ 275.00	1103	Title Examination	$
804	Credit Report	$ 50.00	1105	Document Preparation Fee	$
805	Lender's Inspection Fee	$	1106	Notary Fee	$ 35.00
806	Mortgage Insurance Application Fee	$	1107	Attorney's Fee	$
807	Assumption Fee	$	1108	Title Insurance	$ 618.75
808	Mortgage Broker Fee	$			$
810	Tax Related Service Fee	$ 98.00			$
811	Application Fee	$			$
812	Commitment Fee	$			$
813	Lender's Rate Lock-In Fee	$ 200.00			$
814	Processing Fee	$ 250.00			$
815	Underwriting Fee	$ 400.00			$
816	Wire Transfer Fee	$			$

900	ITEMS TO BE PAI DIN ADVANCE ;		1200	GOVERNMENT RECORDING AND TRANSFER CHARGES	
901	Interest for 1 days @ $13.78 day	$ 13.78	1201	Recording Fee	$ 33.50
902	Mortgage Insurance Premium	$	1202	City/County Tax/Stamps	$ 80.00
903	Hazard Insurance Premium	$ 420.00	1203	State Tax/Stamps	$ 80.00
904	County Property Taxes	$1320.00	1205	Intangible Tax	$
905	Flood Insurance	$			$
		$			$

1000	RESERVES DEPOSITED WITH LENDER		1300	ADDITIONAL SETTLEMENT CHARGES	
1001	Hazard Ins 3 Mo @ $ 35 Per Mo	$ 105.00	1201	Survey	$
1002	Mortgage Ins. Mo@$ Per Mo	$	1202	Pest Inspection	$
1004	Tax & Assmt. 7 Mo@$110 Per Mo	$ 770.00	1203		$
1006	Flood Insurance	$	1205		$
		$		TOTAL ESTIMATED SETTLMENT CHARGES	$

S/B designates these costs to be paid by Seller / Broker   A designates those costs effecting APR

TOTAL ESTIMATED MONTHLY PAYMENT		TOTAL ESTIMATED FUNDS TO CLOSE	
Principal & Interest	$ 616.00		
Real Estate Taxes	$ 110.00	Down Payment	$
Hazard Insurance	$ 35.00	Estimated Closing Costs (not financed)	$7743.03
Flood Insurance	$	Estimated Prepaid Items/Reserves	$
Mortgage Insurance	$	Total Paid Items (subtract)	$
Other	$	Other	$
TOTAL MONTHLY PAYMENT	$ 761.00	CASH FROM BORROWER	$

APPROVED SERVICE PROVIDER LIST

Some mortgage lenders will use specific service providers when completing the processing and closing of a loan application. If the mortgage lender uses a specific service provider and the borrower will be responsible for the billing that is incurred as a result of this use, the lender must provide a disclosure to the borrower detailing this use so that the borrower has the opportunity to make an informed decision applicable to the costs that they will incur.

APPROVED SERVICE PROVIDER LIST
Addendum to the standard "Good Faith Estimate" of Settlement Costs

_____ requires the use of certain providers in the processing and settlement of your loan. These providers are chosen from an approved list and we require that you pay for all portions of the services provided from these providers. The costs of these services are based on the charges of these providers or industry standards. Please refer to your attached Good Faith Estimate form for an estimate of each proposed charge. The following providers have been repeatedly used for the designated services within the last 12 months.

1. CREDIT REPORTING AGENCIES:

2. APPRAISAL SERVICES:

3. PRIVATE MORTGAGE INSURANCE PROVIDERS:

4. OTHER:

I/we acknowledge that we received a copy of this notice:

_____   _____
Borrower Signature   Date

_____   _____
Co-Borrower Signature   Date

2:12 Sample Form– Approved Service Provider List – HUD Release

RATE LOCK OR FLOAT OPTION

The borrower must complete a rate lock or float option form. This form specifies the borrower's determination as to whether they wish to lock in the offered interest rate now or wait on the chance that the interest rate will change for the better during the loan processing stage.

The upper section of the form should provide identifying details relating to the borrower, the property, and the loan. The form will have two areas. The borrower should complete and sign the area that relates to their choice.

If they wish to lock in the currently offered interest rate, they will complete the RATE LOCK section of the form. The rate lock section will show the offered rate, any points associated with the obtainment of this rate, and the number of days that the rate lock offer is applicable.

The borrower will sign and date the form to illustrate their acceptance of the offered rate and terms.

If the borrower wishes to wait to lock the rate in the hopes that the market will improve thus improving the interest rate that they can obtain, the borrower will complete the DO NOT LOCK section of the form by signing and dating the applicable area.

The borrower should receive a copy of the completed rate lock form.

RATE LOCK/RATE FLOAT OPTION

Loan Amount $ _____
Property Address _____
City, State, Zip _____

This is to certify that I DO want to exercise my interest rate lock option at this time.

A. My guaranteed interest rate will be _____ %.
B. The total points paid at settlement will not exceed _____ . This total does not include settlement costs such as title insurance, homeowners insurance, transfer taxes, etc.
C. This agreement will end _____ days from today. This date is called the ending date.

ACKNOWLEDGEMENT

_____   _____
Signed   Date

This is to certify that I DO NOT want to exercise my interest rate lock option at this time.

A. I understand that my lender cannot predict interest rate changes.
B. If I want to obtain an interest rate commitment in the future, I may do so at any time up to ___ days before the closing of my mortgage loan.
C. I understand that I must sign an interest rate lock-in agreement to obtain a guaranteed interest rate lock.
D. I understand that it is my responsibility to advise the lender of my desire to obtain interest rate commitment.

ACKNOWLEDGEMENT

_____   _____
Signed   Date

2:13 Sample Form– Rate Lock / Float Option – HUD Release

KENNEY

AFFILIATED BUSINESS ARRANGEMENT NOTICE

If the lender has a business arrangement or interest in one of the service providers associated with the loan process or closing, the lender must give the borrower notice of this arrangement or interest. An Affiliated Business Arrangement Notice should be provided to the borrower, and a signature obtained that acknowledges the borrowers understanding of this business arrangement or interest. The borrower should receive a copy of this notice.

Affiliated Business Arrangement Notice

This is to give you notice that   has a business relationship with
(Describe the nature of the relationship between the referring party and the provider(s) including percentage of ownership interest, if applicable). Because of this relationship, this referral may provide a financial or other benefit.

(A.) Set forth below is the estimated charge or range of charges for the settlement services listed. You are NOT required to use the listed provider(s) as a condition for (settlement of your loan) (or) (purchase, sale or refinance of) the subject property. THERE ARE FREQUENTLY OTHER SETTLEMENT SERVICE PROVIDERS AVAILABLE WITH SIMILAR SERVICES. YOU ARE FREE TO SHOP AROUND TO DETERMINE THAT YOU ARE RECEIVING THE BEST RATE FOR THESE SERVICES.

_____

_____

(B.) Set forth below is the estimated charge or range of charges for the settlement services of an attorney, credit reporting agency, or real estate appraiser that we, as your lender, will require you to use, as a condition of your loan on this property, to represent our interests in this transaction.

_____

_____

ACKNOWLEDGMENT

I/we have read this disclosure form and understand that (referring party) is referring me/us to purchase the above described settlement service(s) and may receive a financial benefit as a result of this referral.

2:14 Sample Form– Affiliated Business Arrangement Notice – HUD Release

---

MAILING ADDRESS CONFIRMATION

The lender who provides the funds for the closing will often ask the borrower to sign a statement confirming their mailing address and understanding of the monthly payment dictated through the mortgage and note documents. This statement will

- Detail the correspondence information of the borrower

- State the monthly payment breakdown specifics including breakdown information for PMI, school and county taxes, insurance premiums and any reserves required under the mortgage agreement

- Define any mortgage servicing information known to the mortgage lender at the time of closing

- Detail the mailing address and other contact information of the mortgage lender

The borrower will be asked to review all of the entries on this document and confirm a receipt of a copy of the statement. The mailing address and payment confirmation is a snapshot of all of the data pertaining to the loan that was included on the previous pages and it is critical that you ensure the borrower receives a copy of this statement in their closing package.

MAILING ADDRESS CONFIRMATION / PAYMENT LETTER

From:

Re: Loan #   *** IMPORTANT, PLEASE READ THROUGHOULY ***
       Property Address

To:

Dear Homeowner:

A.   All mortgage servicing correspondence will be mailed to the above referenced property address. In order to ensure proper receipt of all mortgage servicing notifications (i.e. monthly statement, Q&A booklets, etc.) please indicate the correct mailing address if it is different from the property address. The address to mail payments and the phone number to call for customer service are listed below.

    Please indicate (X):

    ( )   The property address is correct as referenced above and should be used for correspondence.

    ( )   The proper mailing address is: _____

                                                    _____

B..   The monthly payments on the above loan are to begin on   , and will continue monthly until

    Your monthly payment will consist of the following:

    MONTHLY PAYMENT ....$_____
    MMI/PMI INSRUANCE .... _____
    RESERVE FOR COUNTY TAXES .... _____
    RESERVE FOR HAXARD INSURANCE................................ _____
    RESERVE FOR FLOOD INSURANCE.................................... _____
    RESERVE FOR CITY TAXES.. _____
    RESERVE FOR ANNUAL ASSESSMENT............................. _____
    RESERVE FOR SCHOOL TAXES.. _____
    _____..................................... _____
            TOTAL MONTHLY PAYMENTS.........$_____

*** Please be aware that if you have an impound account, you may see a change in your initial monthly payment figure due to information available after the closing of your loan.

               Engages the services of   as its servicer. You will be receiving a billing notice from   within two weeks of your loan funding.   has the right to collect your payments and this in no way affects the terms and conditions of the mortgage instruments, other than the terms directly related to the servicing of your loan. If you do not receive a payment booklet or have other questions about the servicing of your loan, please call:

2:15 Sample Form – Mailing Address Confirmation Letter – HUD Release

MORTGAGE SERVICING TRANSFER NOTIFICATION

In today's market, mortgage-servicing rights are often bought and sold. The Real Estate Settlement and Procedures Act provide the borrower with certain rights regarding the servicing of the mortgage and escrow accounts.

The servicing of a mortgage loan means the continued collection of payments, management of escrow, and the handling of all post close activity relating to the mortgage loan until the loan is paid in full.

Many lenders will sell the servicing rights of a mortgage to another company after the closing of the transaction. At the closing, information pertaining to how often the mortgage lender transfers servicing rights, the handling of such a transfer, and the effects of such transfer on the buyer will be disclosed. It is important that the buyer understand these documents and receive a copy so that they may refer to the inclusions if, at some point, the loan servicing is transferred.

If a loan is transferred to a new servicer, the loan servicer is required to notify the borrower in writing at least 15 days before the servicing of the loan is transferred to a new servicer.

The notice must include

- The effective date of the transfer.

- The date the new servicer will begin accepting payments.

- The name, address, and toll-free or collect telephone number for the new servicer.

- Information concerning the continuance of any optional insurance, such as mortgage, life, or disability insurance.

- A statement that the transfer of the loan servicing does not affect any term or condition of the mortgage documents other than the terms directly related to the servicing of the loan.

- An explanation that the payment may not be treated as late during the 60-day period beginning on the effective date of the transfer if it is mistakenly sent it to the old mortgage servicer instead of the new one.

KENNEY

Mortgage Servicing Disclosure

NOTICE TO MORTGAGE LOAN APPLICATNS: THE RIGHT TO COLLECT YOUR MORTGAGE LOAN PAYMENTS MAY BE TRANSFERRED. FEDERAL LAW GIVES YOU CERTAIN RELATED RIGHTS. READ THIS STATEMTN AND SIGN IT ONLY IF YOU UNDERSTAND ITS CONTENTS.

Because you are applying for a mortgage loan covered by the Real Estate Settlement Procedures Act (RESPA), you have certain rights under that Federal law. This statement tells you about those rights. It also tells you what the chances are that the servicing for this loan may be transferred to a different loan servicer. "Servicing" refers to collecting your principal, interest and escrow account payments, if any. If your loan servicer changes, certain procedures must be followed. This statement generally explains those procedures.

Transfer Practices and Requirements
If the servicing of your loan is assigned, sold or transferred to a new servicer you must be given notice of that transfer. The present loan servicer must send you notice in writing of the assignment, sale, or transfer of the servicing not less than 15 days before the effective date of the transfer. The present servicer and the new servicer may combine this information in one notice so long as the notice is sent to you within 15 days before the effective date of the transfer. The 15-day period is not applicable if a notice of prospective transfer is provided to you at settlement. The law allows a delay in the time (not more than 30 days after a transfer) for servicers to notify you under certain limited circumstances, when your servicer is changed abruptly. This exception applies only if your servicer is fired for cause, is in bankruptcy proceedings, or is involved in a conservatorship or receivership initiated by a Federal Agency.

Notices must contain certain information. They must contain the effective date of the transfer of the servicing of your loan to the new servicer, the name, address and toll-free or collect call telephone number of the new servicer, and toll-free or collect call telephone numbers of a person or department for both your present servicer and your new servicer to answer your questions about the transfer of servicing. During the 60-day period following the effective date of the transfer of the loan servicing, a loan payment received by your old servicer before its due date may not be treated by the new servicer as late and a late fee may not be imposed on you.

Complaint Resolution
Section 5 of RESPA gives you certain consumer rights *whether or not your loan servicing is transferred.* If you send a qualified written request to your loan servicer concerning the servicing of your loan, your servicer must provide you with a written acknowledgement within 20 business days of receipt of your request. A "qualified written request" is a written correspondence other than notice on payment coupon or other payment medium supplied by the servicer that includes your name and account number and your reasons for the request. Not later than 60 Business Days after receiving your request, your servicer must make any appropriate corrections to your account or must provide you with a written clarification regarding any dispute. During this 60-Business Day period, your servicer may not provide any information to a consumer reporting agency concerning any overdue payment related to such period or qualified written request.

A business day is any day excluding public holidays, State or Federal, Saturday or Sunday.

Damages and Costs
Section 6 of RESPA also provides for damages and costs for individuals in circumstances where servicers are shown to have violated the requirements of that section.

Servicing Transfer Estimated by Lender

1.   The following is the best estimate of what will happen to the servicing of your loan:

        We may assign, sell, or transfer the servicing of your loan sometime while the loan is outstanding. We are able to service your loan and we presently intend to service your loan.

2.   For all mortgage loans that we make in the 12-month period after your mortgage loan is funded, we estimate that the percentage of mortgage loans for which we will transfer servicing is between:

        ___ and ___%

        This is only our best estimate and it is not binding. Business conditions or other circumstances may affect

3.   This is our record of transferring the servicing of mortgage loans we have made in the past:

        Year   Percentage of Loans Transferred

ACKNOWLEDGEMENT OF MORTGAGE LOAN APPLICANT

I/We have read this disclosure form and understand the contents as evidenced by my/our signature(s) below. I/We understand that this acknowledgement is a required part of the mortgage loan application.

2:16 Sample Form – Mortgage Servicing Disclosure – HUD Release

RIGHT TO RECEIVE A COPY OF THE APPRAISAL

When an appraisal has been conducted as a part of the transaction, the borrower has a right to obtain a copy of the appraisal if they have paid for the completion.

- The appraisal will often be delivered directly to the lender during the course of the loan process.

- The loan officer should provide instructions to the buyer on how to obtain a copy of the appraisal if they desire one at or before the settlement meeting.

- These instructions must be signed and witnessed during the closing process.

NOTICE REGARDING YOUR
UNIFORM RESIDENTIAL APPRAISAL REPORT

You are advised that you have the right, under the Equal Credit Opportunity Act, to obtain a copy of your *Uniform Residential Appraisal Report.*

If you wish a copy, please write us at the address shown below. We must hear from you no later than 90 days after we notify you about the action taken on your credit application or you withdraw your application.

Please send your written request to:

In your letter, give the following information:

      Loan or application number (if known)

      Date of application

      Name(s) of loan applicant(s)

      Property address

      Current mailing address

A copy of your Uniform Residential Appraisal Report shall be mailed to you within 30 days after receipt of your request.

2:17 Sample Form – Right to Receive a Copy of Appraisal – HUD Release

RIGHT OF RECISSION/RIGHT TO CANCEL

Some transactions must include a right for the borrower to rescind or cancel the loan after the closing date.

Any credit transaction that involves a security interest in the borrower's primary residence must provide the borrower with the right to rescind the transaction.

RIGHT OF RECISSION LENDER RESPONSABLITY

The lender has certain responsibilities that help to protect these rights.

- Lenders are required to provide two copies of the right to cancel or rescind to the borrower.

- The notice must be on a separate document that identifies the rescission period available to the borrower.

- The notice must clearly disclose the fact that the borrower's primary residence will be held as a security instrument because of the transaction.

- The notice must state the borrower's right to rescind or cancel the transaction.

- The notice must state how the borrower may exercise the right to rescind or cancel.

- The notice must designate the address of the lender or the place of business to which the rescission or cancellation must be delivered.

- The borrower will receive a refund of all money or property provided to the lender within twenty days of delivery of the decision to rescind or cancel the transaction.

RIGHT OF RESCISSION BORROWER RESPONSIBILITY

The borrower also has certain responsibilities with regard to the right to cancel a credit transaction.

- The borrower must notify the lender of the decision to rescind or cancel the transaction in writing.

- The decision must be delivered to the lender by mail, telegram, or another available communication method that allows for the written delivery of the signature of the borrower.

- The borrower may exercise the right to rescind or cancel the transaction until midnight on the third day after the transaction.

- When more than one borrower in a transaction has the right to rescind or cancel, the exercise of the right of rescission or cancellation by one borrower shall be binding upon all borrowers.

- When a borrower rescinds or cancels the transaction the security interest resulting from the transaction becomes void.

- The borrower will receive a refund of all money or property provided to the lender within twenty days of delivery of the decision to rescind or cancel the transaction.

- The borrower may waive the right to rescind by completing the applicable notice.

NOTICE OF RIGHT TO CANCEL

Your Right to Cancel

You are entering a transaction that will result in a mortgage on your home. You have a legal right under Federal Law to cancel this transaction without cost until midnight of the third business day after, whichever of the following events occurs last

(1.)   the date of the closing of the transaction

(2.)   the date you received your Truth in Lending disclosure

(3.)   the date you received this notice of your right to cancel

If you cancel the transaction, the mortgage is also canceled. Within 20 calendar days after we receive your notice we must take the steps necessary to reflect the fact that the mortgage on your house has been cancelled, and we must return to you any money or property you have given to us or to anyone else in connection with this transaction.
You may keep any money or property we have given you until we have completed the items mentioned above, but you must return the money or property upon completion of the described actions. If it is impractical or unfair for you to return the property, you must offer its reasonable value. You may offer to return the property at your home or at the location of the property. Money must be returned to the address below. If we do not take possession of the money or property within 20 calendar days of your offer, you may keep it without further obligation.

How to Cancel

If you decide to cancel this transaction you may do so by notifying

_____

_____

You may use any written statement that is signed and dated by you and states your intention to cancel, or you may use this notice by dating and signing below. Keep one copy of this notice because it contains important information about your rights.

If you cancel by mail, you must send the notice no later than midnight of _____, 20___ (or midnight of the third business day following the latest of the events listed above.) If you send or deliver your written notice to cancel in some other manner, it must be delivered to the above address no later than that time.

2:18 Sample Form –Notice of Right to Cancel – HUD Release

SETTLEMENT STATEMENT

The settlement statement is the statement that itemizes all of the closing costs payable at the closing or settlement meeting.

The settlement statement will contain details derived from the good faith estimate, the sales agreement, payoff and billing information, and other specific figures supplied to the closing agent's office.

You will typically not be responsible for the completion of the settlement statement, but you should understand the inclusions and gain the ability to compare the financial details of the settlement statement to the loan specifics offered to the borrower. It will be a part of your function to review the settlement statement prior to the settlement meeting. You should confirm that the numbers included match the loan strategy and details that the borrower expects.

The borrower's portion of the settlement statement should mirror the initial Good Faith Estimate.

The seller's portion of the settlement statement breaks down all items on the seller's behalf. Included in the seller's portion will be:

- Any liens or mortgages that must be paid to secure a clear title to the property

- Any seller concession toward the buyers closing costs as negotiated in the Sales Agreement and any additional charges for which the seller is responsible.

- Any prorated items the seller has agreed to pay as negotiated in the sales agreement.

- Any other costs the seller has incurred that must be paid at the closing table.

You will wish to review the seller's portion to ensure that any concessions, assumed loans, or costs that the seller has agreed to pay as part of the purchase negotiations are correctly debited from the seller and credited to your borrower. An error in the allocation of concessions or costs will affect the figures on the borrower's side of the settlement statement.

The settlement statement contains the final figures pertaining to the loan. It is your duty to review the settlement statement before the closing meeting. You should confirm that all of the details set forth on the settlement statement are in agreement with the loan program structured for the borrower.

Page one section 100 will contain the total of all costs involved with the loan process. These will include:

- The sales price

- Any Settlement charges allocated to the borrower.

- Any pro-rated taxes due from the borrower

Section 200 will contain all amounts, which are paid on behalf of the borrower. These will include:

- Any deposit or earnest money the borrower paid at the time of the Sales Agreement negotiation.

- Any additional deposits or payments made by the borrower in the course of the loan processing.

- The loan amount as negotiated with the lender.

- Any assumed loans the borrower is taking.

- Any seller financing as negotiated at the time of the sales agreement.

- Any closing costs to be paid by the seller as negotiated at the time of the Sales Agreement.

- Any additional adjustments that the Title Company has determined must be made to the finances of the package.

The figures will be calculated, taking the amount paid on behalf of the borrower and the amount due from the borrower to determine the exact figure the borrower is required to bring to the closing table.

You should review the final settlement statement to confirm that all of the figures match the loan as it has been structured and that the cash to or from the borrower matches the estimate of charges on the initial good faith estimate. A very small amount of change is expected due to the pro-rata of exact charges. However, if the figures vary greatly from the initial estimate, the Settlement Statement will need to be reviewed with more care to determine exactly where the error has occurred.

Page two of the settlement statement contains a more detailed breakdown of the charges included in the section titled settlement charges to borrower. The fees and costs being charged on the loan will be included in this section. These figures will mirror the good faith estimate making an error relatively simple to find.

Upon confirming that the Settlement Statement is in agreement with the Good Faith Estimate and the planned structuring of the loan, you should inform the Settlement Company that the Settlement Statement is approved. The closing can then go forward.

F. Type of Loan				
1__ FHA 2 __ FmHA 3__ Conv 4 __ VA 5 __ Conv Ins	6. File Number:	7. Loan Number:	8. Mortgage Insurance Case Number	
G. Note: This form is furnished to give you a statement of actual settlement costs. Amounts paid to and by the settlement agent are shown. Items marked "(P&C)" were paid outside the closing; they are shown here for informational purposes and are not included in the totals.				
D. Name & Address of Borrower.		E. Name & Address of Seller	F. Name & Address of Lender	
G. Property Location		H. Settlement Agent Place of Settlement:	I. Settlement Date	

J. Summary of Borrower's Transaction		K. Summary of Seller's Transaction	
100. Gross Amount Due From Borrower		**400. Gross Amount Due To Seller**	
101. Contract Sales Price		401. Contact Sales Price	
102. Personal Property		402. Personal Property	
103. Settlement Charges to borrower (line 1400)		403.	
104.		404.	
105.		405.	
Adjustments for items paid by seller in advance		Adjustments for items paid by seller in advance	
106. City / Town Taxes for		406. City / Town Taxes for	
107. County Taxes for		407. County Taxes for	
108. Assessments for		408. Assessments for	
109.		409.	
110.		410.	
111.		411.	
112.		412.	
120. Gross Amount Due From Borrower		**420. Gross Amount Due To Seller**	
200. Amounts Paid By Or In Behalf Of Borrower		**500. Reductions In Amount Due To Seller**	
201. Deposit or earnest money		501. Excess deposit (see instructions)	
202. Principal amount of new loan(s)		502. Settlement charges to seller (line 1400)	
203. Existing loan(s) take subject to		503. Existing loan(s) taken subject to	
204.		504. Payoff of first mortgage loan	
205.		505. Pay off of second mortgage loan	
206.		506.	
207.		507.	
208.		508.	
209.		509.	
Adjustments for items unpaid by seller		Adjustments for items unpaid by seller	
210. City / Town Taxes for		510. City / Town Taxes for	
211. County Taxes for		511. County Taxes for	
212. Assessments for		512. Assessments for	
213.		513.	
214.		514.	
215.		515.	
220. Total Paid By/For Borrower		**520. Total Reduction Amount Due Seller**	
300. Cash At Settlement From/To Borrower		**600. Cash at Settlement To/From Seller**	
301. Gross amount due from borrower (line 120)		601. Gross amount due to seller (line 420)	
302. Less amounts paid by/for borrower (line 220)	( )	602. Less reductions in amt due seller (line 520)	( )

2:19 Sample Form – HUD 1 Settlement Statement Page 1 – HUD Release

		Paid From Borrowers Funds at Settlement	Paid From Seller's Funds at Settlement
700. Total Sales/Brokers commission based on price $ @ %			
Division of Commission (line 700) as follows:			
701. $ to			
702. $ to			
703 Commission paid at Settlement			
704.			
800. Items Payable in Connection with Loan			
801. Loan Origination Fee %			
802. Loan Discount %			
803. Appraisal Fee to			
804. Credit Report to			
805. Lender's Inspection Fee			
806. Mortgage Insurance Application Fee to			
807. Assumption Fee			
808.			
809.			
810.			
811.			
900. Items Required By Lender To Be Paid In Advance			
901. Interest from to @$ / day			
902. Mortgage Insurance Premium for months to			
903. Hazard Insurance Premium for years to			
904.			
905.			
1000. Reserves Deposited With Lender			
1001. Hazard Insurance months @$ per month			
1002. Mortgage Insurance months @$ per month			
1003. City Property Taxes months @$ per month			
1004. County Property Taxes months @$ per month			
1005. Annual Assessments months @$ per month			
1006. months @$ per month			
1007. months @$ per month			
1008. months @$ per month			
1100. Title Charges			
1101. Settlement or closing fee to			
1102. Abstract or title search to			
1103. Title examination to			
1104. Title insurance binder to			
1105. Document preparation to			
1106. Notary fees to			
1107. Attorney's fees to			
(includes above items numbers:)			
1108. Title Insurance to			
(includes above items numbers:)			
1109. Lender's coverage $			
1110. Owner's coverage $			
1111.			
1112.			
1200. Government Recording and Transfer Charges			
1201. Recording fees: Deed $: Mortgage $: Releases $			
1202. City/county tax/stamps: Deed $: Mortgage $			
1203. State tax/stamps: Deed $: Mortgage $			
1204.			
1205.			
1300. Additional Settlement Charges			
1301. Survey to			
1302. Pest Inspection to			
1303.			
1304.			
1400. Total Settlement Charges (enter on lines 103, Section J and 502, Section K)			

2:20 Sample Form – HUD1 Settlement Statement Page 2 – HUD Release

ESCROW ACCOUNT DISCLOSURE STATEMENT

When the loan is being structured, one element that must be considered is whether to impound property tax and insurance payments or to allow the borrower to pay these billings themselves as they come due.

- At times, the buyer will pay a portion of these bills each month as part of their monthly payment.

- The funds will then be placed into an escrow account until the billings become due.

- The lender then uses the payments made by the borrower throughout the year to make payment for these billings.

- At other times, the buyer may agree to pay the billings themselves as they become due.

This is known as impounding, not impounding, escrowing, or not escrowing payments.

Whichever method is chosen, a document will often be presented at closing that details handling of the tax and insurance payments. You must obtain the proper signature on these documents, as the payment of such billings can be critical to maintaining the rights of the parties.

BORROWER(S):

PROPERTY ADDRES:

NON IMPOUND NOTICE

I DO UNDERSTAND THAT THE LENDER FOR THIS MORTGAGE WILL NOT IMPOUND FOR REAL ESTATE TAXES AND HOMEOWNERS INSURANCE COVERAGE ON THE ABOVE REFERENCED ACCOUNT.

THE MONTHLY PAYMENT I WILL BE MAKING ONLY COVERS PRINCIPAL AND INTEREST ON THE LOAN.

I AM FULLY RESPONSIBLE TO PAY FOR REAL ESTATE TAXES AND HOMEOWNERS INSURACE POLICY PREMIUMS WHEN THEY BECOME PAYABLE.

2:21 Sample Form – Non Impound Notice – HUD Release

INITIAL ESCROW ACCOUNT DISCLOSURE STATEMENT

Borrower Name and Address	*Lender's Name and Address*
Loan No.	*Telephone No.*

___ Your mortgage payment for the coming year will be $_____ of which $_____ will be for principal and interest and $_____ will go into your escrow account.

___ Your first monthly mortgage payment for the coming year will be $_____ of which $_____ will be for principal and interest and $_____ will go into your escrow account.

The terms of your loan may result in changes to the principal and interest payments during the year.

This is an estimate of activity in your escrow account during the coming year based on payments anticipated to be made from your account.

Month/ Payment No.	*Payments to* Escrow Acct.	*Payment from* Escrow Acct.	*Description*	*Escrow Acct.* Balance

Please keep this statement for comparison with the actual activity in your account at the end of the escrow accounting computation year. Cushion selected by the servicer is $_____.

2:22 Sample Form – Initial Escrow Account Disclosure Statement – HUD Release

PRO-RATA CALCULATIONS

The act of completing the pro-rata calculations will often be assigned to the title agent in charge of the loan file or to the closing agent who works for the mortgage lender. While the completion of the final pro-rata calculations will typically not be a part of your functions, you should gain an understanding of the methodology behind these calculations. You will need apply these figures in your functions and when creating the good faith estimate and reviewing the HUD 1.

Prorating allows for the buyer and seller to split the costs and income related to the property fairly according to the term of ownership. These prorations may be based on the date of closing or another date as negotiated within the sales contract.

Items subject to pro-rata may include

- Real estate taxes

- Homeowner's insurance premiums

- Accrued interest on assumed loans

- Rents received on income producing property

- Other income received from an income producing property

- Expenses incurred on an income producing property

- Oil or other fuel tank filling costs

- Any utility billing for any utility not turned off and paid in full prior to the date of closing

- Any other negotiated matter

These are the most common items subject to pro rata calculations, but as each transaction is different, the items to be pro-rated may be different. It is important that any financial matter that may be subject to a split between the buyer and the seller be negotiated, in writing, on the sales agreement. This written negotiation ensures that all parties understand the income and expenses that may be assessed. The written negotiations also provide the settlement company with the information necessary to prorate the applicable items according to the wishes of the buyer and the seller. You will enter an estimate of any pro-rated items in the good faith estimate before you provide the estimate to the borrower.

30-DAY MONTH

It is customary to complete the pro rata calculations based on a 30-day month rather than altering the figures to the exact number of days within the closing month. This 30-day month is used when prorating

- Mortgage Interest

- Property Taxes

- Water Bills

- Insurance Premiums

- And other items as determined by the specific transaction

If the use of the customary 30-day month creates a significant financial impact on either the buyer or the seller, they can agree to prorate using the exact number of days in the applicable month or to use the 365-day year to find the daily pro rata calculation rate. Any negotiation of this sort will be incorporated into the sales contract or written as an addendum to the sales contract.

REAL ESTATE TAXES

To understand how pro-rata calculations affect the financial figures associated with the closing, we will define the figures for an example real estate property tax calculation.
Prorating real estate property taxes is a common element in nearly every real estate transaction. The date basis for the calculation will depend on

- The number of times taxes are assessed per year

- The due date of each tax billing cycle

- The status of the payments of the taxes

- The period each payment covers

In some parts of the country, it is customary for property owners to receive and pay two sets of real estate taxes per year.

Regardless of the number of times payments are required, the method of prorating the tax payments will be the same. The only change that will occur will be that the final tax figures will be based on two separate sets of calculations.

To prorate taxes, you must first determine the due date of each tax payment.

- We will assume that the tax-billing period is due April 1.

You will next determine the period this billing covers.

- We will assume that the tax-billing due on April 1 is for the period of January 1 through December 31.

The status of the payment dictates whether the seller receives a tax payment reimbursement from the buyer or if the seller is required to remit tax funds for the payment of the tax billing at the time of closing.

- We will assume the tax payment was made as required by the seller on or before the due date.

Using a closing date of May 20 and the assumptions, you would perform the calculations to determine the monthly and daily tax rate by taking the total of the yearly taxes. In our example the

➢ Yearly Taxes total $585.00. You will divide this total figure by 12 months to determine the monthly tax costs of the property. In our example that total is $48.75 per month

$585.00 / 12 = $48.75 per month

➢ We have determined that the Monthly Taxes equal $48.75. Since we are using a 30-day month, we will divide the monthly figure by 30 to determine that the daily tax rate equals $1.625.

$ 48.75 / 30 = $ 1.625 daily rate

➢ The Seller Portion of the taxes covers the period of January 1 though May 20.

You will take the $48.75 monthly figure and multiply it by the four months allocated to the seller to total $195.00.

$48.75 x 4 = $195.00

You will then take the $1.625 daily figure and multiply it by the 20 extra days allocated to the seller to total $32.50.

$ 1.625 x 20 = $ 32.50

You will add the total of the monthly calculations and the daily calculations to determine that the total taxes assessed to the seller equals $227.50.

$195.00   +   32.50   = $227.50

➢   This example leaves the buyer's portion of the taxes to cover the period of May 21 through December 31.

You have the baseline figures for both the monthly and daily tax rate from your seller allocation calculations.

You will use again use the $48.75 monthly figure but this time you multiply it by the 7 months allocated to the buyer. The monthly total allocated to the buyer equals $341.25.

$48.75   x   7   = $341.25

You will then take the daily figure of 1.625 and multiply it by the 10 days remaining in the month. 10 days plus the 20 days already accounted for on the sellers side equals the 30-day month. This calculation example has the buyer paying $16.25 to cover the daily allocation of the taxes.

$ 1.625   x   10   = $ 16.25

You will then add the $341.25 monthly figure to the $16.25 daily figure to determine that the total taxes assessed to the buyer equals $357.50.

$341.25   + $16.25 = $357.50

➢   You may confirm that your calculations are correct by adding the buyer portion and the seller portion and then comparing it to the total taxes due on the property.

If the tax payments are due twice yearly, you will calculate the second payment in the same manner and add both figures to achieve a total allocation of the taxes.

The figures will be entered as either a positive or a negative on the good faith estimate depending on the status of the payment.

➢   In other words, payment for the taxes due has been made by the seller, the borrower will repay the seller for their portion at the settlement table.

➢   If taxes due have not been paid by the seller, the sellers tax portion will be given back to the borrower as part of the settlement process.

This figure can be entered as a positive figure on the good faith estimate.

The ability to enter a positive in this column may make a difference to the ability to close the transaction if the borrower is extremely cash poor.

HAZARD INSURANCE

Hazard insurance is typically paid in advance based on the billing received from the hazard insurance company providing the coverage. At the beginning of each year of the policy, the premium for that year's coverage must be paid. At times, a billing cycle such as monthly or quarterly payment may be negotiated with the insurance company. When real estate is sold, the borrower may ask the seller to transfer the current insurance coverage or may obtain new coverage through the insurance company of their choice. If the existing coverage is transferred, the premiums required to maintain coverage will be allocated to the borrower and seller respectively based upon the date of the closing or other date as negotiated in the sales contract.

You will need to obtain information pertaining to the insurance coverage to begin the process of prorating the premiums. This might include

- The frequency of payment for the policy

- The total premium of the policy

- The exact term covered by the policy premium

    Example: A payment is made one time of year.

                  The total premium is $660 per coverage period.

                  The coverage period extends from November 1 to October 31.

                  The sales contract negotiates that:

    - the borrower will assume the sellers insurance policy from the date of closing

    - closing is held on May 1

    Both the buyer and the seller will be responsible for 50% of the total premium.

    The seller has paid the premium in full in advance

    The buyer owes the seller exactly $330 for the insurance coverage

Closings dates typically do not occur on a neat, evenly divided basis. Therefore, the pro-rata calculations will often require more in-depth calculations than those described in the example. It is typically necessary to divide the premium coverage year into months and then divide the months into days to complete the calculations.

Using the previous example, suppose the closing occurred on April 30 instead of May 1. This would give the buyer 6 months and 1 day of coverage.

The first step in calculating the exact figure the borrower owes the seller is to divide the total premium into 12 monthly premium figures.

$660 premium   /   by 12 months   = $55.00 per month

The next step is to divide the monthly premium into a daily cost basis.

$55.00 monthly figure /   30 days in a month   = $1.8333 per day

Next, you will multiply the monthly rate by the term the buyer will obtain

6 months   x $55.00 monthly figure = $330.00

Then, you will multiply the daily rate by the daily term the buyer will obtain

1 day   x   the daily figure $1.8333 = $ 1.83

The Total buyer premium is $331.83

All of the figures will be rounded up or down to the nearest 1 cent.

Truth-In-Lending Act Regulation Z

The Truth-in-Lending act is a part of the Consumer Credit Protection Act. The Truth-in-Lending act is meant to protect and inform the consumer by requiring disclosures regarding loan terms and costs. This regulation applies to all institutions offering credit to a consumer.

- The Truth-in-Lending act allows the borrower to compare the cost of a cash transaction against the costs of a credit transaction.

- The Truth-in-Lending act also provides an easy to understand format for borrowers when comparing one lending institutions terms against those of another lending institution.

The regulations require lenders to

- Disclose the maximum, potential interest rate for all variable rate transactions.

- Limit home equity plans that incorporate the costs of financing into the principal balance of the loan.

- Adhere to disclosure standards for advertisements that refer to credit terms.

- Provide borrowers with fair rights of rescission.

You should provide your borrower with specific disclosures to comply with Regulation Z. These include

- Arm Loan disclosure

- Right of rescission notice

- Advertising practice disclosures

The Truth-in-Lending act also requires that lenders make certain disclosures concerning the Real Estate Settlement and Procedures Act. These disclosures must be provided with in three days of an application for credit. The initial disclosures will be partially based upon information provided by the borrower. A final series of disclosures will be provided at the time of settlement. These final disclosures will contain the confirmed and final information regarding the loan and loan terms.

DEFINITION OF TRUTH-IN-LENDING TERMS

ANNUAL PERCENTAGE RATE
The Annual Percentage Rate is not the Note rate or the quoted interest rate for which the borrower applied. The Annual Percentage Rate is the cost of the loan in percentage terms.

The Annual Percentage Rate takes into account a variety of loan charges; interest is only one of these charges. Other charges that are used in the calculation of the Annual Percentage Rate are private mortgage insurance costs (when applicable) and any Prepaid Finance Charges including loan discount, origination fees, prepaid interest and any other credit costs added to the loan package.

The Annual Percentage Rate is calculated by spreading the cost of these charges over the life of the loan. Adding these charges results in a higher rate than the interest rate quoted to the borrower. If interest were the only Finance Charge, the interest rate and the Annual Percentage Rate would be the same. When creating the Good Faith Estimate, it is important to consider charges that will affect the Annual Percentage Rate.

PREPAID FINANCE CHARGES

Prepaid Finance Charges are charges made in connection with the loan that must be paid at the closing of the loan. The Federal Reserve Board Regulation Z defines these charges. The borrower must pay these charges. Some examples of the charges are Origination Fee, Discount Fee, PMI, and Tax Service Fee. Some loan charges such as appraisal fees and credit report fees are excluded from the Prepaid Finance Charges.

FINANCE CHARGE

The **Finance Charge** is the amount of interest, prepaid finance charges and certain insurance premiums that the borrower is expected to pay over the life of the loan.

AMOUNT FINANCED

The **Amount Financed** is the loan amount the borrower is obtaining less any prepaid finance charges. The Prepaid Finance Charges are found on the Good Faith Estimate.

For example, if the borrowers note is for $100,000 and the prepaid finance charges are $5,000 then the amount financed is equal to $95,000.

The Amount Financed is the amount on which the Annual Percentage Rate is based.

TOTAL OF PAYMENTS

The **Total of Payments** figure represents the total of all of the payments that will be made toward principal, interest and mortgage insurance over the life of the loan.

PAYMENT SCHEDULE

The figure represented in the **Payment Schedule** includes principal, interest, plus private mortgage insurance payments that will be made over the life of the loan. These figures do not reflect taxes and insurance escrows or any buy down payments that were contributed by the seller.

2:23 TIL Definitions

Adjustable Rate Mortgage Disclosure

If a borrower's primary dwelling is going to be secured by an Adjustable Rate or Variable Rate loan, the Truth-in-Lending act requires that additional disclosures be provided to the borrower with regard to the Adjustable Rate Mortgage.

An adjustable rate mortgage is a mortgage program that carries a variable interest rate that can change over the life of the loan. The interest rate applied to an adjustable rate mortgage may go up or down depending on the status of the index to which it is linked.

Adjustable-rate mortgage programs are created with a pre-set margin. The margin base is set on a major mortgage index such as the Libor. An adjustable rate mortgage program has the ability to affect the borrower's monthly payments through the application of the new interest rate occurring at each adjustment period. This adjusted rate could place some borrowers at risk if economic conditions dictate that the rate goes up and the borrower's debt to income ratio is unable to bear the payment applied because of the increased interest rate.

When working with a borrower that is obtaining an adjustable rate mortgage, you must provide the borrower with educational notices and disclosures that assist them in understanding the loan program that they are obtaining.

- The Consumer Handbook on Adjustable Rate Mortgages

- A disclosure for each variable rate program offered to the borrower.

The disclosures must contain all the necessary information required by Regulation Z.

The Truth-in-Lending Act also requires loan services to provide disclosures to consumers each month an adjustment to the interest rate occurs.

ADJUSTABLE RATE MORTGAGE DISCLOSURE STATEMENT

IMPORTANT MORTGAGE LOAN INFORMATION - PLEASE READ CAREFULLY

PROGRAM NAME: _____

You have expressed an interest in applying for an Adjustable Rate Mortgage loan (ARM). This disclosure contains information regarding the differences between this ARM and other mortgage loans. This disclosure describes the features of the specific ARM that you are considering. Upon request, we will provide you with information about any other Adjustable Rate Mortgage programs we have available.

ADJUSTABLE RATE MORTGAGE LOAN: This loan is an Adjustable Rate Mortgage loan. The interest rate may change based upon movements of a specific interest rate index. Changes in the interest rate will be reflected by increases or decreases for payments. The date or dates on which changes can occur will be specified in the ARM loan documents. This ARM is based on the terms and conditions of the program in which you have expressed an interest. We have based this disclosure on recent interest rates, index and margin values, and fees.

THIS DISCLOSURE: This disclosure is not a contract or loan commitment. The matters discussed in this disclosure are subject to change by us at any time without notice. DETERMINING THE INTEREST RATE: Your interest rate will be determined by means of an index that is subject to change.

Your interest rate is based on the Index value plus a margin. A change in the index generally will result in a change in the interest rate. If the Index rate change since the previous adjustment is less than _____, the interest rate will not change. The amount that your interest rate change may also be affected by periodic interest rate change limitations and the lifetime interest rate limits set forth in your loan program.

Interest Rate Adjustments Your interest rate under this ARM can change every _____ years.

Your interest rate cannot increase or decrease more than ____ percentage points at each adjustment.

Your interest rate cannot increase or decrease more than ____ percentage points over the term of your loan.

Rate adjustments under this ARM will be reflected in higher or lower payments.

DETERMINING THE PAYMENTS: Your initial monthly payment of principal and interest will be determined based on the interest rate, loan term, and loan balance when your loan is closed. Your payment will be set to amortize the loan over a period of ____ payments.

Frequency of Payment Changes: Based on increases or decreases in the Index, payment amounts under this ARM loan can change every _____ years. Your monthly payment amount could change more frequently if there is a change in other loan factors not relating to the ARM. These factors may include taxes, assessments, insurance premiums, or other charges required when creating an escrow or impound account.

Limitations on Payment Changes: Your payment can change every ___ years based on changes in the interest rate, loan term, or loan balance.

Adjustment Notices: You will be notified if interest rate changes occur. If an interest rate change effects your monthly payment, you will be notified at least 25 calendar days before the changed payment is due. The notice will indicate the adjusted payment amount, interest rate, Index value, and the outstanding loan balance at that time.

** INSERT AN EXAMPLE AND INDEX TABLES AS THEY APPLY TO THE ARM UNDER DISCUSSION.

I/we acknowledge that we have received a copy of this disclosure:

Borrower Signature   Date   Co-Borrower Signature   Date

2:24 Sample Form –ARM Disclosure – HUD Release

Homeownership Equity Protection Act (HOEPA)

The Homeownership Equity Protection Act of 1994 is designed to protect the borrower against unfair and abusive lending tactics. This act was created as an amendment to the Truth-in- Lending Act Regulation Z.
The Homeownership Equity Protection Act establishes requirements regarding interest rates and fees. The loans covered under the Homeownership Equity Protection Act include

- First mortgage transactions where the Annual Percentage Rate exceeds 8% of the current prime rate as established by the Treasury securities of comparable maturity

- Second mortgage transactions in which the Annual Percentage Rate exceeds 10% of the current prime rate as established by the Treasury securities index of comparable maturity.

- Loans where the total fees and points paid by the borrower exceed 8% of the total loan amount or the fixed figure established yearly. The greater of the two costs is used to establish the requirements.

The loans affected by this act are generally termed high-rate or high-fee loans. This type of loan is seen more frequently within the sub-prime industry than the prime industry.

The Act does not include provisions regarding construction loans, reverse mortgage transactions, or equity lines of credit.

You must provide specific disclosures to the borrower regarding the loan terms and fees:

- Right to cancel

- Specific information regarding Annual Percentage Rate, monthly payment amounts, and the loan amount

- Variable rate or Adjustable rate mortgages require an additional disclosure that states the monthly payment and the interest rate are subject to change. The disclosure must state the maximum amount of change that may occur.

Homeowners Protection Act of 1998

In 1998, additional homeowner protection regulations were put into place. These regulations are designed to assist the borrower in understanding and minimizing the private mortgage insurance costs accrued.

Private mortgage insurance is used to allow more individuals to purchase homes with a minimal amount of cash down payment. Private mortgage insurance is required by most lenders until the borrower obtains an equity position in the home of greater than 20%.

> Private mortgage insurance benefits the borrower in that the placement of the insurance enables the borrower to obtain home financing without a large cash down payment.

> Private mortgage insurance requirements can be removed if the borrower is able to pay 20% of the sales price in down payment.

Since some borrowers are unable to provide 20% of the sales price in cash at the time of closing, purchasing the Private mortgage insurance policy enables the lender to provide financing while minimizing risk.

Once a borrower reaches an equity position of 20% of the property value Private mortgage insurance, premiums are no longer needed to protect the position of the lender. At this point borrowers are no longer required to continue making yearly premium payments. Processes have been put into place to enable the borrower to cancel the Private mortgage insurance policy when the required equity position in the property has been reached.

Borrower Initiated Cancellation

The Homeowner Protection Act of 1998 provides remedies for the cancellation of the Private Mortgage Insurance coverage and an end to the yearly premium payments. A homeowner who has a 20% equity position in the property and a good payment history on their loan may request that their Private mortgage insurance be cancelled.

A borrower may initiate a cancellation request if:

- The loan has reached an 80% LTV based upon the initial amortization schedule provided to the borrower. Adjustable rate mortgages are based on Adjustable Amortization Schedules.

- The borrower has a good payment history.

  A good payment history dictates that No mortgage payments were made more than 60 days late with in the preceding 24-month period.

  The borrower must be able to illustrate that no mortgage payments were made more than 30 days late within the proceeding 12-month period

- The mortgage holder must approve the valuation of the property through verified methods such as the appraised value.

- The equity position must be free and clear.

  No subordinate liens may be held against the equity position of 20%.

Automatic Cancellation

The borrower is not required to take action to cancel the policy. Under the act, the policy will be subject to Automatic Cancellation when certain pre-set conditions have been met.

- The Homeowner Protection Act requires that the Private Mortgage Insurance be automatically cancelled when the borrower's equity position reaches 22%.

- When a mortgage, which is subject to Private Mortgage Insurance reaches a 78% Loan to value, based upon the initial amortization schedule, the Private Mortgage Insurance must be automatically terminated if the borrower is current on mortgage payment obligations.

- If the borrower is not current on mortgage payment obligations, the Private Mortgage Insurance must be terminated when the borrower brings their balance current.

High-Risk Mortgages

Certain high-risk mortgages may be subject to an alteration in the rules of cancellation for private mortgage insurance policies.

The Homeowner Protection Act bases the determination of a high-risk loan on the guidelines defined by Fannie Mae and Freddie Mac. The Private Mortgage Insurance payments on a high-risk loan are automatically terminated when the loan reaches a 77% loan to value or the term reaches half-life. The cancellation is based upon whichever level occurs first.

PMI Disclosure Requirements

Loans that carry Private Mortgage Insurance have additional disclosure requirements.

If you conduct a transaction that is subject to Private Mortgage Insurance, you must provide certain specific disclosures to the borrower in relationship to the transaction.

- A written initial amortization schedule based on loan terms at the time of the loan.

- The date the borrower may cancel based on the Initial Amortization Schedule only.

- Notice that the borrower may request cancellation in accordance with the requirements set forth in the borrower cancellation portion of the Act.

- Notice that Automatic Cancellation will occur at the termination date as defined by the Initial Amortization Schedule.

- Notice concerning exemptions to the cancellation pertaining to High-Risk loans

---

PRIVATE MORTGAGE INSURANCE INITIAL DISCLOSURE

Borrower:_____ Co-Borrower:_____

Property Address:_____

PRIVATE MORTGAGE INSURANCE TERMINATION DISCLOSURE

We SAMPLE MORTGAGE COMPANY require that you BORROWER NAME maintain private mortgage insurance ("PMI") in connection with your mortgage loan. PMI protects lenders and others against financial loss in case of borrower default. Federal law provides you with the right to cancel PMI under certain circumstances. Federal law establishes when PMI must be terminated. This Disclosure describes those cancellation and termination rights.

____1. We have provided you with an initial amortization schedule. Federal Law basis the cancellation and termination terms on this initial amortization schedule.

____2. Borrower Initiated Cancellation: A borrower may initiate cancellation if certain requirements are satisfied.

Term Requirements of Cancellation:

You have the right to request cancellation of PMI at any time on or after:

The date that the principal balance of the loan, based on the initial amortization schedule, reaches 80% of the original value (lesser of sales price or appraised value) of the property securing the loan.

The date that the principal balance of the loan, based on actual payments made, reaches 80% of the original value (lesser of the sales price or appraised value) of the property securing the loan.

Status Requirements for Cancellation:

PMI may be cancelled when you reach the stated percentage if you meet all of the following requirements:

You must submit your cancellation request in writing to the servicer of your loan.

You must have a good payment history on your loan.

A good payment history is described as a history where you have not made a mortgage payment that was 60 days or longer past due during the 24 months preceding the cancellation date.

The description of a good payment history also requires you have not made a mortgage payment that was 30 days or longer past due during the 12 months proceeding the cancellation date.

You must have provided the note holder with

Evidence that the value of the property securing the not has not declined below its original value

Certification that you do not have a subordinate lien on the equity in the property

___3. Automatic Termination: If mortgage loan payments are current, PMI will automatically terminate when the principal balance of the loan is scheduled to reach 78% of the original value (lesser of sales price or appraised value) of the property based on the initial amortization schedule.

The loan servicer will notify you when the automatic cancellation of PMI occurs.

___4. Exemptions

There are certain exemptions to the right to cancellation and automatic termination of PMI. These exemptions relate to certain mortgage loans with higher risks associated with the extension of credit. These exemptions do not apply to your loan transaction.

I/We have received a copy of this Private Mortgage Insurance Termination Disclosure.

Borrower Signature   Date   Co-Borrower Signature   Date

2:25 Sample Form – Private Mortgage Insurance Initial Disclosure – HUD Release

Flood Disaster Protection Act of 1973

Because of increased losses to homeowners from floods and mudslides, the Flood Disaster Protection Act implemented a National Flood Insurance Program that increased limits of insurance coverage and the amount of insurance outstanding in flood prone communities.

The need for a revision of the flood insurance system was created because of population growth and the need to establish community centers in areas of the country with a higher flood potential.

- The Act increased the limits of coverage under the National Flood Insurance Program.

- The Act provides for identification concerning flood prone areas.

- The Act requires State and Local communities to participate in flood insurance programs and to adopt flood plain ordinances.

- The Act requires the purchase of flood insurance by property owners who own or acquire land located in areas identified as having special flood hazards.

Each borrower must fully understand his rights and obligations under the Flood Disaster Protection Act.

NOTICE OF SPECIAL FLOOD HAZARDS
NOTICE OF AVAILABILITY OF FEDERAL DISASTER RELIEF ASSISTANCE

The property securing the loan for which you have applied is located in an area identified as having special flood hazards.

The area is identified by FEMA as a special flood hazard area using FEMA's Flood Insurance Rate Map or the Flood Hazard Boundary Map for the following community:

This area has at least a one- percent chance of a flood equal to or exceeding the base flood elevation or 100-year flood plain in any given year. During the live of a 30-year mortgage loan, the risk of a 100-year flood in a special, flood hazard area is twenty-six percent.

Federal law allows the lender and the borrower to request the Director of FEMA to review the determination of the location as a special, flood hazard area. If you would like to make such a request please contact our offices at

The community in which the property is located participates in the National Flood Insurance Program (NFIP). Federal law does not allow us to make the loan you have applied for if you do not purchase flood insurance. The flood insurance purchased must be maintained for the life of the loan. If you fail to purchase or renew the flood insurance on the property, Federal Law authorizes and requires us to purchase the flood insurance for you at your expense.

Flood insurance must cover the lesser of

The outstanding principal balance of the loan

The maximum amount of coverage allowed for this type of property under NFIP.

Federal disaster-relief assistance may be available for damages incurred in excess of your flood insurance coverage. TO qualify for Federal Disaster Relief, your community must participate in the NFIP in accordance with NFIP requirements.

Borrower(s) agree to furnish at the borrower(s) expense, a flood insurance policy that meets the lender's requirements on or before closing of the loan.

2:26 Sample Form – Notice of Special Flood Hazards – Notice of Availability of Federal Disaster Relief Assistance – HUD Release

CHAPTER 3

BORROWER PRE-QUALIFICATION

From the moment you first speak with a prospective borrower, you should be gathering information and planning how you will structure the loan. Many Loan Officers fail to achieve their goals for the simple reason that they are afraid to ask for information.

Information is your most valuable tool in planning a loan strategy. Obtaining information is quite simple if you just get over the natural shyness of asking strangers for personal information. You will find that, as a professional, people will answer almost any question you ask. However, you must ask!

On the next page, you will find a "Pre-approval Questionnaire" that we recommend using for each prospective borrower. Most of your initial contacts will be over the telephone. If you have this form handy, preferably bound in a notebook, you will always be able to lead the conversation exactly where you, as the loan officer, need it to go.

The pre-approval questionnaire is your most important ally. Most of the information required when pre-certifying a loan package is included in the questionnaire. In fact, much of the basic information that will be required for the residential mortgage application is included. This allows you to pre-fill some information, subject to verification during the application interview.

Pre-filling saves time and allows you and the borrower to focus on the loan process requirements.

Pre-Qualification Questionnaire Date: _____

Referral: _____ Phone: _____

Borrower Name: _____ Co-Borrower Name: _____

Home Phone: _____ Other Phone: _____ Best time(s) to call: _____

DOB: _____ SSN: _____ DOB: _____ SSN: _____

May I run a credit report?___ Yes ___ No   May I run a credit report? ___ Yes ___ No

Employer: _____ Employer: _____

Address: _____ Address: _____

Phone: _____ No yrs. ___ Position: _____ Phone: _____ No yrs. ___ Position: _____

Current Address: _____ Check? ___ Yes ___ No

Landlord/Mortgage Holder: _____ Phone: _____

Rent _____ Own ___ No. Yrs: ___ Have you chosen a home to purchase? ___ Yes ___ No Value$_____

___ 1st ___2nd ___Rate/Term Refi ___ C/O Refi ___ Special: _____

Gross Income		Debt	
Borrowers Mthly	$_____	Mortgage/Rental Payment	$_____
Prev Year	$_____	Auto Payment	$_____
Co-Borrowers Mthly	$_____	Auto Payment #2	$_____
Prev Year	$_____	Installment Debt / Type _____	$_____
Other Income _____	$_____	Installment Debt / Type _____	$_____
Other Income _____	$_____	Other _____	$_____
Total Income	$_____	Total Debt	$_____

DTI _____%

Explanation of Credit Situation/Notes: _____
_____
_____
_____

Outcome:

Taken By: _____
L/O: _____

Pre- qualification Questionnaire Key

Date
You will always want to date the query.

You may need to 'shelve' a query until an issue has seasoned.

It is our recommendation that you bind each month's questionnaires in a master folder for tracking of referral sources, inquiries vs. applications and other numbers that will affect your career.

You will want to keep a copy of any query that does not lead to a full application for follow-up marketing.

Referral
You will want to have referral information available so you may provide follow-up information.

Tracking referral source information will allow you to assess your branches marketing and advertising effort effectiveness.

Telephone Number
You will want to have the referral partner's telephone number handy to assist you in maintaining communication.

Look these up yourself, DO **NOT** require your borrower to find the number for you.

Keeping referral partners informed of the progress of a package is one of your greatest assets.

These updates provide a fabulous reason for a face-to-face 'call' on a referral partner and their office.

Referral partners appreciate frequent updates. Referral partners are reluctant to work with a loan officer who does not consistently provide status information concerning the status of a borrower's application.

Borrower Name
You will need the full name including middle initial and any additional information Jr., Sr., II

Do not use nicknames.

Note any aliases that the borrower commonly uses.

Names, especially among family, can be very similar.

The more identifying information you can acquire the more pure your credit report will be.

Co-Borrower Name	Some applications will not have a co-borrower.

When a co-borrower exists, it is important to acquire correct identifying information for this person to ensure sufficient pre-qualification data is available.

If the co-borrower information is not readily available at the time of the call, complete the primary borrower information and request the applicant telephone you later the same day with the co-borrower information.

Date of Birth/Social Security Number etc This information is important for the loan application and vital when you are pulling a credit report.

Always pull credit reports separately.

Even if the borrower and co-borrower are married, you will want to have separate reports.

There are times you will want to drop one borrower in an effort to improve loan grades.

May I run a credit report? It is imperative that you obtain permission to pull a borrower's credit report.

You will have the borrower sign the credit consent forms later in the loan process.

Consent must be available before you may run the report.

You may not run a credit report on any individual without their consent.

Employer This information aids you in determining some of the issues that may arise during the course of the loan.

If there is a history of job changes or there is not a 2-year employment history a problem may exist during documentation. Issues such as these are red flags.

Number of years at present employment You are looking for a minimum of two years employment history.

If the borrower/co-borrower has not been in their current employment two years, you will need to trace back under comments until you acquire a complete two-year history.

This is an excellent reference when you have an application that requires an exception. A common compensating factor is 'at current employment more than 5 years'.

Current Address	This is identifying information you will want to have to clarify identity on the credit report.
Do you rent or own?	This allows you to determine potential source of funds, loan product possibilities and additional documentation that you may require from the borrower.
Landlord/Mortgage Holder	It is important to determine from the start if the borrower pays an entity or an individual for their housing expense.

You can verify payments to an entity via VOR/VOM but an individual will typically require checks for verification of payment history.

Do you pay by check? This question is important if the borrower or co-borrower rents or is purchasing from an individual.

If your borrower or co-borrower rents or is buying from an individual and does not pay by check, you will typically need to acquire alternate documentation as proof of rental/mortgage payment history.

Number of years at Present address? You will need a two-year residence history for each borrower on the application.

If the borrower has been at the current residence less than two years, you will need to add in comments any additional residence history until you obtain two full years.

This is an excellent reference when you have an application that requires an exception. A common compensating factor is 'at current residence more than 5 years'.

Have you chosen a home to purchase? You will want to determine the urgency of the query and if the borrower is currently working with an Agent.

KENNEY

If no Agent is working with the borrower, you will want to take the opportunity to refer the borrower to an affinity member with whom you would like to establish a referral relationship.

Perform all referrals after you have the borrower commitment to your programs. Since you do not have a referring relationship built with the referral partner, they may refer these borrowers to another lender if you do not obtain the commitment before sending the borrower to the partner.

Value   This question pertains to the package even if they have not chosen a home to purchase.

You will want to get an idea of their expectations and the price range they are considering.

You will use this figure to determine if the buyer's expectations are reasonable and fit into their DTI.

Often borrowers are very high or very low in their estimate of what they are able to afford.

You will want to pre-qualify the borrower for the highest amount they feel comfortably fits their budget.

Type of Loan: 1st Mortgage, 2nd Mortgage, Rate or Term Refinance, Cash-out Refinance.

Knowing the type of loan the borrower or co-borrower believes they desire, allows you to begin planning the loan structure and matrix placement from the moment of query.

You will find some product approvals vary greatly depending on the type of loan.

Income Information   In order to pre-qualify a package you must have complete income information.

Many loan denials occur due to excessive DTI Ratios.

All income should be entered even if the borrower does not wish to use all income as qualifying income or if not all the income can be used as qualifying income. This is an excellent reference when you have an application that requires an exception. Income is a part of many compensating factors.

Debt Information   Debt load will be visible on the Credit Report but it is important to ask a borrower this information. There may be new debt, which is not yet showing on the report but may crop up before closing the loan.

Child support and alimony payments do affect the debt load.

Explanation of credit situation?	This is the opportunity for notes.
	Your borrowers will usually explain any information that is present on their credit report.
	Gathering this information now allows you to pre-plan the loan package, request any additional documentation that you may need and is an excellent reference if problems appear later in the loan process.
Outcome	You will want to note what happened with the query.
	Some queries will lead to an application.
	You will file other queries for follow-up when an issue is resolved.
	Keeping a file of this information allows you to track your numbers in future months.
	Outcome is important if the borrower's are working with an agent.
	You will want immediate documentation if the package dies at query so your agent is not spending valuable time working with borrower's who you cannot qualify at this time.

Lending is a service business. The final analysis shows that our most important "product" is our professionalism, attentiveness, and responsiveness to our borrowers. Much of our communication is on the telephone.

Whether you are communicating with a borrower, prospect, or others on the telephone or in person, the impression that you convey creates an image in the person's mind. This image will affect your future relationship with that person. For those reasons, it is important that your conversations are controlled and concise. A complete course on telephone and conversational control is available in our advanced program offerings. For now, you must focus on learning career basics. To assist you we have provided a script to allow you to flow smoothly through the pre-qualification process.

The pre-approval questionnaire offers an excellent tool for structuring your first contact.

The proper way to use the questionnaire is as follows:

L/O:	Good morning/afternoon/evening, <u>Your Company Name</u> this is <u>YourName</u>, may I help you?
Borrower:	They will state the reason for there call and very likely explain their situation.
L/O:	Do you have a few minutes to answer a couple of questions?
Borrower:	Since they made the call to you, they will typically have a few minutes to spare while they determine if you have a program to fit their situation.
L/O:	Could you tell me how you were referred to us? (DO NOT ask for details such as telephone number of referral source – you can look this information up yourself).
L/O:	What is your name?
L/O:	Will you be on loan alone or with someone else? (Keep in mind that it is occasionally prudent to cut either the borrower or co-borrower from the loan later in the process. This is a decision will be made based on credit scores and/or income and debt ratios.
L/O:	What is your Date of Birth?
L/O:	What is your Social Security Number?
L/O:	May I run a credit report?
	You are looking for a yes. None of the other information you acquire will aid you in any way if you cannot see what type of credit situation you are dealing with. The approval to run a credit report signifies a commitment on the part of the borrower to your loan program.
L/O:	Where are you employed?
L/O:	How long have you been there?
	If they have been at their current employment less than two years, you will need to acquire two full years' employment history before completing the application.
L/O:	What is your position?
L/O:	Ask for the same information for the co-borrower.
L/O:	What is your current address?
L/O:	How long have you lived there?

L/O: Do you rent or own the home?

L/O: Who is your landlord or mortgage holder?

If the landlord or lender is a company there is no need for further documentation, it will typically appear on the credit report. However, if the landlord/mortgage holder is an individual, more documentation   will be required to prove a mortgage/rental history.

L/O: Do you pay by cash or check?

This question only applies in the event that their landlord/mortgage holder is an individual.

L/O: Have you chosen a home to purchase?

This will allow you to rate the urgency of the file. A borrower who has not begun the home search process will be less urgent than a borrower with a sales contract in hand.

L/O: Do you know the amount you are looking to spend?

This question allows you to determine from the start if their spending expectations are set too high for some of the loan products and place them accordingly.

L/O: What is your monthly income?

You will frequently need to do the math yourself. Accept the income they give you whether they provide yearly, monthly, or weekly income figures.

L/O: Do you have income you wish use from any other source: rental property, alimony, child support etc?

A borrower is not required to use additional income as part of the approval criteria. If the borrower wishes to use other income, it is allowable.

L/O: Obtain the same information for the co-borrower.

L/O: What is your monthly rent/mortgage payment?

L/O: What is your car payment?

L/O: Do you have a second car?

L/O: Do you have any credit cards or personal loans?

L/O: What are the monthly payments?

              A borrower's debt load will be visible on the credit report but it is advisable to review
              the debts with the borrower to limit surprises later in the process.

Throughout the questionnaire, the borrower will be giving you information that you will want to note
in the explanation of credit situation section. This aids you in determining the special circumstances
surrounding this loan package.

Upon completion of the questionnaire, you will want to assure the borrower that they ARE your
borrower and that you plan to pre-qualify their questionnaire later that same day. You should set an
appointment to meet face-to-face with the borrower to give you the opportunity to obtain the
necessary documentation, verify their information, and discuss their loan options. A sample of how to
do this smoothly is as follows:

L/O: Ok, I plan to pass this information over to _____. They will be working
              with us to during the early stages of your loan. We will review your information
              tonight to see what programs will work best for your situation. Are you available <u>date
              not more than two days away</u>?

Borrower: Answers positive or negative

L/O: Set up an appointment.

L/O: Ok, when you come I will need you to bring a few things. I will need (below are the
              most common items to request – you will need to refer to documenting a loan package
              for detailed information):

              ▪   W-2's from the last two years
              ▪   Proof of any additional income you want me to consider – child support order,
                   divorce decree
              ▪   Any proof you have concerning (whatever their special credit situation BK,
                   Divorce Decree, etc.)
              ▪   12 months cancelled rent checks (if paying an individual)

L/O: Ok then, I will see you on <u>date</u> at <u>time</u> if there are any problems, please give me a call.

Upon completion of the questionnaire, you will be able to pre-qualify the borrower. Providing you
have obtained their permission, your next step is to pull a credit report and begin the process of
determining the initial purchase levels and possible loan programs available for the borrower.

CHAPTER

4

READING THE CREDIT REPORT

Every action that a consumer takes affects their credit report. These actions can have a negative or a positive effect.

Credit reports are an overview of a person's entire history of spending and payment habits. Almost everything that a person does financially is collected, reported, and stored in the credit profile. The primary concern of during the mortgage process is any action that had a negative or derogatory impact on a borrower's credit history.

Debt   is the term describing any situation in which funds are borrowed under an agreement to make repayment.

Debt Load   is the amount of debt an individual is carrying or the amount that the individual owes to another.

Debt load may include many items. The most common being:

- Credit card debt

- Department store debt

- Charge accounts

- Auto loans

- Student loans

- Mortgages

The ability to borrow more money or to have additional credit extended is affected by how much debt a potential borrower currently carries.

You will be concerned with the debt-to-income ratio of the borrower.

Debt-to-Income Ratio's   are the amount of open debt a borrower has available weighed against the borrower's monthly income.

The higher the DTI the greater the potential risk of a borrower default on the loan.

The credit report will provide a relatively accurate view of the borrowers current debt load. You must document the borrower's income in order to have the information necessary to calculate the debt-to-income ratio.

Late payments: Any payments that have been paid more than 30-days past the due date are considered to be late payments.

Late payments can be a severe blemish on the credit report.

You will need to rate late payments based on how late the payment was made and the frequency with which the late payments occurred.

- Prime lenders are typically reviewing the previous two-year payment history.

- Sub-prime matrixes will typically assess the preceding 12-month payment history.

A late payment will appear on the credit report for two years, though credit bureaus may keep them in the credit file for up to seven years.

Bankruptcy   actions can remain on the credit report for as long as 10 years.

A bankruptcy is a significant factor the must be considered when choosing a loan program for a borrower.

A borrower in the prime market may have to wait up to four years to attempt to qualify for some prime loans after completing a bankruptcy process. The borrower must re-establish a credit history during that time. This re-establishment of credit will aid in showing that the borrower is no longer a credit risk.

The sub-prime market is more lenient as to time that must elapse after a bankruptcy. The sub-prime market is also more lenient concerning the amount credit the borrower must establish before seeking mortgage financing. The sub-prime market gains their security in the borrower through higher interest rates and fees.

Collection accounts are accounts that a borrower has failed to pay as agreed.

These accounts are turned over to a collection department within the structure of the original creditor, a collection agency, or another service in the attempt to collect the payments owed. The initial creditor and the collection agencies report these accounts to the bureaus.

At times, you may find collection accounts, or other accounts, entered more than one time on a borrower's credit profile. You should remit a credit supplement request to the credit bureau asking that these duplicate entries be condensed to reflect that the entries all refer to one account. This may assist in raising the credit score of the borrower and helps to minimize issues during underwriting.

If your borrower has paid these debts in full, have them obtain a letter from the creditor stating that the debt has been satisfied and no further action on their part is necessary.

Loan program guidelines handle collection accounts differently. Some will allow a certain dollar amount of collections to remain open while others will require all of the collection accounts to be paid in full before the loan can close. Some underwriting guidelines will handle medical collection accounts differently than other accounts.

You will want to consider the type and amount of collections that your borrower has open and place the loan with the program that has the most beneficial guidelines for your borrower's profile.

Medical collections are accounts owed to medical service providers that the borrower has failed to pay.

Medical Collection Accounts are often treated differently than other collection accounts.

You will need to consider the type of collection accounts in the profile and review the underwriting guidelines to determine how to handle each type of account.

Credit inquiries are accesses to a borrower's credit profile.

These inquiries are visible on the credit report.

Underwriter training teaches them to note if a borrower appears to be on a credit-gathering spree.

- A credit-gathering spree means that the borrower is out to expand their credit quickly for a specific purchase.

A series of inquiries could also indicate that new credit obligations are present but not visible on the report.

If you can illustrate that a number of recent inquiries on the credit report pertain to the search for a home mortgage, the underwriting team will consider that information.

Credit Bureau Scores are the scores generated based solely on the data contained within the credit report. A Fair, Isaac Credit Bureau Score, is sometimes referred to as a FICO score. The FICO Score is calculated using a system of scorecards.

Credit Bureau Scores are one of the many elements that are reshaping today's mortgage industry.

Credit scoring has been around since the 1950's and Credit Bureau Scores became widely available in the 1980's.

Credit Scores are now used extensively in such industries as mortgage lending, auto lending, and bankcards.

A Credit Bureau Score is a scientific way of assessing how likely a borrower is to pay back a loan.

Score Range: The approximate range of the Fair, Isaac Credit Bureau Scores range is between 450 to 850 points.

Repositories: Credit scores are available through three national repositories.

The scoring programs of these credit bureaus are called:

BEACON	at EQUIFAX (CBI)
EMPIRICA	at TRANS UNION
TRW/FAIR, ISAAC	at TRW

The credit score is calculated at the repository and is based on the data within that repositories credit file.

How is the CBS Calculated? A Credit Bureau Score is based on the data available with in the borrower's credit report.

The score measures the relative degree of risk a potential borrower represents to the lender or investor.

A credit bureau score is not a measure of a borrower's income, assets, or bank account.

- These factors are taken into consideration by lenders and investors independent of credit scores.

In developing the credit scorecards, Fair, Isaac uses actual credit data from millions of consumers. They apply complex mathematical methods and perform extensive research into credit patterns that enable them to forecast credit performance.

Through this process, the repository identifies distinctive credit patterns. Each pattern corresponds to a likelihood that a consumer will make his or her loan payments as agreed.

This score is based on all of the credit-related data in the credit bureau report, not just negative data such as a missed mortgage payment or a bankruptcy.

The score will consider the amount of credit a borrower has available, the amount of credit the borrower is using compared to these limits, the types of credit a borrower has available, and the borrowers payment performance on their credit obligations among other factors.

Score Data: The types of credit information used in the credit bureau scorecards are typically the same items that the underwriter will use to make a credit decision. These can include

Payment history

Public records and Collection Items

Severity, recentness, and frequency of delinquencies noted in the trade line section

Outstanding Debt

Number of balances recently reported

Average balance across all trade lines

Relationship between total balances and total credit limits on revolving trade lines

Credit History

Age of oldest trade line

Inquiries and new account openings

Number of inquiries in the last year

Number of new accounts opened in the last year

Amount of time since the most recent inquiry

Types of credit in use

Number of trade lines for each type pf credit

> Bankcard
> Travel and Entertainment cards
> Department Store cards
> Personal Finance Company references
> Installment Loans
> Other credit

Fair, Isaac observes tens of thousands of credit report histories to determine which credit report items or combination of items are the most predictive of future risk. This data indicates the amount of weight each item should contribute to a credit decision.

THE FAIR ISAAC CREDIT BUREAU SCORES DO NOT USE RACE, COLOR, RELIGION, NATIONAL ORIGIN, SEX, MARITAL STATUS, OR AGE AS PREDICTIVE CHARACTERISTICS.

OCCUPATION AND LENGTH OF TIME IN PRESENT HOUSING ARE NOT USED IN THE SCORECARDS.

ANY INFORMATION THAT IS NOT PRESENT IN THE CREDIT FILE IS NOT USED IN CREATING A CREDIT BUREAU SCORECARD.

Understanding a score's impact

The credit report will contain one or multiple credit scores followed by a series of score factor reason codes. This numerical score is often termed a fair isaac credit bureau score and it is a means of rank ordering potential borrowers based on the likelihood that they will pay their credit obligations as agreed.

A higher score indicates a better credit quality. If all other things in the borrower profile were equal, a borrower with a credit score of 642 is more likely to pay their debts as agreed than a borrower with a score of 537.

The Fair Isaac Credit Bureau Score models at each credit repository are of similar design. The scores are scaled to indicate a similar level of risk across all three repositories. In other words, a score of 660 at one bureau will represent a similar level of risk as a score of 660 at another bureau.

The risk denoted by the credit score is defined as the number of accounts remaining in good standing compared to those accounts that contain derogatory data or that have gone into default.

Sample credit score ranges for new mortgage borrowers from a national sample	
Score Range	Number of good loans for each bad loan showing delinquency or foreclosure (# of good to 1 bad)
Below 600	8 to 1
700 – 719	123 to 1
Above 800	1,292 to 1

Credit bureau scores will rank order potential borrowers based on risk or the number of good loans to bad loans denoted by the score. This rank order is likely to fluctuate depending on changes in the economy, regional differences, changes in credit guidelines and other reasons.

A lender who uses scores for rank order potential borrower is basing their guideline tiers of risk on historical data related to the files that they have processed and closed in the past. The levels or approval tier that the lender uses is likely to fluctuate over time due to changes in the economy. The lender will create approval tiers and loan product offerings by comparing the performance of their loans over time. This enables them to determine the relationship of borrower performance by market environment, credit score, and other details.

Report Appearance

Credit reports can take multiple visual forms depending on the bureau that issued the report and the type of record being requested. Regardless of the initial visual variations, all credit reports contain the same basic elements. These include borrower details and data, a summary of all of the credit inclusions, and a detailed breakdown of the borrower's current and historical credit transactions. Each section of the report will contain details that will assist you in determining if the potential borrower will qualify for one of your loan programs.

The upper portion of credit report will typically include identifying information including your name or company name as the individual, who requested the report.

Information relating to the individual within the credit bureau who pulled the report and the internal case ID # assigned to the report will be defined in the header of the report. This information will be important if you must request updates to the report or address a discrepancy in the report with the credit bureau.

Report type will usually be included in the header. Report type may be individual or joint.

MERGED INFILE CREDIT REPORT

Prepared For:	Property Address:	Prepared By:	Date Rec:
Attention:	Loan Type:	Computer ID:	Date Comp:
	Purpose of Loan:		
	Report Type:	Lender Case #:	Date Revised:

APPLICANT		CO-APPLICANT	
Name:		Name:	
SSN:	DOB:	SSN:	DOB:
Marital Status:	Dependents:	Marital Status:	Dependents:
:		:	
Home Phone:		Home Phone:	
Present Address:		Present Address:	
Since:	Own / Rent	Since:	Own / Rent
Previous Address:		Previous Address:	

Date data will be included within the report. Date data can include the date the request was received by the credit bureau, the date the credit bureau completed the report, and the date of any revisions created by the credit bureau in relationship to the report.

Date is important because underwriting typically stipulates that the report must be current, or within a certain date range, in order to be used for closing.

If the report is out of date, underwriting will request a new report in order to ensure that no changes have occurred in the borrower's credit profile during the processing stage of the loan. You should caution your borrower not to make any large purchases or take any action that may alter the contents of the report until after the loan has closed.

KENNEY

Borrower Information

The credit report will contain details relating to the individual or individuals to whom the credit report applies.

This portion includes specifics such as full name, social security number, and date of birth. Information relating to the borrowers address and employment may be included in this segment of the report. It is important that you remember that information you have gained directly from the borrower may be more up-to-date than information contained within the credit report.

Variations in borrower address and employment are common within the report. You should note any discrepancy between the report and your file information and verify with the potential borrower to ensure that the report does not contain entries that relate to another individual with a similar name. If you note a discrepancy, you must address these differences before the package is submitted to underwriting.

MERGED INFILE CREDIT REPORT			

Prepared For:	Property Address:	Prepared By:	Date Rec:
Attention:	Loan Type: Purpose of Loan: Report Type:	Computer ID: Lender Case #:	Date Comp: Date Revised:

APPLICANT | CO-APPLICANT

Name:
SSN: DOB:
Marital Status: Dependents::
Home Phone:

Present Address:

Since: Own / Rent

Previous Address:

Name:
SSN: DOB:
Marital Status: Dependents:
Home Phone:
Present Address:

Since: Own / Rent

Previous Address:

Borrower and Co-Borrower identifying information is entered in this section.

You should verify that all details entered match the information included on the loss mitigation summary.

Credit Summary

The credit report will contain a segment that summarizes the details contained within the actual report. You should review this area to ensure that the inclusions do not bring to mind a red flag issue. You may need to question the homeowner more closely regarding these matters.

CREDIT SUMMARY

	PAYMENTS	BALANCES	LIMITS	TRADES	30+	60+	90+
REVOLVING	0	2061	2200	4	4	4	17
INSTALLMENT 1307	1307	79365	90610	25	34	8	27
REAL ESTATE	378	35384	36600	1	2	0	0
OPEN/OTHER	991	1041	1041	5	0	0	0
TOTAL	2676	117851	129451	38	40	12	44

# INQUIRIES	50	# PUBLIC RECORDS	0	# BANKRUPTCIES	0
WORST TRADE	9	OLDEST DATE	07/01/89	# SATISFACTORIES	17

The summary will contain details identifying the types of credit that the borrower has available. You wish to ensure that the types and amount of credit available to the homeowner is exported into the DTI Analysis Form.

If you are using a system that does not automatically export report data into the Analysis Forms, you will need to enter each credit account, payment, and status by hand.

Credit payment totals and current balances will appear within the credit summary portion of your report.

You will confirm the payment information when you review the report inclusions.

Then you will use this information to confirm the debt ratio information and begin isolating potential loss mitigation options for the homeowner.

A summary data analysis of the details of the report will be included within the summary. This analysis will assist you in completing the scoring key. Much of the data you will use during credit scoring and mitigation screening will be summarized within this section. Before you export the data into the credit-scoring key, debt-to-income ratio form, or loss mitigation application, you must review the report with the homeowner to ensure that all of the inclusions of the summary are correct and relate to active accounts. You will confirm the status of each account by reviewing the detail pages of the credit report.

CREDIT SUMMARY

	PAYMENTS	BALANCES	LIMITS	TRADES	30+	60+	90+
REVOLVING	0	2061	2200	4	4	4	17
INSTALLMENT 1307	1307	79365	90610	25	34	8	27
REAL ESTATE	378	35384	36600	1	2	0	0
OPEN/OTHER	991	1041	1041	5	0	0	0
TOTAL	2676	117851	129451	38	40	12	44

# INQUIRIES 50	# PUBLIC RECORDS 0	# BANKRUPTCIES 0
WORST TRADE 9	OLDEST DATE 07/01/89	# SATISFACTORIES 17

The number of inquiries into credit profile will be totaled and entered into the summary.

A detailed breakdown of the companies that made credit inquiries will be included at the end of the report.

The homeowner may be required to provide an explanation for any excessive inquiries.

Credit inquiries may indicate that the homeowner has already attempted to remedy the delinquency through outside measures, such as a refinance.

You should review the data relating to these inquiries and discuss the results of any outside efforts the homeowner has made.

Specifics regarding public records, bankruptcy, and the worst trade payment history that you will encounter in the report will be included within the credit summary.

You should note these entries to ensure that you locate the applicable data within the report relating to any bankruptcy, late payment, or public record detailed within the summary.

Public records could relate to liens placed against the property not related to a mortgage or refinance. These liens could become a factor in loss mitigation negotiations where the surrender of the property is being considered.

If a judgment or public record exists in the borrower profile, the details of that record will be included within the report.

This data could include bankruptcy or foreclosure actions as well as judgments and other public records.

CREDIT SUMMARY

	PAYMENTS		BALANCES	LIMITS	TRADES	30+	60+	90+
REVOLVING	0		2061	2200	4	4	4	17
INSTALLMENT	1307	1307	79365	90610	25	34	8	27
REAL ESTATE	378		35384	36600	1	2	0	0
OPEN/OTHER	991		1041	1041	5	0	0	0
TOTAL	2676		117851	129451	38	40	12	44

# INQUIRIES	50	# PUBLIC RECORDS	0	# BANKRUPTCIES	0
WORST TRADE	9	OLDEST DATE	07/01/89	# SATISFACTORIES	17

The oldest date field indicates the date that the borrower fist obtained credit.

This inclusion allows you to ensure that an adequate credit history is available to the borrower. Many underwriting guidelines will require the potential borrower have at least a two-year credit history with at least three open active trade lines. If your potential borrower does not have a sufficient credit history or quantity of accounts, you may need to take alternative actions to aid the borrower in creating a credit profile that meets the minimum requirements of the loan guidelines.

It is important to address any issues early in the prequalification process. Proactively addressing issues early in the process helps to minimize stipulation requests, speeds the loan process, and facilitates positive relationships with borrowers, referral partners, and affinity service providers. This positive relationship building activity helps to ensure that your office gains the reputation as the office that can get the job done.

If a judgment or public record exists in the borrower profile, the details of that record will be included within the report.

This data could include bankruptcy or foreclosure actions as well as judgments and other public records.

You should scrutinize any inclusion within this section thoroughly to determine the status of the public record, the age of the public record, and the manner that the record will affect your borrower's approval status.

The type of public record will be named.

This typing will indicate to you the specific handling of the matter per the loss mitigation option that is being considered for the homeowner.

The report will include the dates pertaining to the specific public record.

The opened date will indicate the age of the judgment.

The last active date may affect the handling of the record depending upon the specific loss mitigation option being considered for the homeowner.

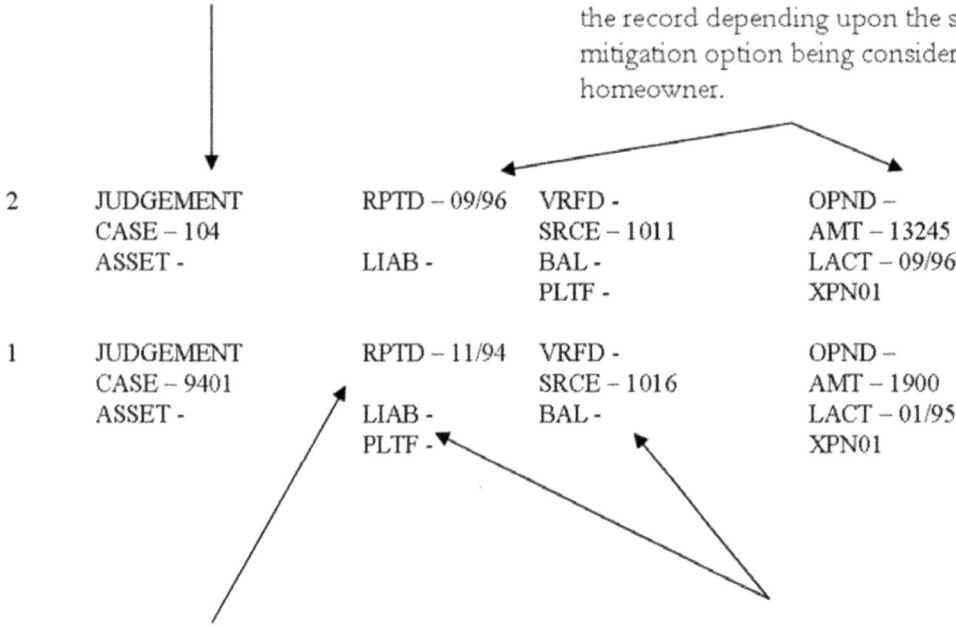

2	JUDGEMENT	RPTD – 09/96	VRFD -	OPND –
	CASE – 104		SRCE – 1011	AMT – 13245
	ASSET -	LIAB -	BAL -	LACT – 09/96
			PLTF -	XPN01

1	JUDGEMENT	RPTD – 11/94	VRFD -	OPND –
	CASE – 9401		SRCE – 1016	AMT – 1900
	ASSET -	LIAB -	BAL -	LACT – 01/95
		PLTF -		XPN01

Data regarding the status of the record will be included.

A satisfied judgment or closed bankruptcy will affect your file differently than an open or active record.

The liability or balance of the record will be included.

You will want to verify these figures and compare them to the specific
Underwriting Guidelines of the chosen loan program.

Underwriting guidelines will vary regarding the age requirements of a public record.

Score Factors

The name of the repository issuing the credit score included with the report will be included.

The lender negotiating the loss mitigation workout will designate the repository score that will be used for the process.

This designation is a result of regional

The code of the applicable agency will be entered to confirm the source of the score.

EFX = Equifax

8   BEACON SCORE   EFX01
519
SERIOUS DELINQUENCY AND DEROGATORY PUBLIC RECORD OR COLLECTION FILED
AMOUNT OWED ON DELINQUENT ACCOUNTS
PROPORTION OF BALANCES TO CREDIT LIMITS TOO HIGH ON REVOLVING ACCOUNTS
LENGTH OF TIME ACCOUNTS HAVE BEEN ESTABLISHED

8   EMPIRICA SCORE   TRU01
493
SERIOUS DELINQUENCY, AND PUBLIC RECORD OR COLLECTION FILED
LEVEL OF DELINQUENCY ON ACCOUNTS
TIME SINCE DELINQUENCY IS TOO RECENT OR UNKNOWN
PROPORTION OF REVOLVING BALANCES TO REVOLVING CREDIT LIMITS IS TOO HIGH

8   FAIR ISAAC SCORE   XPN01
529
SERIOUS DELINQUENCY AND PUBLIC RECORD OR COLLECTION FILED
PROPORTION OF BALANCES TOO HIGH ON REVOLVING ACCOUNTS
NUMBER OF ACCOUNTS DELINQUENT
LENGTH OF TIME SINCE LEGAL ITEM FILED OR COLLECTION ITEM REPORTED

The factors that affect the score will be included on the report. This information is often referred to by a score factor code.

KENNEY

Score Factors – Reason Codes

 To understand why a credit report scored the way it did, you must review the reason codes given within each score. These reason codes provide the top reasons why a profile did not score higher. These codes only indicate the top reasons and other factors probably contribute to the overall score. You should review both the score and the reasons the score ranks where it does with your customer.

To find the scores you should locate a number or a letter followed by a brief description.

For example, a score of 540 may have the following factors

- 02 – Delinquency on accounts

- 01 – Amount owed on accounts is too high

- 09 – Too many accounts opened in the last 12 months

- 19 – Too few accounts currently paid as agreed

Score factors are less meaningful for higher scoring credit records as they merely point to the reasons why a very good credit report was not perfect.

Examples of adverse factors that may appear on the report as a consideration in the score calculation are

- Current outstanding balances on accounts

- Delinquency report on accounts

- Accounts not paid as agreed

- Too few open accounts

- Too many open accounts

- Too many bank accounts with outstanding balances

- Too many finance company accounts

- Payment history too new to rate

- Number of inquiries within the last 12 months

- Number of accounts opened within the last 12 months

- Balance too high

- Length of credit history

- No recent account information

- Too few accounts rate as current

- Amount past due on accounts

- No adverse factors

- Recent derogatory public record or collection

This is not an all-inclusive listing. The items listed are examples of issues you may find in the score coding section of a report. You should review each report carefully to determine the factors specific to that credit profile.

FRAUD ALERT

The fraud alert field is becoming increasingly filled field within today's environment. Any data that indicates possible fraud activity will be included with in this section. The information will often become a warning entry because of some action taken by the borrower but any entry other than "*available and clear*" should be reviewed and discussed with the potential borrower.

Basic information noted by the credit bureau as potential fraud will be flagged.

If the entry is not related to an action taken by the borrower, the borrower may be a victim of identity theft and all entries in the body of the report should be scrutinized to ensure that all of the accounts do belong to the borrower.

An example of a fraud alert entry would be the number of inquiries in the last 60 days.

Excessive inquiries may be a result of the mortgage shopping process. In this case, there is little cause for concern as the alert is related to an action taken by your borrower. However, excessive inquiries could indicate access to the credit profile by another party who is seeking to open fraudulent accounts in your borrower's name.

FRAUD ALERT

| 1 | TRANS ALERT | TRU01 |

INQUIRIES IN LAST 60 DAYS: 04
RECORDED INQUIRIES ALTER

| 1 | HAWK ALERT | TRU 01 |

HAWK AVAILABLE AND CLEAR

Details regarding any activity that may indicate fraud will be included.

AVAILABLE AND CLEAR =   No information found

inquiries in the last 60 days =   potential credit gathering spree.

At times, this could indicate a stolen profile but more often, this insert is related to the search current loan search.

CREDIT HISTORY DETAILS

The main body of the report will contain details of each account contained within the borrower's credit history. You will wish to scrutinize each entry within this section to determine the status of the borrower's credit, gain an understanding of the borrower payment and spending habits, and complete the credit history-scoring key.

The credit history-scoring key will be explained later and is included within the appendix section of your workbook. This key will assist you in extracting the necessary details from the credit profile.

CREDIT HISTORY

E C O A	CREDITOR ACCOUNT NO	DATE RPTED	DATE LAST ACT	DATE OPND	LIMIT / HIGHEST CREDIT	PRESENT STATUS		TERMS	PAY AMT	TYPE AND ACCT STATUS	HISTORICAL STATUS			
						BALANCE OWING	AMOUNT PAST DUE				NO MOS HIIS T REV	3 0	60	9 0
8	AFM-BLOOM #APRINTLO COLLECTION	02/99	04/94		425	425				OPN05				

The name of the creditor and the account number will be included within the report.

Account numbers are often shortened on the credit report and the full account number may not appear. You can obtain the full account number directly from your borrower if it is a necessary element of the loan process.

For example, a refinance transaction may require certain bills to be paid in full as part of the transaction. You will need to obtain the full account number for each account to confirm the pay off amount and to ensure that all payments are allocated correctly at the closing.

CREDIT HISTORY

E C O A	CREDITOR ACCOUNT NO	DATE RPTED	DATE LAST ACT	DATE OPND	LIMIT / HIGHEST CREDIT	PRESENT STATUS							
						BALANCE OWING	AMOUNT PAST DUE						
8	AFM-BLOOM #APRINTLO COLLEC-TION	02/99	04/94		425	425							

The date reported is the last reporting date for a particular account.

Not all creditors report on a monthly basis.

You may be required to bring the data pertaining to a specific account up to date to comply with specific underwriting requirements and to ensure that no derogatory data exists for the last months of the account.

The date last active provides you with information relating to the last date the account was in use.

Some accounts will be closed and will not effect of the transaction.

You should review the last active date before including the account in your history score.

The opening date of the account allows you to review the historical status with more accuracy.

The date opened may also help you to define when the homeowner began to have financial issues. This information is helpful when proving that the loss mitigation need is a result of a specific financial hardship and not an indication of poor planning or credit use on the part of the homeowner.

The present status details the current balances and any amounts currently due or past due for each account.

You should scan this column to note any issues that may arise during qualification and workout processes.

Past due accounts may lead to a lien against the subject property and should be considered during the workout planning.

The terms field shows you the original and the current agreement relating to the payments and terms of the account.

A revolving account or credit card will typically not provide you with an end date for the payments as these amounts will fluctuate depending on the borrower's spending actions.

If the account is an installment note, the column will give you the payment terms agreed upon for the account.

Payment amount will provide you with the minimum payment that is due on the account.

You will export these payment amounts into the debt-to-income ratio calculation form.

If the account has no payment entered, it may be an inactive account or it may be a revolving account that does not currently have a balance.

Even if an account does not have a balance, if credit is available to the borrower you must factor a minimum payment into the debt ratio for that account.

The underwriting guidelines will define the payment amount you will use.

E C O A	CREDITOR ACCOUNT NO	DATE RPTED	DATE LAST ACT	DATE OPND	LIMIT / HIGHEST CREDIT	PRESENT STATUS		TERMS	PAY AMT	TYPE AND ACCT STATUS	HISTORICAL STATUS			
						BALANCE OWING	AMOUNT PAST DUE				NO MOS HIIST REV	3 0	6 0	9 0
8	AFM-BLOOM #APRINTLO COLLEC-TION	02/99	04/94		425	425				OPN05				

HISTORICAL STATUS details allow you to review the credit history as well as determine if a specific credit issues exists in relationship to a particular account.

NO MOS HIST REV indicates the number of months detailed within the historical data section.

The numerical entries indicate the status of the payments to be found within the report.

Each account history will contain numbers indicating the status of a particular month's payment.

1 = on time
2 = 30 days late
3 = 60 days late
X = same as previous month

Read the history from LEFT to RIGHT.

Type and account status will provide you with the type of account and its present status.

- Revolving   REV
- Installment   Ins
- Mortgage   Mtg
- Consumer   Cons

This field could also contain derogatory accounts such as collections, charge offs or judgments.

- The number of month's history shows the numbers of months reported on the history of the account.

  Underwriting guidelines will dictate the number of months that must be reviewed for each account.

- When you review the account, you will be seeking the status of the account.

  In other words, you will review the account to determine whether the payments were made on time or if any late payment exists within the history.

- You will also look for the date of each payment reference.

  Minimal account history requirements may also exist.

  This column will enable you to determine if the borrower can meet these minimum credit requirements of the loan program you are considering.

- The historical status and late payments section provides you with numerical entries that indicate any late payments that will be found within the report.

  Each account history will contain numbers indicating the status of a particular month's payment.

  1 = on time

  2 = 30 days late

  3 = 60 days late

  X = the same status as the previous month

  This section of the history summary will provide you with the number of times a borrower has been on time, 30 days, and 60 days late during the reported credit history.

  An account shows a 1 indicates that the account was paid on time within the history.

  ➢   When you note an account that contains derogatory information or a credit blemish, you should first confirm that the account is active and that the derogatory account is recent and the entry applies to the process.

> You will then determine the last date that the account is reported and begin counting backwards from the last entry.

You will review account details by moving from left to right.

Example: The reporting of this account begins in July.

The first entry is July. Moving backwards from Left to Right the next entries are

June	=	On Time
May	=	30 Days Late
April	=	On Time

and then backwards through time all of the payments were made on time.

Example: The next account was reported in June so the backwards counting will begin with the month of June.

You will need to obtain an update for this account that illustrates the payment in July to bring this account current with the other entries on the report.

When you locate an account that illustrates a late payment, you will enter a 1x30 day late into the status section of your credit history-scoring key.

You will complete this process for every account in the report that contains a derogatory entry. You will export any credit blemish or derogatory entry you find on the credit report into your credit history.

Many people find it helpful to note any derogatory or important data directly on the report prior to exporting this information onto the credit history-scoring key. This helps to ensure that you do not skip any important factors during the export processes.

Increasing the Score

Over time, a borrower can improve the information in his or her credit report by paying credit obligations as agreed and using credit wisely. As derogatory data in the credit report gets older, it affects the score less. A missed payment from four years ago will not count as much as a missed payment from six months ago. As the borrower uses their credit in a more controlled manner, keeping debt load well below their maximum credit limits, their score is also likely to increase.

A credit score, like a credit report, is a snapshot of an individual's changing credit record. If you make a request for a second repository report to get an updated score, the score is likely to change for many reasons.

The credit items on the report are updated often, so new items are likely to have been added since the previous report. Repeatedly requesting a borrower's credit report may substantially increase the number of inquiries on the repository report, which may affect the score adversely.

You can assist your borrower in understanding how they can improve their overall credit rating by reviewing the score factor reason codes with them an providing them with the direction that they need to use their credit wisely in the future.

The number of inquiries may or may not be a factor in the score. When inquiries are a factor, they are typically not a strong one. If a borrower is very close to the score threshold for a particular loan product, you may receive a score based exception from underwriting. To do this you must show that one or more inquiries appearing on the report are related to this particular loan process. You must also show that the number of inquiries appear as one of the score factor reason codes of the report.

The law requires the credit repository keep a record of all credit inquiries in the file. This means an inquiry cannot be removed from the credit report. Consumer disclosure inquiries are not used in determining score. It is up to the lender, as in all circumstances, to decide what constitutes a sufficient credit risk.

Removing Erroneous Information

Consumers who want to address what they believe is erroneous information on a credit report should contact the credit repository that developed the report.

The Fair Credit Reporting Act (FCRA) allows the credit-reporting agency a "reasonable period of time", generally not to exceed 30 days, to investigate consumer disputed items.

A significant number of credit grantors use an automated system for investigating the disputes and respond to the dispute within a few days. Most credit reporting agencies make a special effort to resolve disputed information affecting a mortgage decision. The lender can weigh these factors and documentation provided by the borrower when deciding whether a disputed item will be counted as a derogatory matter during the credit approval process.

** Special Note: As a Lender, you will have the ability to request a credit supplement. This is typically done by completing the last page of the credit report requesting further information. Most repositories will allow you to fax the supplement request, along with the Consent for Credit Check signed by the borrower, to the office creating the credit report.

Upon receipt of the supplement request, a staff member of the Credit Reporting Office will verify the validity and status of the debt. The staff member will issue a credit supplement. This supplement will show the true status of the account as of the date that the supplement was printed. The new data will often not show up on the borrower's credit report in time for loan closing, but this supplement will allow underwriting to underwrite the loan based on the supplemented information.

Because the score uses all of the credit-related data on the credit bureau report and takes into account all contributing factors, removing or changing one specific, derogatory item will not guarantee an increase in Credit Bureau Score. In some cases, a change in the credit bureau report will have little or no effect on the score. Because there are many scorecards and the score is calculated using a complex mathematical formula, it is not possible to estimate how much the score will change if specific derogatory information is removed.

MERGED INFILE CREDIT REPORT

Prepared For:	Property Address:	Prepared By:	Date Rec:
Attention:	Loan Type:	Computer ID:	Date Comp:
	Purpose of Loan:		
	Report Type:	Lender Case #:	Date Revised:

APPLICANT / CO-APPLICANT

APPLICANT	CO-APPLICANT
Name:	Name:
SSN: DOB:	SSN: DOB:
Marital Status: Dependents:	Marital Status: Dependents:
Home Phone:	Home Phone:
Present Address:	Present Address:
Since: Own / Rent	Since: Own / Rent
Previous Address:	Previous Address:

CREDIT SUMMARY

	PAYMENTS	BALANCES	LIMITS	TRADES	30+	60+	90+
REVOLVING	0	2061	22004	4	4	4	17
INSTALLMENT	1307	79365	90610	25	34	8	27
REAL ESTATE	378	35384	36600	1	2	0	0
OPEN/OTHER	991	1041	1041	5	0	0	0
TOTAL	2676	117851	129451	38	40	12	44

# INQUIRIES	50	# PUBLIC RECORDS	0	# BANKRUPTCIES	0
WORST TRADE	9	OLDEST DATE 07/01/89		# SATISFACTORIES	17

2	JUDGEMENT	RPTD – 09/96	VRFD -	OPND –
	CASE – 104		SRCE – 1011	AMT – 13245
	ASSET -	LIAB -	BAL -	LACT – 09/96
			PLTF -	XPN01

1   JUDGEMENT   RPTD – 11/94   VRFD -   OPND –
        CASE – 9401   SRCE – 1016   AMT – 1900
        ASSET -   LIAB -   BAL -   LACT – 01/95
                                      PLTF -   XPN01

8   BEACON SCORE   EFX01
        519
        SERIOUS DELINQUENCY AND DEROGATORY PUBLIC RECORD OR COLLECTION FILED
        AMOUNT OWED ON DELINQUENT ACCOUNTS
        PROPORTION OF BALANCES TO CREDIT LIMITS TOO HIGH ON REVOLVING ACCOUNTS
        LENGTH OF TIME ACCOUNTS HAVE BEEN ESTABLISHED

8   EMPIRICA SCORE   TRU01
        493
        SERIOUS DELINQUENCY, AND PUBLIC RECORD OR COLLECTION FILED
        LEVEL OF DELINQUENCY ON ACCOUNTS
        TIME SINCE DELINQUENCY IS TOO RECENT OR UNKNOWN
        PROPORTION OF REVOLVING BALANCES TO REVOLVING CREDIT LIMITS IS TOO HIGH

8   FAIR ISAAC SCORE   XPN01
        529
        SERIOUS DELINQUENCY AND PUBLIC RECORD OR COLLECTION FILED
        PROPORTION OF BALANCES TOO HIGH ON REVOLVING ACCOUNTS
        NUMBER OF ACCOUNTS DELINQUENT
        LENGTH OF TIME SINCE LEGAL ITEM FILED OR COLLECTION ITEM REPORTED

CREDIT HISTORY

ECOA	CREDITOR ACCOUNT NO	DATE RPTED	DATE LAST ACT	DATE OPND	LIMIT / HIGHEST CREDIT	PRESENT STATUS		TERMS	PAY AMT	TYPE AND ACCT STATUS	HISTORICAL STATUS			
						BALANCE OWING	AMOUNT PAST DUE				NO MOS HIIST REV	30	60	90
8	AFM-BLOOM #APRINTLO COLLECTIO	02/99	04/94		425	425				OPN05	132111111 TRU01			
8	BENEFICL-HFC #7101702	07/00	04/00	03/97	0	0	0	39M 125		INS 01	37 XX1111111X1111111111X XXX1111111111111111111 TRU01	0	0	0
8	CAPTIAL 1 BK 05291071382	04/00	01/00	06/96	592	0	0			REV01	41 1111111111111111111111 1111111111111111111111 TRU01	0	0	0
8	CCB 42270972 CREDIT CARD	07/00	02/00	07/98	950	0				REV01	24 EFX01	0	0	0
1	CITIBANK 54241800	06/00	06/00	12/99	3500	3516	0	72	72	REV01	8 11111111 TRU01	0	0	0

ECOA	CREDITOR ACCOUNT NO	DATE RPTED	DATE LAST ACT	DATE OPND	LIMIT / HIGHEST CREDIT	PRESENT STATUS		TERMS	PAY AMT	TYPE AND ACCT STATUS	HISTORICAL STATUS			
						BALANCE OWING	AMOUNT PAST DUE				NO MOS HIIST REV	30	60	90
8	CORNER STONE S0000070010	09/00	06/96	09/94	4374	0	0	18M 223		INS00	1	0	0	0
											TRU01			
8	DIRECT MERCH BK 54580000114	07/00	07/00	11/95	2600	2496		83	83	REV01	25	0	0	0
											111111111111111111111 111111111111111111111 XPN01			
8	AFM-BLOOM #APRINTLO COLLEC CLOSED – CONS	02/99	04/94		425	425				OPN05				
											132111111 TRU01			
8	BENEFICL-HFC #7101702 CLOSED	07/00	04/00	03/97	0	0	0	39M 125		INS 01	37	0	0	0
											XX1111111X1111111111X XXX1111111111111111111 TRU01			
8	CAPTIAL 1 BK 05291071382 CLOSED – CONS	04/00	01/00	06/96	592	0	0			REV01	41	0	0	0
											111111111111111111111 111111111111111111111 TRU01			
8	CCB 42270972 CREDIT CARD CREDIT CARD	07/00	02/00	07/98	950	0				REV01	24	0	0	0
											EFX01			
1	CITIBANK 54241800 CREDIT CARD	06/00	06/00	12/99	3500	3516	0	72	72	REV01	8	0	0	0
											11111111 TRU01			
8	CORNER STONE S0000070010 CLOSED AUTO	09/00	06/96	09/94	4374	0	0	18M 223		INS00	1	0	0	0
											TRU01			
8	DIRECT MERCH BK 54580000114 CREDIT CARD	07/00	07/00	11/95	2600	2496		83	83	REV01	25	0	0	0
											111111111111111111111 111111111111111111111 XPN01			
1	FCNB/NEWP 4220507 CHARGE ACCOUNT	07/00	06/00	09/99	900	888		30	30	REV01	10	0	0	0
											111111111111111111111 111111111111111111111 TRU01			
3	FIRST USA BANK NA 5417623 CREDIT CARD	07/00	07/00	12/99	3000	2602	0	65	65	REV01	8	0	0	0
											11111111 TRU01			
2	FNANB 15230035125 CREDIT CARD	09/00	09/00	12/99	3000	1976		79	79	REV01	9	0	0	0
											111111111111111111111 11111 EPN01			
1	FNANB VISA 54063555013	06/00	06/00	06/98	700	0				REV01	27	1	0	0
											X112111111111111111111 EFX01			

FRAUD ALERT

1 TRANS ALERT   TRU01
 # INQUIRIES IN LAST 60 DAYS: 04
 RECORDED INQUIRIES ALTER

1 HAWK ALERT   TRU 01
 HAWK AVAILABLE AND CLEAR

Credit History (12 months)
Borrower

Mortgage Last 12 Months	Consumer Last 12 Months	Bankruptcy NOD/Foreclosure	Charge offs/Judgments
_____ X 30	_____ X 30	Chapter _____	# Filed _____
_____ X 60	_____ X 60	Discharge Date:	$ Amount _____
_____ X 90	_____ X 90	_____	$ to remain open _____
_____ X 120	_____ X 120	Balances: _____	$ to be paid _____
_____ Level	_____ Level	_____ Level	_____ Credit Score

Estimated Credit Level:_____

Credit History (12 months)
Co-Borrower

Mortgage Last 12 Months	Consumer Last 12 Months	Bankruptcy NOD/Foreclosure	Charge offs/Judgments
_____ X 30	_____ X 30	Chapter _____	# Filed _____
_____ X 60	_____ X 60	Discharge Date:	$ Amount _____
_____ X 90	_____ X 90	_____	$ to remain open _____
_____ X 120	_____ X 120	Balances: _____	$ to be paid _____
_____ Level	_____ Level	_____ Level	_____ Credit Score

Estimated Credit Level:_____

Credit History Scoring Key

You now have a better understanding of the inclusions of a credit report. You must learn to score each credit report to determine the loan availability for each barrower. The credit history-scoring key provides a simple method of extracting necessary information from the report and organizing the information for credit rating functions.

To begin the credit scoring process, you should locate the credit history-scoring key in the credit report section of your workbook. This key will assist you and organizing the information found in the credit report into a format that you can easily use when placing the loan.

➤ The first item of importance in the credit report is the mortgage history.

Locate the mortgage for the borrower's primary residence on the report.

Review the entries within the status segment to determine if any late payments exist over the last 12 to 24 months.

Conforming or government loans typically use the last 24 months credit history.

Some programs will use the last 12 months.

You should refer to the underwriting guidelines for specific loan program you are considering for the borrower to determine the time period that must be used for scoring purposes.

Most product matrix is interested only the worst trading rating that exists during the specified time.

Example: If the borrower was one time 60 days late then the quantity of payments that were 30 days late is unimportant.

If the borrower does not have a mortgage or rental history showing on their credit report, you will need to acquire other documentation in order to determine the residence payment history.

If the borrower has additional real estate beyond their primary residence, you will need to determine how the loan product guidelines require you to handle these housing payments. Most programs will define non-owner occupied mortgage payments as consumer credit rather than mortgage. A nonresident mortgage is often rated as consumer debt and you will need to rate the payments accordingly.

➤ Consumer history is the next field you will review.

You will tally all of late payments falling into the consumer debt category. These will include personal loans, credit card debt, revolving lines of credit, nonresident mortgage loans, and any other report items that indicate the borrower makes monthly payments toward the payment of a debt.

Consumer data typically tallied based on the worst piece of history over the last 12 to 24 months.

The rating term you will use depends on the loan guidelines for the product you are considering.

You will tally the worst consumer payment status that appears on the credit report. In other words if the borrower has paid a debt one time 60 days late, this payment makes any 30-day consumer late payments appearing on the report unimportant.

➢ In addition to reviewing the body of the report to determine the status of the payments on each account, you will need to review the section relating to public records.

The public records field will contain information relating to any bankruptcy, foreclosure, or judgment against the borrower.

You will typically become aware to look for these issues during the pre-qualification processes. The borrower will usually define any derogatory debt that exists.

You should review the dates of all derogatory entries to determine if it is within the review period of the credit report.

At times, a derogatory debt may be showing in the columns that has been discharges as part of a bankruptcy proceeding.

> If an item is showing on the report as an open account but has been discharged as part of a bankruptcy proceeding, you will need to obtain a credit supplement from the credit-reporting agency verifying that the debt is fully discharged.

> You may also be required to submit full bankruptcy discharge paperwork as supporting documentation.

➢ Each product matrix has different criteria concerning charge-offs.

You will need to have an idea of which loan product you will use for the borrower before determining what charge off accounts will need to be paid in order to close the loan.

For the present, you will include all charge off, judgment and collection history in the total number and total account balances in the credit history-scoring key.

Any account related to a bankruptcy should be noted as discharged and left off of the form.

You will complete the section of the scoring key related to accounts to be left open and the amount to be paid prior to or at closing later in the process.

Some credit matrix allows certain charge off accounts to be left open. An example is an account that is less than $200 and over four-year old.

Early in your career, you may wish to complete a separate credit scoring form for each program until you become familiar with the requirements of each loan program and can determine the possible loan programs from a single form.

➢ The final element that you will export into the credit scoring history key is the credit score.

Some programs will use the middle of the three credit scores on a tri-merged report, while others will require you to use a specific repository score depending on which repository is considered the most complete for the borrower's particular area.

You should review the underwriting guideline manual for each loan program you have available to determine which credit score will be applicable for the borrower.

➢ Each piece of credit history will denote a level on the corresponding credit matrix.

A sample product matrix is included later in the course.

It is important for now that you understand that some programs will provide blending approvals while others will use the lowest level denoted by the credit history for approval. This is information you will obtain from the lender guidelines for the each program you have available.

Once you have completed all of the rating activity for the borrower, you will follow the same rating system for the co-borrower. You should score each credit report separately so that you can gain an approval level for each applicant. If you do complete a separate credit scoring history assessment for each applicant, you should be aware that joint accounts may be reported on both reports and be careful not to count these accounts twice during the scoring process.

If you tally an account twice, it will affect the debt to income ratio of the applicant, may affect the overall credit placement, and could alter the loan program you choose for the borrower.

It is sometimes beneficial to review the reports side by side and cross off any duplicate accounts on one of the reports, typically the co-borrower's report.

If it becomes beneficial to remove one borrower later in the process, you should review the reports and ensure that you have counted these duplicate accounts for the applicant who will be obtaining the loan.

Once you have completed the credit history-scoring key, the elements of the key will be compared to the product matrix of the loan programs that are available for the borrower. Each lender's method of rating a potential borrower is different. You will wish to review multiple matrixes, compare the program requirements and approval levels to the borrower's profile, and choose the best product to suit your borrower's loan goals.

When reviewing the matrix, you will note that some lender's will use a blended approval process that takes every element of the credit and borrower profile into account, other lender's will issue an approval level based only on the credit score while still others will use the worst rating within the borrower profile to determine a loan offering.

CHAPTER 5

COMPENSATING FACTORS AND DEBT-TO-INCOME

You will occasionally come across a borrower that falls on the edge of a credit tier. In these cases, you can attempt to use compensating factors to request an exception from the underwriting team.

When a borrower's situation exceeds the normal guidelines set forth by underwriting, the borrower may obtain a higher approval or exception to the applicable guideline with compensating factors.

It is your job to make a strong case for your borrower. You will base your case on any piece of information that you gather that reflects favorably on your borrower. Some compensating factors include:

112

- Less than 10% increase for old rent/housing payments, to the new housing expense.

- A decrease from the old rent/housing payments to the new housing expense

- A borrower's excellent savings ability (as shown by savings accounts, etc)

- 3 or more months cash reserves.

- Borrower has income that is not qualifying income.

- Larger than minimum down payment

- Residual income (excess after expense) of $500 per adult and $250 per child

- Time at current residence exceeds 5 years.

- Time at current employment exceeds 5 years.

- Debt-to-income ratios below maximum guideline as set forth for that approval level.

- Credit scores fall within a few points of next highest level.

- A perfect mortgage or rental history proven through the credit bureau

5:1 Example – Common Compensating Factors

These are only examples of the most commonly used factors. Each loan package has a different set of circumstances and it is up to you to make the best case to the underwriting team on behalf of your borrowers.

DEBT-TO-INCOME RATIO'S

The debt ratio is what will determine "how much" loan a borrower can afford.

There are two types of debt ratios that will be used during the borrower qualification.

Front-End Ratio   The front-end ratio is the gross income divided by the new PITI mortgage payment.

This standard guideline is 29%.

Non-conforming loan programs often use only the back-end debt ratio.

Ratio guidelines will vary depending on the loan product.

Back-End Ratio   The back-end ratio is the gross income divided by the new PITI mortgage payment and the minimum monthly payments from all of the borrowers other liabilities.

The standard guideline is 41%.

The non-conforming guideline can be as high as 55%.

The typical debts used to determine the qualifying ratios include:

Front-End Ratios

- the current and or future house payment

Back-End Ratios

- the minimum required monthly payments on all of the following:

  Auto Loans (unless there is less than 10 months left to pay)

  Student Loans (unless there is less than 10 months left to pay)

  Personal Loans (unless there is less than 10 months left to pay)

  Charge Cards - minimum required payments only (all open credit accounts will be counted at the minimum payment even if there is no balance outstanding. The availability of the credit line requires a payment to be factored.)

  Child Support (unless if there is less than 10 months left to pay)

  Alimony (unless there is less than 10 months left to pay)

  Federal Tax Lien Repayment Schedules (unless there is less than 10 months left to pay)

  State Tax Lien Repayment Schedules (unless there is less than 10 months left to pay)

  Other open debt may be a consideration if it is an open line, with regular monthly payments and is not a part of housing or personal maintenance.

Common monthly liabilities that you will not use to calculate debt ratios:

Utility Bills
Car & Health Insurance
Cell Phone Bills

This is not to be considered an all-inclusive list. The lists included for review are for example purposes only. Other debt may exist in the borrower profile.

The percentage of debts to income is called the debt-to-income ratio. An example of the income to debt calculation is as follows:

Income	= $3,000
New Mortgage Payment	= $900.
Minimum Monthly Payments	= $300

FRONT END CALCULATION:

Mortgage	/	Income	=	30%
900	/	3,000	=	30%

BACK END CALCULATION

Mortgage	+	Monthly Payments	=	Debt Load
900	+	300	=	1200

Debt Load /	Income		=	40%
1200	/	3000	=	40%

In this scenario, your front-end ratio is 30% and back-end ratio is 40%, which is acceptable for many conforming loan programs.

These ratios can also be adjusted or exceeded if there are item(s) that can be paid-off, if you are able to lower the interest rate, or you can lower the loan amount for the borrower.

Additional debt ratio exercises are included in the Workbook.

DEBT TO INCOME RATIO (DTI%)

Monthly Income

Borrower
$_____ Base Pay/ _____
$_____ Commission/ _____
$_____ Other _____
$_____ Other _____
$_____ Total Monthly Income

Co-Borrower
$_____ Base Pay/ _____
$_____ Commission/ _____
$_____ Other _____
$_____ Other _____
$_____ Total Monthly Income

Combined Monthly Income $_____

Monthly Debt

Borrower
$_____ House/Rent Payment
Automobile Payment
$_____ Credit Card _____
$_____ Credit Card _____
$_____ Credit Card _____
$_____ Personal Loan _____
$_____ Other_____
$_____ Other_____
$_____ Total Monthly Debt

Co-Borrower
$_____ House/Rent Payment(factor once) $_____
$_____ Automobile Payment
$_____ Credit Card _____
$_____ Credit Card _____
$_____ Credit Card _____
$_____ Personal Loan _____
$_____ Other_____
$_____ Other_____
$_____ Total Monthly Debt

Combined Monthly Debt $_____

Take combined debt $_____ (factor each debt only once – if it is a joint debt list under the primary income earner only) and divide by the combined income $_____. The percentage _____% is your monthly debt-to-income ratio. This number should be below the maximum set forth in the loan matrix for the product level you have chosen for your borrowers. You can change the housing expense ratio to enable the borrower to fit your matrix. Just remember to alter the purchase price on your application to match or your underwriting team will decline the loan package for excessive ratios.

CHAPTER 6

THE LOAN APPLICATION

The proper completion of the loan application, or 1003, is a critical element in the creation of loan packages that will move smoothly to closing. The underwriting team will scrutinize each entry on the loan application and issue a loan approval based on these inclusions.

The documentation that you gather over the course of the loan process will support the entries on the loan application.

The completion of the loan application and obtainment of the necessary file documentation that will support these entries is critical to the structure, process, and closing of the loan.

You must gain a comprehensive understanding of each element on the loan application and of how each entry on the application will affect the loan approval terms.

KENNEY

Uniform Residential Loan Application

This application is designed to be completed by the applicant(s) with the Lender's assistance. Applicants should complete this form as "Borrower" or "Co-Borrower", as applicable. Co-Borrower information must also be provided (and the appropriate box checked) when ___ the income or assets of a person other than the "Borrower" (Including Borrower's spouse) will be used as a basis for loan qualification or ___ the income or assets of the Borrower's spouse will not be used as a basis for loan qualification, but his or her liabilities must be considered because the Borrower resides in a community property state, the security property is located in a community property state or the borrower is relying on other property located in a community property state for repayment of the loan.

I. TYPE OF MORTGAGE AND TERMS OF LOAN

Mortgage Applied for:	___ VA ___ Conventional ___ Other ___ FHA ___ FmHA		Agency Case Number	Lender Case Number
Amount $	Interest Rate %	No of Months	Amortization Type	___ Fixed Rate ___ Other (explain) ___ GPM ___ ARM (type)

II. PROPERTY INFORMATION AND PURPOSE OF LOAN

Subject Property Address (street, city, state, & zip code)	No Of Units
Legal Description of Subject Property (attach description if necessary)	Year Built

Purpose of Loan ___ Purchase ___ Construction ___ Other (explain) ___ Refinance ___ Construction-Permanent	Property will be: ___ Primary ___ Secondary ___ Investment Residence Residence

Complete this line if construction or construction-permanent loan

Year Lot Acquired	Original Cost $	Amount Existing Liens $	(a) Present Value of Lot	(b) Cost of Improvements	Total (a-b)

Complete this line if this is a refinance loan

Year Acquired	Original Cost $	Amount Existing Liens $	Purpose of Refinance	Describe Improvements ___ made ___ to be made Cost $

Title will be held in what Name(s)	Manner in which Title will be held	Estate will be held in ___ Fee Simple
Source of Down Payment, Settlement Charges, and / or Subordinate Financing (explain)		___ Leasehold (show expiration date)

III BORROWER INFORMATION

Borrower	Co-Borrower
Borrowers Name (include Jr or Sr if applicable)	Co-Borrowers Name (include Jr or Sr if applicable)

Social Security Number	Home Phone	Age	Yrs School	Social Security Number	Home Phone	Age	Yrs School

___ Married ___ Unmarried (include single ___ Separated divorced, widowed)	Dependents (not listed by co-borrower)		___ Married ___ Unmarried (include single ___ Separated divorced, widowed)	Dependents (not listed by borrower)	
	No	Ages		No	Ages

Present Address (street, city, state, zip code) ___ Own ___ Rent No Yrs	Present Address (street, city, state, zip code) ___ Own ___ Rent No Yrs

If residing at present address less than two years, complete the following

Former Address (street, city, state, zip code) ___ Own ___ Rent No Yrs	Former Address (street, city, state, zip code) ___ Own ___ Rent No Yrs

Former Address (street, city, state, zip code) ___ Own ___ Rent No Yrs	Former Address (street, city, state, zip code) ___ Own ___ Rent No Yrs

IV EMPLOYMENT INFORMATION

Borrower	Co-Borrower
Name & Address of Employer ___ Self Employed	Years on this Job	Name & Address of Employer ___ Self Employed	Years on this Job

Name & Address of Employer ___ Self Employed	Years on this Job Years employed in this line of work or profession	Name & Address of Employer ___ Self Employed	Years on this Job Years employed in this line of work or profession
Position/Title/Type of Business	Business Phone	Position/Title/Type of Business	Business Phone

If employed in current position less than two years or if currently employed in more than position, complete the following:

Name & Address of Employer ___ Self Employed	Dates (from-to) Monthly Income $	Name & Address of Employer ___ Self Employed	Dates (from-to) Monthly Income $
Position/Title/Type of Business	Business Phone	Position/Title/Type of Business	Business Phone

Name & Address of Employer ___ Self Employed	Dates (from-to) Monthly Income $	Name & Address of Employer ___ Self Employed	Dates (from-to) Monthly Income $
Position/Title/Type of Business	Business Phone	Position/Title/Type of Business	Business Phone

6:1 Sample Form 1003 – HUD Release

118

I. TYPE OF MORTGAGE AND TERMS OF LOAN			
Mortgage __ VA __ Conventional __ Other Applied for: __ FHA __ FmHA		Agency Case Number	Lender Case Number
Amount $	Interest Rate %	No of Months	Amortization __ Fixed Rate __ Other (explain) Type __ GPM __ ARM (type)

6:2 Sample Form Extraction 1003 – HUD Release

The upper portion of the 1003, *Type of Mortgage and Terms of Loan,* contains file copy data and details relating to type of loan that you have chosen for the borrower.

Type of Mortgage

You will need to check the box for the loan type that you have chosen for your borrower.

This ensures that the proper guidelines are applied to the prequalification and approval processes.

Agency Case Number

The agency case number is the file tracking number assigned by the individuals who underwrite, pre-qualify, and approve the loan package.

Lender Case Number

The lender case number is the internal case number that you office assigns to the file.

Terms of Loan

The terms of loan section of the 1003 refers to the type of mortgage that you are requesting.

These numbers are based on the calculation that you perform using the product matrix charts and borrower needs assessment.

When you submit an application for a pre-approval, you will enter the highest loan amount you and the borrower feel comfortable with given the borrower's specific situation and needs. This will be the pre-approval number and may be subject to a change when the borrower has chosen a home to purchase.

You should ensure that the amount you enter under loan amount is the highest loan the borrower will require to complete the purchasing process.

It is easier to request a loan reduction from underwriting than to request a loan increase later in the process.

If you need to return the file to underwriting to obtain an increase in the loan amount qualification, underwriting will review the entire file and issue a new pre-approval.

KENNEY

Interest Rate   The information you enter relating to interest rate is also preliminary unless your borrower has locked the offered interest rate.

You should ensure that you obtain a completed rate lock/float option form before submitting an application to underwriting for pre-approval or final approval.

Number of Months   The number of months refers to the amortization term of the loan.

You should enter the amortization term agreed to with the borrowers. The amortization term will effect the monthly payments and loan approval. The amortization term should match the current interest rate sheet for the loan program.

Amortization Type   The amortization type is the method that will be applied to the loan.

The amortization type is a vital part of the application because the method and term of amortization dictates the monthly payment. You should also remember that certain amortization methods would require additional disclosures to the borrower.

II. PROPERTY INFORMATION AND PURPOSE OF LOAN					
Subject Property Address (street, city, state, & zip code)					No Of Units
Legal Description of Subject Property (attach description if necessary)					Year Built
Purpose of Loan __ Purchase __ Construction __ Other (explain) __ Refinance __ Construction-Permanent				Property will be: __ Primary __ Secondary __ Investment Residence Residence	
Complete this line if construction or construction-permanent loan					
Year Lot Acquired	Original Cost $	Amount Existing Liens $	(a) Present Value of Lot	(b) Cost of Improvements	Total (a-b)
Complete this line if this is a refinance loan					
Year Acquired	Original Cost $	Amount Existing Liens $	Purpose of Refinance	Describe Improvements __ made __ to be made Cost $	
Title will be held in what Name(s)		Manner in which Title will be held			Estate will be held in __ Fee Simple
Source of Down Payment, Settlement Charges, and / or Subordinate Financing (explain)					__ Leasehold (show expiration date)

6:3 Sample Form Extraction 1003 – HUD Release

Section 3 of the 1003 provides details relating to the *property* that is to be financed and the *purpose of the loan.*

Subject Property   If the borrower has a sales agreement or knows the address of the subject property, you will enter the applicable details into the loan application.

You will extract the information for this section from the sales agreement or property listing form.

If the borrower is requesting a pre-approval, with no property in mind, you will write, "to be decided" on the property address section.

All of the other information concerning the property will be determined once the borrower has chosen a property and the application moves from a pre-approval to an actual loan package.

Number of Units

Federal Housing Acts and Loan Matrix treat properties differently based on the number of units in the property.

Example: You will enter a single-family property as 1.

Example: You will enter a duplex as 2.

Legal Description

The loan package documents will use the legal description of the property.

You can obtain the legal description from the sales agreement, public records system, previous title work, or other documentation provided to you by the borrower or real estate agent.

If the legal description information is too long to fit within the space provided, you will enter "*See Attached Legal Description*" and then attach an addendum page to the application that includes the full legal description of the property.

Year Built

The age of a property will affect various factors ranging from approval status to property valuation. You can obtain information about the age of the property from the Real Estate Agent, the Appraiser, or other sources.

Purpose of Loan

You will always include information about the purpose of the loan.

Understanding the purpose of the loan aids the underwriter in applying the correct underwriting standards to the loan package.

A purchase, refinance, construction, construction to perm, and other types of loan will be handled differently during the underwriting processes.

Property Use/Occupancy

You must include information relating to how the borrower intends to use the property.

- Primary residence

- A vacation home

- Secondary residence

- Investment property

Loan guidelines will vary depending on the use of the property. Owner occupied properties typically obtain a higher LTV status and lower interest rates.

Construction and
Construction to Permanent loans require different processing, approvals, and closing activities.

If the loan is a construction loan, you will incorporate information within the segment that relates to the construction status and costs.

This includes

- The year the borrower obtained the building lot

- The original cost of the lot

- Any existing liens on the property

- The current value of the lot

The details of the building lot added to the costs of the improvements planned using the loan funds enables underwriting to calculate a total property cost and value.

Refinance transactions will require additional information that pertains to the borrower's history with the property.

If the loan is a refinance transaction, you must enter

- The year the property was acquired

- The original cost of the property

- Current liens against the property

- The purpose of the refinance:

  Cash Out
  Interest Rate Reduction
  Other

- You should provide a brief description of any improvements relating to the property.

  Improvements are typically current improvements that are being made or improvements that will be made using the loan funds.

  Many times when individuals apply for a property refinance, they will use some of the funds received during the refinance to complete improvement, renovations, or upgrades to the property.

  These actions will typically improve the property condition or value and should be described within the loan submittal package.

Title

You should include information relating to the title of the property.

The manner that title will be held and the names of the individuals on the property will affect the security of the loan and may alter the individuals who must be included on the loan application.

Most loan guidelines require that any individual who will hold title as an owner of the property also be included on the mortgage loan application.

Source of Funds

The final entry in this section of the application pertains to the source of the down payment, settlement charges, or other financial matters relating to loan.

You should enter the manner that the borrower intends to supply the funds necessary to close.

You may change the source funds details as you move through the loan process.

Example: If the down payment relates to the equity from the sale of a prior property, you will enter that information.

You will include a copy of a Preliminary HUD 1 or other documentation that illustrates the amount of money that will be received from the sale of the other property.

Example: Some loan programs will allow a certain amount of subordinate financing.

Subordinate financing may be a personal loan or a 2nd mortgage held by the seller or other entity.

- Remember that the payments for this financing must fit within the DTI guidelines set by the lender.

If the borrower intends to subordinate financing from the seller or an outside source, you will provide the details of this arrangement within the application package.

All funds that will be used by the borrower to build the amount that they are required to bring to settlement should be defined.

Other common examples of borrower funds to close include

- Seller concessions toward closing costs

- Savings

- 401(k) withdrawals

- A gift from a friend or family member

You should ensure that the information entered in this section matches the funds defined in page two of the 1003, meets the underwriting standards for the loan being requested, and that all sources of funds can be documented.

The underwriter will screen the entries to ensure that the source of funds used matches the guidelines of the particular loan product being obtained.

If you do not document the source of funds inclusions at the time of the initial application, the documentation necessary for each entry will become part of the stipulation list.

It is a part of your job to help the borrower determine the best source of funds to use for their transaction. You must also assist the borrower by telling them what sources are allowed under the guidelines.

Borrower	III BORROWER INFORMATION		Co-Borrower	

Borrowers Name (include Jr or Sr if applicable)				Co-Borrowers Name (include Jr or Sr if applicable)			
Social Security Number	Home Phone	Age	Yrs School	Social Security Number	Home Phone	Age	Yrs School
__ Married __ Unmarried (include single __ Separated divorced, widowed)	Dependents (not listed by co- borrower) No / Ages			__ Married __ Unmarried (include single __ Separated divorced, widowed)	Dependents (not listed by borrower) No / Ages		
Present Address (street, city, state, zip code) __ Own __ Rent No Yrs				Present Address (street, city, state, zip code) __ Own __ Rent No Yrs			
If residing at present address less than two years, complete the following							
Former Address (street, city, state, zip code) __ Own __ Rent No Yrs				Former Address (street, city, state, zip code) __ Own __ Rent No Yrs			
Former Address (street, city, state, zip code) __ Own __ Rent No Yrs				Former Address (street, city, state, zip code) __ Own __ Rent No Yrs			

6:4 Sample Form Extraction 1003 – HUD Release

Much of the borrower information entered into the 1003 will mirror the data you acquired during the completion of the prequalification questionnaire.

You must verify and document this information before submitting the completed application to the underwriter.

Residence History
The borrower should include a residence history that extends back 2 years. If additional space is necessary, they may include the information on the final page of the application.

Employment History
The borrower will enter their employment information into the 1003.

You should verify and document this information through pay stubs, W-2's, and other documentation provided by the borrower during the application meeting.

Employment information must extend back 2-years.
The borrower may use the final page of the application to enter any employment details that do not fit within the designated space.

Additional Income
If the borrower has income that does not relate to direct employment such as disability, child support, or other income, and they wish to use this income for qualifying purposes; they should enter it within the employment history field.

Additional income entries may cause multiple income sources to be entered for the same time period.

You should note this entry on the cover sheet before submitting the application to underwriting.

If the borrower does not wish to use additional or other income for qualifying purposes but still wishes to disclose it on the application as a compensating factor, they should enter the applicable details within the field labeled *"income not to be used for qualifying proposes"*.

The borrower is not required to disclose this income if they do not wish to do so.

Continuation Period

Certain types of income will require a continuation period in order to be considered as qualifying income. This type of income requires that the borrower prove that the income will continue into the future.

Example: Child support income requires documentation proving that the child support payments will continue for two years into the future in order for it to qualify as income used for loan qualification.

Each loan program will have a specified continuation period that they require.

Uniform Residential Loan Application

V. MONTHLY INCOME AND COMBINED EXPENSE INFORMATION

Gross Monthly Income	Borrower	Co-Borrower	Total	Combined Monthly Housing Expenses	Present	Proposed
Self Empl Income *	$	$	$	Rent	$	
Overtime				First Mortgage (P&I)		$
Bonuses				Other Financing (P&I)		
Commissions				Hazard Insurance		
Dividends/Interest				Real Estate Taxes		
Net Rental Income				Mortgage Insurance		
Other (before completing see the notice in describe other income below)				Homeowner Assn Dues		
				Other		
Total	$	$	$	Total	$	$

* Self Employed Borrower(s) maybe be required to provide additional documentation such as tax returns and financial statements.

B/C	Describe Other Income Notice Alimony, child support or separate maintenance income need not be revealed if the Borrower (B) or Co-Borrower (C) doesn't choose to have it considered for repaying this loan.	Monthly Amount
		$
		$
		$

VI. ASSETS AND LIABILITIES

This Statement and any applicable supporting schedule may be completed jointly by both married and unmarried Co-Borrowers if their assets and liabilities are sufficiently joined so that the Statement can be meaningfully and fairly presented on a combined basis; otherwise separate Statements and Schedules are required. If the Co-Borrower section was completed about a spouse, this Statement; and supporting schedules must be completed about that spouse also.

ASSETS Description	Cash or Market Value	Liabilities and Pledged Assets List the creditors name, address and account numbers for outstanding debts including automobile loans, revolving charge accounts, real estate loans, alimony, child support, stock pledges, etc. Use continuation sheet if necessary. Indicate by (*) those liabilities which will be satisfied upon sale of real estate owned or upon refinancing of the subject property.		
Cash deposit toward purchase held by	$	LIABILITIES	Monthly Pmt & Mos Left To Pay	Unpaid Balance
List checking and savings accounts below Name and address of Bank, S&L, or Credit Union		Name and Address of Company	$ Payt / Mos	$
Acct no.	$	Acct No		
Name and address of Bank, S&L, or Credit Union		Name and Address of Company	$ Payt / Mos	$
Acct no.		Acct No		
Name and address of Bank, S&L, or Credit Union		Name and Address of Company	$ Payt / Mos	$
Acct no.	$	Acct No		
Name and address of Bank, S&L, or Credit Union		Name and Address of Company	$ Payt / Mos	$
Acct no.	$	Acct No		
Stocks & Bonds (company name/number & description)	$	Name and Address of Company	$ Payt / Mos	$
Life insurance net cash value Face amount: $	$			
Subtotal Liquid Assets	$	Acct No		
Real estate owned (enter market value) from schedule of real estate owned)	$	Name and Address of Company	$ Payt / Mos	$
Vested interest in retirement fund	$	Acct No		
Net worth of business(es) owned (attach financial statement)	$	Name and Address of Company Acct No	$ Payt / Mos	$
Automobiles owned (make and year)	$	Alimony/Child Support / Separate Maintenance Pmst)	$	
Other Assets	$	Job Related Expense (child care, union dues, etc.)	$	
		Total Monthly Payments	Total Liabilities b	
Total Assets $		Net Worth (a minus b) $		$

6:5 Sample Form 1003 – HUD Release

V. MOTHLY INCOME AND COMBINED EXPENSE INFORMATION

Gross Monthly Income	Borrower	Co-Borrower	Total	Combined Monthly Housing Expenses	Present	Proposed
Self Empl Income *	$	$	$	Rent	$	
Overtime				First Mortgage (P&I)		$
Bonuses				Other Financing (P&I)		
Commissions				Hazard Insurance		
Dividends/Interest				Real Estate Taxes		
Net Rental Income				Mortgage Insurance		
Other (before completing see the notice in describe other income below)				Homeowner Assn Dues		
				Other		
Total	$	$	$	Total	$	$

6:6 Sample Form Extraction 1003 – HUD Release

Page 3 of the 1003 will deal with *income, housing expense and credit related* matters.

Income and Expense

The basic income overtime income, bonus income, commission income, or other income should mirror the income related to the job information that the borrower included on page one of the application.

You must verify and document all of this income before you submit the final application package.

All documentation should be included with the loan package at the time of submittal. This enables underwriting to consider this income as part of the approval process. All of the income that is documented and verified will be totaled and used as a baseline for the DTI ratio calculations and loan approval figures completed by the underwriting department.

B/C	Describe Other Income Notice Alimony, child support or separate maintenance income need not be revealed if the Borrower (B) or Co-Borrower (C) doesn't choose to have it considered for repaying this loan.	Monthly Amount
		$
		$
		$

6:7 Sample Form Extraction 1003 – HUD Release

Additional Income

At times, there may be income that cannot be used as qualifying income. This income will not be entered into the regular income and employment section.

Example: Child support payments that will only continue for 1 ½ years

This income cannot be considered as part of the base DTI income but by including it within the 1003; you strengthen the loan file and set the stage if you must request an exception later in the loan process.

In addition to income and assets, page 3 of the 1003 will address *present rent or mortgage payments* and the *proposed mortgage payment* that will exist after the loan is completed.

You may verify current rent or mortgage payments form the credit report or send a VOR/VOM form to the current property owner or mortgage holder.

Combined Monthly Housing Expenses	Present	Proposed
Rent	$	
First Mortgage (P&I)		$
Other Financing (P&I)		
Hazard Insurance		
Real Estate Taxes		
Mortgage Insurance		
Homeowner Assn Dues		
Other		
Total	$	$

6:8 Sample Form Extraction 1003 – HUD Release

You should enter the

- monthly housing expense

- any housing insurance payments

- the amount of real estate taxes the borrower pays for the present property

- any mortgage insurance premium

- homeowner's association dues

- any other fixed housing expenses related to the property the borrower and co borrower use as their primary residence

The total of all of these figures will be the current housing expense information.

You will enter the proposed mortgage payment based on the

- loan amount

- amortization term

- interest rate

that the borrower is requesting.

You will also calculate

- Insurance

- real estate taxes

- other expenses related to the home

You will total these, and this figure will act as the baseline for the housing expense ratio.

Assets

In addition to income, assets will be considered as part of the approval process.

The borrower and co-borrower will need to inform you of all assets they have available.

The underwriter will often refer to the assets section of the 1003 to verify the availability of the funds that you have indicated will be used as the source of funds to close.

The loan program in which you are placing your borrower will dictate the asset documentation requirements.

Example: Bank accounts and other savings will typically require the use of the VOD form.

VOD forms are included within the documentation section of the coursework.

You should review the use and completion of these forms as well as the other documentation requirements to ensure that you have an understanding of how loan funds and assets will be verified.

ASSETS Description	Cash or Market Value
Cash deposit toward purchase held by	$
List checking and savings accounts below	
Name and address of Bank, S&L, or Credit Union	
Acct no.	$
Name and address of Bank, S&L, or Credit Union	
Acct no.	
Name and address of Bank, S&L, or Credit Union	
Acct no.	$
Name and address of Bank, S&L, or Credit Union	
Acct no.	$
Stocks & Bonds (company name/number & description)	$
Life insurance net cash value Face amount: $	$
Subtotal Liquid Assets	$
Real estate owned (enter market value) from schedule of real estate owned)	$
Vested interest in retirement fund	$
Net worth of business(es) owned (attach financial statement)	$
Automobiles owned (make and year)	$
Other Assets	$
Total Assets	$

6:9 Sample Form Extraction 1003 – HUD Release

130

LIABILITIES	Monthly Pmt & Mos Left To Pay	Unpaid Balance
Name and Address of Company	$ Payt / Mos	$
Acct No		
Name and Address of Company	$ Payt / Mos	$
Acct No		
Name and Address of Company	$ Payt / Mos	$
Acct No		
Name and Address of Company	$ Payt / Mos	$
Acct No		
Name and Address of Company	$ Payt / Mos	$
Acct No		
Name and Address of Company	$ Payt / Mos	$
Acct No		
Name and Address of Company	$ Payt / Mos	
Acct No		
Alimony/Child Support / Separate Maintenance Pmst)	$	
Job Related Expense (child care, union dues, etc.)	$	
Total Monthly Payments	Total Liabilities b	
Net Worth (a minus b) $		

Liabilities and Pledged Assets List the creditors name, address and account numbers for outstanding debts including automobile loans, revolving charge accounts, real estate loans, alimony, child support, stock pledges, etc. Use continuation sheet if necessary. Indicate by (*) those liabilities which will be satisfied upon sale of real estate owned or upon refinancing of the subject property.

6:10 Sample Form Extraction 1003 – HUD Release

Liabilities

The segment relating to recurring debts will often be exported directly from the credit report. You may be required to enter the data regarding debts from the credit report by hand if your company does not use an automated program to conduct this function.

You will verify that all of the debt exported to the liability section of the 1003 is accurate.

If you are aware of any debt that is not included on the credit report, you must enter the information by hand to ensure that underwriting has a clear understanding of the borrower's monthly liabilities.

Example: If child support is paid out to another individual by your borrower or co-borrower, you should attach documentation showing how much the payments are on a monthly basis and how long the payments will continue.

You will then enter this information into the 1003 liability section.

You may be able to discount some of the debt included within the credit report.

Example: A credit card or revolving account that is open enables access to credit by the borrower or co-borrower.

Since these accounts do not have a balance, they will not show a monthly payment.

Since this credit line is available for use, a monthly payment must be factored into the debt ratio even though the account is not presently in use.

Each loan program will set the standards for the amount of payment that will be entered on an open revolving account with a zero balance.

Example: A common practice is to factor a 15-dollar minimum monthly payment for each open revolving account available to the borrower or co-borrower. This ensures that a payment for this account will fit into the debt ratio if the borrower chooses to use this available credit over the life of the loan

VI ASSETS AND LIABILITIES (cont)							
Schedule of Real Estate Owned (if additional properties are owned use continuation sheet)							
Property Address (enter S if sold, PS if pending sale or r if a rental being held for income)		Type of Property	Present Market Value	Amount of Mortgage/Liens	Gross Rental Income	Mortgage Payments	Insurance Maintenance & Taxes	Net Rental Income
			$	$	$	$	$	$
Total			$	$	$	$	$	$

6:11 Sample Form Extraction 1003 – HUD Release

Real Estate   Any additional real estate that the borrower owns but is not selling during this transaction should be defined within the application.

The assets and history from this real estate may be considered a compensating factor.

Underwriting grading processes relating to the mortgage history from non-owner occupied real estate will vary and including the details of this other real estate enables the underwriter to differentiate the entries on the credit report.

List any additional names under which credit has previously been received and indicate appropriate creditor name(s) and account number(s)		
Alternative Name	Creditor Name	Account Number

6:12 Sample Form Extraction 1003 – HUD Release

Aliases   At times, a borrower may have used a different name or a variation of their full name when applying for credit.

Example: A married woman will often establish credit under her maiden name. The name change upon marriage could confuse her credit history report unless you report the maiden name.

Alias information is important to the underwriting team for verification of additional debt and as a combat against fraud.

VII DETAILS OF TRANSACTION	
a. Purchase Price	$
b. Alterations, improvements, repairs	
c. Land (if acquired separately)	
d. Refinance (incl items to be paid off)	
e. Estimated prepaid items	
g. PMI, MIP, Funding Fee paid in cash	
h. Discount (if Borrower will pay)	
i. Total costs (add a through h)	
j. Subordinate Financing	
k. Borrower's closing costs paid by seller	( )
l. Other credits (explain)	
m. Loan amount (exclude PMI, MIP, Funding Fee financed)	
n. PMI, MIP, Funding Fee financed	
o. Loan Amount (add m & n)	
p. Cash from/to Borrower (j, k, l & o from i)	

6:13 Sample Form Extraction 1003 – HUD Release

The *details of transaction* section of the 1003 will summarize all of the mathematical and structural planning that you have completed as part of the application process.

The details of the transaction numbers will automatically export as part of the application process in applications that are computer generated. Hand calculated applications require that you enter these figures manually

Regardless of the method of entry, you should review the details of the transaction carefully to ensure that all entries match the

- structure

- source of funds

- other details you have planned for your borrowers

The underwriter will use this section of the 1003 to gain an understanding of the loan that you are planning for your borrowers and to issue all approval figures. The approval information provided to the borrower from the underwriting team will base all of its inclusions on the entries within the details of the transaction summary.

- You will enter the purchase price of the property or the refinance amount being requested into the 1003.

   If there is no property attached to the loan, and the package is being submitted for a pre-approval, you will want to ask for the highest loan amount your borrowers are eligible to receive based on ratios.

   The loan amount request can be lowered later in the process, however, a higher loan request will require that the underwriting department recalculate all numbers and issue an entirely new approval. New approval documents and disclosures will be issued on a lowered loan amount, but the approval will not need to be re-underwritten to determine if the borrower can afford a higher loan amount.

- Once the borrower has obtained a sales agreement, you will want to verify other details beyond just the purchase price.

   The sales agreement can include any item negotiated between the buyer and the seller.

   A commonly negotiated matter is seller concession toward the buyers closing costs. You will want to ensure that any negotiated financial matter incorporated into the sales agreement is entered into the financial details section of the 1003 AND meets the guideline standards of the loan program.

- Some loan guidelines will require that the borrower pay certain items in advance.

   Any item that will be pre-paid before the date of closing should be entered into the details of transaction.

+ You will enter the closing costs figures directly from the good faith estimate that you provided to the borrower.

   The good faith estimate may need to be revised at the time that the borrower chooses a property. If the good faith estimate is revised, you should ensure that you change the closing costs estimate within the 1003.

+ If the loan program applicable to the transaction requires that the borrower obtain PMI, any cash premium associated with the insurance should be entered into the details of the transaction.

+ At times, the borrower may pay discount points as part of the transaction.

If the funds are available to pay discount points and the borrower chooses to use this option, you should ensure that the quoted interest rate evident on the 1003 and applicable monthly payment reflects these discount points.

You should enter the total amount paid toward discount into the details of the transaction.

=   All costs related tog the loan will be totaled.

-    Subordinate financing or second loans will be added into the details of the transaction.

You should ensure that the terms of the subordinate financing meet the underwriting guidelines and that they payment for this financing falls within the DTI Ratio of the borrower.

+   Any closing costs that the seller has agreed to pay on behalf of the borrower must be documented on the sales agreement and entered as a credit on the details of the transaction.

+   If the are additional credits allocated to the borrower as a part of the process, you should include the amounts within the details of the transaction summary and then provide an explanation for any unusual credit.

-    The loan amount that the borrower will receive because of the transaction should be entered. This loan amount entry should not include any PMI premium that is financed as part of the agreed upon loan terms. You will enter financed PMI premiums under the designated field.

=   All of the figures will then be totaled and a final figure for cash from OR to the borrower will be included within the details of the transaction. Cash to the borrower typically results from a refinance transaction but may result from a higher loan amount and higher up-front payments by the borrower.

•   Cash from the borrower will usually be an included figure in a purchase transaction.

The cash from the borrower is the amount of funds that you must source, usually as the borrowers own money, in order to meet the source of funds guidelines.

•   Cash to the borrower will usually be an included figure in a refinance transaction or in a high LTV transaction if the borrower has placed a higher earnest money deposit or paid a substantial amount of money toward pre-paid items. At times, cash to the borrower might be due to a repair negotiation or other matter negotiated between the seller and the buyer.

You should provide the borrower with a copy of the 1003 and ensure that they understand how the cash from or to the borrower figures were calculated. You should also ensure that they understand that the final figure is the amount of money that they are required to bring to the closing or will receive at the closing.

KENNEY

CREDIT REPORT AUTHORIZATION AND RELEASE

Authorization is hereby granted to _____ to obtain a standard factual data credit report through a credit-reporting agency chosen by _____
_____.

My signature below authorizes the release to the credit-reporting agency a copy of my credit application, and authorizes the credit-reporting agency to obtain information regarding my employment, savings accounts, and outstanding credit accounts (mortgages, auto loans, personal loans, charge cards, credit unions, etc.) Authorization is further granted to the reporting agency to use a Photostatted reproduction of this authorization if necessary to obtain any information regarding the above-mentioned information.

Applicants hereby request a copy of the credit report with any possible derogatory information be sent to the address of present residence, and holds _____
_____ and any credit reporting organization harmless in so mailing the copy requested.

Any reproduction of this credit authorization and release made by reliable means (for example: photocopy or facsimile is considered an original.

_____   _____
Borrower's Signature   Borrower's Signature
Date: Date:
SSN: SSN:

_____   _____
Borrower's Signature   Borrower's Signature
Date: Date:
SSN: SSN:

6:14 Sample Form Credit Authorization and Release – HUD Release

CREDIT DENIAL LETTER

Dear Applicant:

Thank you for your recent mortgage application. Your request for a loan was carefully considered, and we regret that we are unable to approve your application at this time.

This decision is based on the following factor(s):

__ Insufficient income to meet our minimum requirements
__ Insufficient income to sustain payments on the amount of credit requested
__ Income could not be verified
__ Employment history is not of sufficient length to qualify
__ Employment history could not be verified
__ Credit history of timely payments is unsatisfactory
__ Credit history could not be verified
__ Lack of sufficient credit references
__ Lack of acceptable types of credit references
__ Current obligations are excessive in relationship to income
__ Other _____

We will keep your application on file and look forward to working with you in the near future when your situation has changed.

The consumer-reporting agency that provided information that influenced our decision in whole or in part was (*Name, Address, and Telephone Number of Reporting Agency*). The reporting agency is unable to provide specific reasons why we have denied credit to you. You have the right to know the information contained in your credit file under the Fair Credit Reporting Act. Any questions regarding such information should be directed to (Credit Reporting Agency).

6:15 Sample Form – Credit Denial Letter – HUD Release

CHAPTER 7

THE SALES CONTRACT

A sales agreement that is correctly prepared and endorsed is a binding contract that holds each signing party responsible for the terms negotiated within that contract. Once the sales agreement is written and signed, all of the parties are obligated to complete the transaction providing the terms of the contract can be met legally. An essential element of the sales contract and one of the reasons that a sales agreement may become null and void are the clauses relevant to the mortgage-financing portion of the transaction.

The sales agreement will dictate the handling of many matters with regard to both the pre-close activities that you must facilitate to ensure a timely closing and the type and terms of the mortgage loan that are acceptable under the contract. It is critical that you become familiar with all entries on a real estate sales contract and the proper action dictated by each item included within the contract.

A sales agreement may take many forms and include all of the entries on the example included for your review, additional entries created by the parties involved in the transaction or just some of the entries. If a sales agreement is created privately between the buyer and the seller, some information essential to the loan process may not be included. It is up to you to confirm that all of the required details are included in the sales contract or to gain the necessary information from the buyer and the seller prior to proceeding with the loan structure, order of affinity services, or closing processes.

This segment will assist you in understanding the clauses within the standard real estate sales contract that are most critical to the process from your perspective. Additional sections and clauses are included for your review. You should gain a basic familiarity with all areas of a standard residential sales agreement and focus more intensely on those sections that apply directly to the mortgage finance details of the transaction.

It is important to remember that a sales agreement may take many forms and that addenda can be created to the sales agreement. Addenda will typically address items of specific importance to the parties involved and will often create additional requirements or negotiations that will bind the parties. These clauses, requirements, and negotiation elements will alter the handling of the transaction and should be reviewed with care. Any alteration to the sales agreement should be scrutinized to ensure that the applicable party completes each action required according to the expectations of the involved parties.

STANDARD AGREEMENT FOR THE SALE OF REAL ESTATE

SELLERS BUISNES RELATIONSHIP WITH LICENSED BROKER
Broker (company) _____ Phone _____
Address _____ Fax _____
Licensee(s) _____Designated Agent __ Yes __ No
BROKER IS THE AGNET FOR THE SELLER   OR (if checked below):
Broker is NOT the Agent for the seller and is a/an: __ AGENT FOR BUYER __ Transaction Licensee

BUYERS BUISNES RELATIONSHIP WITH LICENSED BROKER
Broker (company) _____ Phone _____
Address _____ Fax _____
Licensee(s) _____Designated Agent __ Yes __ No
BROKER IS THE AGNET FOR THE BUYER   OR (if checked below):
Broker is NOT the Agent for the seller and is a/an: __ AGENT FOR SELLER __ Transaction Licensee

When the same Broker is Agent for Buyer, Broker is a Dual Agent. All of Broker's licensees are also Dual Agents UNLESS there is a separate Designated Agents for Buyer and Seller. If the same Licensee is designated for Seller and Buyer, the Licensee is a Dual Agent.

1. *This Agreement*, dated _____ is between SELLER(S):
   _____, called Seller, and
   BUYER(S): _____ , called Buyer.

2. PROPERTY Seller herby agrees to sell and convey to Buyer, who hereby agrees to purchase:
   ALL THAT CERTAIN lot or piece of ground with buildings and improvements thereon erected, if any, known as:
   _____
   _____
   In the _____ of _____ County of _____ in the State of
   _____. Identification (e.g., Tax ID#, Parcel #; Lot, Block; Deed Book, Page,
   Recording Date): _____
3. TERMS
   (A) Purchase Price _____
   _____ U.S. Dollars
   which will be paid to the Seller by the Buyer as follows:
   1. Cash or check at the signing of this Agreement_____ $ _____
   2. Cash or check within ____ days of the execution of this agreement_____ $ _____
   3. _____ $ _____
   4. Cash or cashiers check at the time of settlement_____ $ _____
                                                              TOTAL $ _____

7:1 Sample Form – Real Estate Purchase Agreement Page 1

(B) Deposits paid by Buyer within _____ DAYS of settlement will be by cash or cashiers check. Deposits, regardless of the form of payment and the person designated as payee, will be paid in U.S. Dollars to Broker for Seller (unless otherwise stated here) _____
_____ who will retain deposits in an escrow account until consummation or termination of this Agreement in conformity with all applicable laws and regulations. Any check tendered as deposit monies may be held uncashed pending the acceptance of this agreement.
(C) Seller's written approval to be on or before _____
(D) Settlement to be on _____ or before if Buyer and Seller agree
(E) Settlement will occur in the county where the Property is located or in an adjacent county, during normal business hours, unless Buyer and Seller agree otherwise.
(F) Conveyance from Seller will be by fee simple deed of Special Warranty unless otherwise stated here _____
_____
(G) Payment of transfer taxes will be divided equally between Buyer and Seller unless otherwise stated here _____
_____
(H) At the time of settlement, the following will be adjusted pro-rata on a daily basis between Buyer and Seller, reimbursing where applicable current taxes (see Information regarding Real Estate Taxes), rents, interest on mortgage assumptions, condominium fees, and home owners association fees, water and or sewer fees together with any other lienable municipal services.

7:1 Sample Form – Real Estate Purchase Agreement Page 1 Continued

1. *This Agreement*, dated _____ is between SELLER(S):
_____, called Seller, and
BUYER(S): _____ , called Buyer.

7:2 Sample Form Extraction – Real Estate Purchase Agreement Page 1

The full names of the buyers and the sellers of the transaction should be included on these lines of the sales agreement.

If the form of the names varies from the names incorporated into the mortgage application, you must discuss this matter with the borrower. The underwriter will wish to have every individual named on the sales agreement placed on the application and loan.

If any individual is named on the sales agreement but is not included within the application, you must have the name of the extra party removed before the sales agreement is remitted to the underwriting team.

All documents pertinent to the transaction should match in all ways. If there is a discrepancy, you must request correction of the document that contains the error.

2. PROPERTY Seller herby agrees to sell and convey to Buyer, who hereby agrees to purchase:
ALL THAT CERTAIN lot or piece of ground with buildings and improvements thereon erected, if any, known as:
_____
_____
In the _____ of _____ County of _____ in the State of
_____. Identification (e.g., Tax ID#, Parcel #; Lot, Block; Deed Book, Page, Recording Date):

7:3 Sample Form Extraction – Real Estate Purchase Agreement Page 1

The property information should be included on the sales contract.

The description of the property including physical address, city name, county name, and deed information should match all of the other documents in the transaction. If there is a discrepancy, you must request correction of the document that contains the error.

The individual overseeing the file and preparing the documents for closing will use the information entered on these forms to complete the closing package and to generate the signature pages that will close the transaction.

---

3. TERMS
(A) Purchase Price _____
_____ U.S. Dollars
which will be paid to the Seller by the Buyer as follows:
1. Cash or check at the signing of this Agreement_____ $ _____
2. Cash or check within _____ days of the execution of this agreement_____ $ _____
3. _____ $ _____
4. Cash or cashiers check at the time of settlement_____ $ _____
TOTAL $ _____

7:4 Sample Form Extraction – Real Estate Purchase Agreement Page 1

Purchase Price

The financial details that have been agreed to between the borrower and seller as the basis of the agreement for the sale will be included on the sales agreement.

The purchase entry details the final sales price agreed upon for the transaction.

This figure will act as the basis for all other transaction calculations during the process.

Cash or check at Signing

The area defined as cash or check at the signing of the agreement will be termed the earnest money deposit on your worksheet.

It is important that you review the handling of the earnest money deposit.

The earnest money deposit is a source of borrower funds to close and should be reflected on both the mortgage application and on the good faith estimate.

If these details are not included, you must gain the necessary agreement information in order to have the funds applied correctly as the transaction progresses.

Additional Funds

At times, the buyer and seller may negotiate a transaction in which the buyer pays more than one deposit. If this is the case, the details of these additional payments should be outlined within the contract and the application of the funds should be defined. If these funds are to be allocated to the buyer as part of the process, you will include them in the details of transaction section of your loan package.

Signing Funds   The amount of money that remains due to the seller after the application of all deposit money will be detailed on the sales agreement. You should review these numbers to confirm that all of the funds listed add up to the sales price detailed on the contract. If there is a discrepancy, you should contact the Real Estate Agent if one is being used, or the buyer and seller to have the discrepancy corrected prior to proceeding.

The financial figures entered into the sales agreement will be the ones that you use as the basis for all of the calculations applicable to the transaction. It is essential that the financial basis you use match the sales agreement, as even a slight variation in figures will alter the borrower's debt-to-income ratio, down payment requirements, loan amount, and all other financial estimates.

You should note that these figures only pertain to the actual sales price money for the property. Details pertaining to the closing costs and other financial matters will usually not appear within this section of the sales agreement. The calculation of the remaining costs will be based upon the completion of the good faith estimate and loan structure that your office creates for the borrower.

(B) Deposits paid by Buyer within _____ DAYS of settlement will be by cash or cashiers check. Deposits, regardless of the form of payment and the person designated as payee, will be paid in U.S. Dollars to Broker for Seller (unless otherwise stated here) _____
_____ who will retain deposits in an escrow account until consummation or termination of this Agreement in conformity with all applicable laws and regulations. Any check tendered as deposit monies may be held uncashed pending the acceptance of this agreement.

7:5 Sample Form Extraction – Real Estate Purchase Agreement Page 1

The method of payment, term for payment and handling of the deposit money, both before and after the offer is accepted will be detailed here.

The contingencies pertaining to the application and / or return of the earnest money deposit were explained earlier.

(C) Seller's written approval to be on or before _____
   (D) Settlement to be on _____ or before if Buyer and Seller agree
   (E) Settlement will occur in the county where the Property is located or in an adjacent county, during normal business hours, unless Buyer and Seller agree otherwise.

7:6 Sample Form Extraction – Real Estate Purchase Agreement Page 1

The dates pertinent to the transaction will be included within this section.

The most important date from your prospective will be

"Settlement to be on 'preferred closing date' or before if buyer or seller agree."

The date entered on this line is the date that you will use to manage the flow of the transaction. All applicable actions and documentation should be completed on or before this date so that the transaction can close in compliance with the agreement. If all if the required items cannot be completed by this date, an extension agreement will need to be made between the buyer and the seller.

F) Conveyance from Seller will be by fee simple deed of Special Warranty unless otherwise stated here _____

7:7 Sample Form Extraction – Real Estate Purchase Agreement Page 1

The specific type of deed that the seller agrees to provide and the buyer agrees to accept will be detailed within the sales agreement.

You should confirm that the type of deed and warranties contained within the deed match the requirements set forth by the underwriting guidelines. The decision to lend money for a specific transaction is contingent on the property specifics as well as the borrower specifics. Any deed limitations could affect the value of the property and would affect the approval terms and loan parameters.

(G) Payment of transfer taxes will be divided equally between Buyer and Seller unless otherwise stated here _____
_____

(H) At the time of settlement, the following will be adjusted pro-rata on a daily basis between Buyer and Seller, reimbursing where applicable current taxes (see Information regarding Real Estate Taxes), rents, interest on mortgage assumptions, condominium fees, and home owners association fees, water and or sewer fees together with any other lienable municipal services.

7:8 Sample Form Extraction – Real Estate Purchase Agreement Page 1

The payment of transfer taxes and pro ration calculations pertaining to other costs of the transaction will be detailed within the sales agreement.

You should note

- The division of transaction expenses outlined within the sales contract.

- The date set for the division of fixed expense.

The individual responsible for the preparation of the HUD 1 will calculate and verify the payments incorporated into this clause before finalizing the closing package. A rough estimate of the calculations should be incorporated into the financial details of the 1003 and disclosed on the good faith estimate.

4. **FIXTURES & PERSONAL PROPERTY**
   (A) INCLUDED in this sale are all existing items, permanently installed in the Property, free of liens, including plumbing, heating, lighting fixtures (including chandeliers and ceiling fans); water treatment systems; pool and spa equipment; garage door openers and transmitters; television antennas; unspotted shrubbery, plantings and trees; any remaining heating and cooking fuels stored on the Property at the time of settlement; sump pumps; storage sheds; mailboxes; wall to wall carpeting; existing window screens, storm windows and screen storm doors, window covering hardware, shades and blinds; awnings; built-in air conditioners, built in appliances; and the range unless otherwise stated. Also included: _____
   (B) LEASED items (not owned by Seller): _____
   (C) EXCLUDED fixtures and items: _____

5. **DATES / TIME IS OF THE ESSENCE**
   (A) The settlement date and all other dates and times referred to for the performance of the obligations of this Agreement are of the essence and are binding.
   (B) For purposes of this Agreement, the number of days will be counted from the date of execution, excluding the day this Agreement was executed and including the last day of the time period. The Execution Date of this Agreement is the date when Buyer and Seller have indicated full acceptance of this Agreement by signing and/or initialing it. All changes to this Agreement should be initialed and dated.
   (C) The settlement date is not extended by any other provision of this Agreement and may only be extended by mutual written Agreement of the parties.
   (D) Certain time periods are pre-printed in this Agreement as a convenience to the Buyer and Seller. All pre-printed time periods are negotiable and may be changed by striking out the pre-printed text and inserting a different time period acceptable to all parties.

6. **MORTGAGE CONTINGENCY**
   ___ WAIVED This sales is NOT contingent on mortgage financing, although Buyer may still obtain mortgage financing.
   ___ ELECTED
   (A) The sale is contingent on Buyer obtaining mortgage financing as follows:

First Mortgage on the Property	Second Mortgage on the Property
Loan Amount $_____	Loan Amount $_____
Minimum Term _____ years	Minimum Term _____ years
Type of Mortgage _____	Type of Mortgage _____
Mortgage Lender _____	Mortgage Lender _____
Interest Rate _____% however, Buyer agrees to accept the interest rate as may be committed by the mortgage lender, not to exceed a maximum interest rate of _____%. Discount points, loan origination, loan placement, and other fees charged by the lender as a percentage of the mortgage loan (excluding any mortgage insurance premiums or VA funding fee) not to exceed _____% (1% if not specified)	Interest Rate _____% however, Buyer agrees to accept the interest rate as may be committed by the mortgage lender, not to exceed a maximum interest rate of _____%. Discount points, loan origination, loan placement, and other fees charged by the lender as a percentage of the mortgage loan (excluding any mortgage insurance premiums or VA funding fee) not to exceed _____% (1% if not specified)

The interest rate(s) and fee(s) provisions in paragraph 6(A) are satisfied if the mortgage lender(s) gives Buyer the right to guarantee the interest rate(s) and fee(s) at or before the maximum levels stated. Buyer gives Seller the right at Seller's sole option and as permitted by law and the mortgage lender(s) to contribute financially, without promise of reimbursement to the buyer and or the mortgage lender(s) to make the above mortgage terms available to the Buyer.
   (B) Within _____ days (10 if not specified) from the Execution Date of this Agreement, Buyer will make a completed, written mortgage application for the mortgage terms stated above to the mortgage lender(s) defined in paragraph 6(A), if any, otherwise to a responsible mortgage lender(s) of Buyer's choice. Broker for Buyer, if any, otherwise Broker for Seller, is authorized to communicate with the mortgage lender(s) to assist in the mortgage loan process.
   (C) Should Buyer furnish false or incomplete information to Seller, Broker(s), or the mortgage lender(s) concerning Buyer's legal or financial status, or fail to cooperate in good faith in processing the mortgage loan application, which results in the mortgage lender(s) refusing to approve a mortgage loan commitment, Buyer will be in default of this Agreement.
   (D) 1. Mortgage commitment date: _____ if Seller does not receive a copy of Buyer's mortgage commitment by this date, Buyer and Seller agree to extend the mortgage commitment date until the Seller terminated this Agreement buy written notice to the Buyer
   2. Upon receiving a mortgage commitment, Buyer will promptly deliver a copy of the commitment to the Seller.
   3. Seller may terminate this Agreement, in writing, after the mortgage commitment date, if the mortgage commitment
      a. is not valid until the date of settlement , OR
      b. is conditional upon the sale and settlement of any other property, OR
      c. does not satisfy all the mortgage terms as stated in paragraph 6(A), OR
      d. Contains any other conditions not specified in this Agreement that is not satisfied and or removed in writing by the mortgage lender(s)
   4. If this Agreement is terminated pursuant to paragraph 6(D)(1) or (3), or the mortgage loan(s) is not obtained for settlement, all deposit monies will be returned to Buyer according to the terms of paragraph 30 and this Agreement will be VOID. Buyer will be responsible for any costs incurred by Buyer for any inspections or certifications obtained according to the terms of this Agreement and any costs incurred by Buyer for (1) Title search, title insurance and or mechanics' lien insurance, or any fee for cancellation. (2) Flood insurance and or fire insurance with extended coverage, mine subsidence insurance or any fee for cancellation (3) Appraisal fee and charges paid in advance to mortgage lender(s)

7:9 Sample Form – Real Estate Purchase Agreement Page 2

---

4. **FIXTURES & PERSONAL PROPERTY**

   (A) INCLUDED in this sale are all existing items, permanently installed in the Property, free of liens, including plumbing, heating, lighting fixtures (including chandeliers and ceiling fans); water treatment systems; pool and spa equipment; garage door openers and transmitters; television antennas; unspotted shrubbery, plantings and trees; any remaining heating and cooking fuels stored on the Property at the time of settlement; sump pumps; storage sheds; mailboxes; wall to wall carpeting; existing window screens, storm windows and screen storm doors, window covering hardware, shades and blinds; awnings; built-in air conditioners, built in appliances; and the range unless otherwise stated. Also included: _____

   (B) LEASED items (not owned by Seller): _____

   (C) EXCLUDED fixtures and items: _____

7:10 Sample Form Extraction – Real Estate Purchase Agreement Page 2

Specific details pertaining to the fixtures and personal property that will be included in the sale of the real estate will be shown on the sales agreement. The removal or addition of fixtures and personal property will affect the value of the property and may alter the approval terms of the loan. Many loan guidelines will require the removal of any value assessed to personal property transferring as part of the transaction. This value removal will lower the basis for the loan amount provided to the borrower.

Example: If the sales agreement sets the sales price of a property at $150,000 and the loan approval dictates an eight percent loan to value, the loan amount for the transaction would be $120,000.

                 The borrower would need to provide the $30,000 shortfall between the sales price and the loan amount as part down payment funds.

                 If the same sales agreement dictates that the buyer keeps $10,000 worth of furnishings, decorations, and other personal property as part of the negotiations, the value of these items is not a part of the value of the property and underwriting will deduct this value from the overall sales price.

                 That would mean that the loan amount would now be based on $140,000 ($150,000 sales price - $10,000 furniture and goods = $140,000 property purchase price).

                 Using the same 80% loan to value, the new loan amount would be $112,000.

                 The borrower would now need to prove that they have $38,000 to use as down payment funds.

---

5.   **DATES / TIME IS OF THE ESSENCE**

(A)   The settlement date and all other dates and times referred to for the performance of the obligations of this Agreement are of the essence and are binding.
(B)   For purposes of this Agreement, the number of days will be counted from the date of execution, excluding the day this Agreement was executed and including the last day of the time period. The Execution Date of this Agreement is the date when Buyer and Seller have indicated full acceptance of this Agreement by signing and/or initialing it. All changes to this Agreement should be initialed and dated.
(C)   The settlement date is not extended by any other provision of this Agreement and may only be extended by mutual written Agreement of the parties.
(D)   Certain time periods are pre-printed in this Agreement as a convenience to the Buyer and Seller. All pre-printed time periods are negotiable and may be changed by striking out the pre-printed text and inserting a different time period acceptable to all parties.

7:11 Sample Form Extraction – Real Estate Purchase Agreement Page 2

When the sales agreement negotiations are finalized, specific dates for action will be incorporated into the contract.

These dates set the timeline expectations for the transaction.

Some dates are listed based upon industry standard expectations and may be open to negotiation such as the term for a pest inspection.

Other dates are negotiated dates between the buyer and the seller and as such are considered fixed dates that must be met.

If a specifically negotiated date cannot be met for any reason, an alteration to the contract, signed by all parties, must be created. This type of date includes items such as the mortgage application and approval dates and the expected close date.

It is very important that you use these dates to set the timeline for the transaction and ensure that all required activity is finalized by the expected close date. Additional details pertaining to the expected time flow of a transaction and potential delays to the closing date and methods that you may use to overcome these potential delays are included later in the course.

---

6.   **MORTGAGE CONTINGENCY**

___   WAIVED This sales is NOT contingent on mortgage financing, although Buyer may still obtain mortgage financing.
___   ELECTED

7:12 Sample Form Extraction – Real Estate Purchase Agreement Page 2

The borrower may elect to incorporate a mortgage contingency clause into the sales agreement. This clauses states that the offer to purchase is contingent on your offices ability to structure a loan that enables the borrower to purchase the property. The mortgage contingency clause is one of the most common reasons that an offer to purchase will be cancelled. It is critical that you ensure that you complete all of the functions related to the obtainment of the mortgage in a timely manner and in compliance with the terms set forth in the sales agreement.

First Mortgage on the Property	Second Mortgage on the Property
Loan Amount $ _____	Loan Amount $ _____
Minimum Term _____ years	Minimum Term _____ years
Type of Mortgage _____	Type of Mortgage _____
_____	_____
Mortgage Lender _____	Mortgage Lender _____
_____	_____
Interest Rate _____% however, Buyer agrees to accept the interest rate as may be committed by the mortgage lender, not to exceed a maximum interest rate of _____%. Discount points, loan origination, loan placement, and other fees charged by the lender as a percentage of the mortgage loan (excluding any mortgage insurance premiums or VA funding fee) not to exceed _____% (1% if not specified)	Interest Rate _____% however, Buyer agrees to accept the interest rate as may be committed by the mortgage lender, not to exceed a maximum interest rate of _____%. Discount points, loan origination, loan placement, and other fees charged by the lender as a percentage of the mortgage loan (excluding any mortgage insurance premiums or VA funding fee) not to exceed _____% (1% if not specified)

7:13 Sample Form Extraction – Real Estate Purchase Agreement Page 2

Specific parameters under which the buyer may decline mortgage funding or must accept mortgage funding will often be included in the sales agreement. The minimum and maximum terms of the mortgage that the borrower believes will be acceptable will be outlined. You should review this clause and compare it to the financing that the borrower may actually obtain. If there is a discrepancy between the approval that the borrower receives and the terms outlined in the sales agreement, the sales contract may need to be modified. This modification of the borrower's expectations ensures that the mortgage clause matches the true loan terms and limits the probability that the transaction will be cancelled later in the process. A late cancellation can be expensive to all of the parties involved and will be frustrating to you because you will have invested a great deal of time and effort into the completion of the loan package.

Timelines for application and approval of mortgage funding will be included in the contract. These dates will assist you in setting the time flow and activity sheets for the application remittal, documentation needs, and other preparations you must undertake to meet the expected close date.

Additional details that may be applicable to your transaction such as costs, fees, and other matters may be incorporated. Any detail included within the sales agreement under the mortgage contingency clause should be transferred to your loan package.

KENNEY

(E) If the mortgage lender(s), or an insurer providing property and casualty insurance s required by the mortgage lender(s), requires repairs to the Property, Buyer will, upon receiving the requirements, deliver a copy of the requirements to the Seller. Within ___ DAYS of receiving the copy of the requirements, Seller will notify Buyer whether Seller will make the required repairs at Seller's expense.

    1. If Seller makes the required repairs to the satisfaction of the mortgage lender(s) or insurer, Buyer accepts the Property and agrees to the RELEASE in paragraph 27 of this Agreement.
    2. If Seller will not make the required repairs, or if Seller fails to respond within the time given, Buyer will, within ___ days, notify Seller of Buyer's choice to:
       a. Make the required repairs, at Buyer's expense, with permission and access to the Property given by Seller; permission and access may not be unreasonably withheld by Seller, OR
       b. Terminate this Agreement by written notice to Seller, with all deposit monies returned to Buyer according ot the terms of paragraph 30 of this Agreement.

(F) **Seller Assist**
  __ NOT APPLICABLE
  __ APPLICABLE, Seller will pay:
    $_____, or _____% of Purchase Price, maximum, toward Buyer's costs as acceptable to the mortgage lender(s)

FHA/VA, IF APPLIABLE

(G) It is expressly agreed that notwithstanding any other provisions of this contract, Buyer will not be obligated to complete the purchase of the Property described herein or to incur any penalty by forfeiture of earnest money deposits or otherwise unless Buyer has been given, in accordance with HUD/FHA or VA requirements, a written statement by the Federal Housing Commissioner, Veterans Administration, or a Direct Endorsement Lender setting forth the appraised value of the Property of not less than $_____ (the dollar amount to be inserted is the sales price as stated in this Agreement). Buyer will have the privilege and option of proceeding with consummation of the contract without regard to the amount of the appraised valuation. The appraised valuation is arrived at to determine the maximum mortgage the Department of Housing and Urban Development will insure. HUD does not warrant the value nor the condition of the Property as acceptable.
Warning: Section 1010 of Title 18, U.S.C., Department of Housing and Urban Development and Federal Housing Administration Transactions, provides, "Whoever for the purpose of... influencing in any way the action of such Department, makes, passes, utters or publishes any statement, knowing the same to be false... shall be fined under this title or imprisoned not more than two years or both."

(H) **U.S. Department of Housing and Urban Development (HUD) NOTICE TO PURCHASERS: Buyer's Acknowledgement**
  __ Buyer has received the HUD Notice "For Your Protection: Get a Home Inspection." Buyer understands the importance of getting an independent home inspection and has thought about this before signing this Agreement. Buyer understands that FHA will not perform a home inspection nor guarantee the price or condition of the Property.

(I) **Certification** We the undersigned, Seller(s) and Buyer(s) party to this transaction each certify that the terms of this contract for purchase are true to the best of our knowledge and believe, and that any other agreement entered into by any of these parties in connection with this transaction is attached to this Agreement.

7. **WAIVER OF CONTINGENCIES**
If this Agreement is contingent on Buyer's right to inspect and/or repair the Property, or to verify insurability, environmental conditions, boundaries, certifications, zoning classification or use, or any other information regarding the Property, Buyer's failure to exercise any of Buyer's options within the times set forth in this Agreement is a WAIVER of that contingency and Buyer accepts the Property and agrees to the RELEASE in paragraph 27 of this Agreement.

8. **PROPERTY INSURANCE AVAILABILITY**
  __ WAIVED. This Agreement is NOT contingent upon Buyer obtaining property and casualty insurance for the Property, although Buyer may still obtain property and casualty insurance.
  __ ELECTED. Contingency Period: ___ DAYS (15 if not specified) from the Execution Date of this Agreement.
  Within the Contingency Period, Buyer will make application for property and casualty insurance for the Property to a responsible insurer. **Broker for Buyer, if any, otherwise Broker for Seller, may communicate with the insurer to assist in the insurance process.** If Buyer cannot obtain property and casualty insurance for the Property on terms and conditions reasonably acceptable to Buyer, Buyer will, within the Contingency Period:
  (A) Accept the Property and agree to the RELEASE in paragraph 27 of this Agreement, OR
  (B) Terminate this Agreement by written notice to Seller, with all deposit monies returned to Buyer according to the terms of paragraph 30 of this Agreement, OR
  (C) Enter into a mutually acceptable written agreement with Seller.
  If Buyer and Seller do not reach a written agreement during the Contingency Period, and Buyer does not terminate this Agreement by written notice to Seller within that time, Buyer will accept the Property and agree to the RELEASE in paragraph 27 of this Agreement.

9. **INSPECTIONS**
  (A) Seller will provide access to insurers' representatives and, as may be required by this Agreement, to surveyors, municipal officials, and inspectors. If Buyer is obtaining mortgage financing, Seller will provide access to the Property to appraisers and others reasonably required by the mortgage lender(s). Buyer may attend any inspections.

7:14 Sample Form– Real Estate Purchase Agreement Page 3

(E) If the mortgage lender(s), or an insurer providing property and casualty insurance s required by the mortgage lender(s), requires repairs to the Property, Buyer will, upon receiving the requirements, deliver a copy of the requirements to the Seller. Within ___ DAYS of receiving the copy of the requirements, Seller will notify Buyer whether Seller will make the required repairs at Seller's expense.

1. If Seller makes the required repairs to the satisfaction of the mortgage lender(s) or insurer, Buyer accepts the Property and agrees to the RELEASE in paragraph 27 of this Agreement.
2. If Seller will not make the required repairs, or if Seller fails to respond within the time given, Buyer will, within ___ days, notify Seller of Buyer's choice to:
a. Make the required repairs, at Buyer's expense, with permission and access to the Property given by Seller; permission and access may not be unreasonably withheld by Seller, OR
b. Terminate this Agreement by written notice to Seller, with all deposit monies returned to Buyer according ot the terms of paragraph 30 of this Agreement.

7:15 Sample Form Extraction – Real Estate Purchase Agreement Page 3

The loan commitment provided by underwriting will detail any repairs that must be made to the property in order for the loan to be completed. These repairs are typically based on the inclusions and descriptions contained within the appraisal report and will include any matter that must be remedied in order to stabilize the value and condition of the property.

If such stipulations exist, you must ensure that the borrower negotiates an addendum to the sales contract that dictates who will make said repairs and bear the cost of the repairs.

(F) **Seller Assist**
___ NOT APPLICABLE
___ APPLICABLE, Seller will pay:
$_____, or _____% of Purchase Price, maximum, toward Buyer's costs as acceptable to the mortgage lender(s)
_____

7:16 Sample Form Extraction – Real Estate Purchase Agreement Page 3

The practice of requesting assistance toward the payment of closing costs from the seller in a transaction is becoming more common.

Many standard real estate sales agreements have incorporated a specific clause pertaining to this negotiation.

Seller concessions are the specific amount of funds a seller will allocate toward paying buyers closing costs out of the sellers closing proceeds.

The amount of seller assistance must comply with the maximum amount set forth in the underwriting guidelines for the loan program. Many programs have maximum amounts of seller assistance that they will allow.

If seller assistance is incorporated into the sales agreement, these figures should be included within the financial details section of the ten o three. Any financial modification that you make to the ten o three will carry with it a requirement that you remit the application package to the underwriter so that they may review and approve the changes.

Many borrowers require assistance in obtaining all of the required funds for closing and seller assistance is one tool that will enable the borrower to secure adequate funds. It is important that you understand that seller assistance funds come from the transaction. What this means is that the funds appear as a credit from the seller, but the money used will actually come from the loan funds and down payment money that the borrower brings to the table.

You should verify all of the seller assistance details, allowed costs offsets, and the inclusion of such assistance on the HUD 1 prior to beginning the settlement meeting. All of the entries relating to closing cost assistance must comply with the requirements of the loan guidelines. If any wording or allocation agreement relating to the closing cost assistance does not meet the requirements of the loan guidelines, the sales agreement will need to be modified to bring the negotiations into line with the mortgage approval terms.

At times, errors in the calculations or application of the seller assistance funds can occur during the preparation of the closing documents. It is important that all allowable seller assistance be credited to the borrower at the closing and that the assistance is credited in the correct location on the HUD 1.

Example: The loan guidelines dictate that the seller assistance may be applied to non-recurring closing costs, the allocation of seller assistance on the HUD 1 must be in entries related to non-recurring closing costs.

If the closing agent preparing the settlement statement was to enter some of the seller assistance money in the area detailing payment for homeowners insurance a problem may arise that delays the closing.

Homeowner's insurance premiums are recurring closing costs.

The entry of the seller assistance funds in this area may cause underwriting to invalidate the transaction until the funds are applied according to the guidelines.

The ability to review all documentation before the commencement of closing will enable you to isolate and correct issues before the parties arrive to close the transaction. Gaining a reputation for processing loan packages that lead to a smooth closing is one element that will assist you in growing your business and ensuring referral business from each loan that you close.

Certain specific inspections of the property may be written into the agreement. It is important for you to know some basic facts pertaining to these inspections. You will need to locate the

- Information detailing who will pay for the inspection

- And the specific agreement regarding when the payment for the inspections will be made

The payment for any required inspections may be made outside of closing or these payments may become part of the closing costs paid at the settlement meeting.

All billings pertaining to the transaction that are not paid prior to close must be addressed at the closing table so that the transaction may close without additional obligations coming to the surface for either the buyer or the seller at some point in the future.

When inspections are completed, specific items may become known that must be addressed or corrected prior to the closing of the loan.

Example: If a termite inspection is completed and termites are found on the subject property, one party will likely be responsible for having the problems relating to the termites corrected.

This could cause closing delays while the problem is corrected.

Any matter that must be corrected may also result in additional costs.

The handling of deficiencies should be written into the contracts and all inspections should be ordered early in the loan process. Addressing these items early helps to ensure that there is adequate time to remedy any issues that are discovered.

10. INSPECTION CONTINGENCY OPTIONS

The inspection contingencies elected by Buyer in paragraphs 11-15 are controlled by the Options set forth below. The time periods in these Options will apply to all inspection contingencies in paragraphs 11-15 unless otherwise stated in this Agreement.

Option 1. Within the Contingency Period, as stated in paragraphs 11-15, Buyer will:

1. Accept the Property with the information stated in the report(s) and agree to the RELEASE in paragraph 27 of this Agreement, OR
2. If Buyer is not satisfied with the information stated in the report(s), terminate this Agreement by written notice to the Seller, with all deposit monies returned to the Buyer according to the terms of paragraph 30 of this Agreement, OR
3. Enter into a mutually acceptable written agreement with the Seller providing for any repairs or improvements to the Property and or any credit to Buyer at settlement, as acceptable to the mortgage lender(s), if any.

If Buyer and Seller do not reach a written agreement during the specified Contingency Period, an Buyer does not terminate this Agreement by written notice to Seller within that time, Buyer will accept the Property and agree to the RELEASE in paragraph 27 of this Agreement.

Option 2. Within the Contingency Period, as stated in paragraphs 11-15, Buyer will:

1. Accept the Property with the information stated in the report(s) and agree to the RELEASE in paragraph 27 of this Agreement, OR
2. If Buyer is not satisfied with the information stated in the report(s), present the report(s) to Seller with a Written Corrective Proposal ("Proposal") listing corrections and/or credits desired by Buyer. The Proposal may, but is not required to, include the name of a properly licensed or qualified professional to perform the corrections requested in the Proposal, provisions for payment, including retests, and a projected date for completion of the corrections. Buyer agrees that Seller will not be held liable for corrections that do not comply with mortgage lender or governmental requirements if performed in a workmanlike manner according to the terms of Buyer's Proposal, or by a contractor selected by Buyer.

   a. Within ___ days (7 if not specified) of receiving Buyer's Proposal, Seller will inform Buyer in writing of Seller's choice to:
      1. Satisfy the terms of Buyer's Proposal, OR
      2. Credit Buyer at settlement for the cost to satisfy the terms of Buyer's Proposal, as acceptable to mortgage lender(s), if any, OR
      3. Not satisfy the terms of Buyer's Proposal or to credit Buyer at settlement for the costs to satisfy the terms of Buyer's Proposal.
   b. If Seller agrees to satisfy the terms of Buyer's Proposal or to credit Buyer at settlement as specified above, Buyer accepts Property and agrees to the RELEASE in paragraph 27 of this Agreement.
   c. If seller chooses not to satisfy the terms of Buyer's Proposal and not to credit Buyer at settlement as specified above, of if Seller fails to choose any option within the time give, Buyer will within ___ days (5 if not specified);
      1. Accept the Property with the information stated in the report(s) and agree to the RELEASE in paragraph 27 of this Agreement, OR
      2. Terminate this Agreement by written notice to Seller, with all deposit monies returned to Buyer according to the terms of paragraph 30 of this Agreement, OR
      3. Enter into a mutually acceptable written agreement with Seller providing for any repairs or improvements to the Property and/or any credit to Buyer at settlement, as acceptable to the mortgage lender(s) if any.

11. **PROPERTY INSPECTION CONTINGENCY** (See Property and Environmental Inspection Notices)

Buyer understands that property inspections, certifications and/or investigations can be performed by professional contractors, home inspectors, engineers, architects and other properly licensed or otherwise qualified professionals, and may include, but are not limited to: structural components; roof; exterior windows and exterior doors; exterior siding, fascia, gutters and downspouts; swimming pools, hot tubs and spas; appliances; electrical, plumbing, heating and cooling systems; water penetration; environmental hazards (e.g., mold, fungi, indoor air quality, asbestos, underground storage tanks, etc.); electromagnetic fields; wetlands inspection; flood plain verification; property boundary/square footage verification; and any other items Buyer may select. Buyer is advised to investigate easements, deed and use restrictions (including any historic preservation restrictions or ordinances) that apply to the Property and to review local zoning ordinances. Other provisions of this Agreement may provide for inspections, certifications and/or investigations that are not waived or altered by Buyer's election here.

___ WAIVED Buyer has the option to conduct property inspections, certifications, and/or investigations. Buyer WAIVES THIS OPTION and agrees to the RELEASE in paragraph 27 of this agreement.

___ ELECTED Contingency Period: ___ days (15 if not specified) from the Execution Date of this Agreement.

(A) Within the Contingency Period, Buyer, at Buyer's expense, may have inspections, certifications and/or investigations completed by properly licensed or otherwise qualified professionals. If Buyer elects to have a home inspection of the Property, as defined in the Pennsylvania Home Inspection Law (see Information Regarding the Home Inspection Law), the home inspection must be performed by a full member of a national home inspection association, in accordance with the ethical standards and code of conduct or practice of that association, or by a properly licensed or registered professional engineer, or a properly licensed or registered architect. This contingency does not apply to the following conditions or items: _____

(B) If Buyer is not satisfied with the condition of the Property as stated in the written inspection report(s), Buyer will proceed under one of the following Options as listed in paragraph 10 within the Contingency Period:

   ___ Option 1
   ___ Option 2 For the purposes of Paragraph 11 only, Buyer agrees to accept the Property with the results of any report(s) and agrees to the RELEASE in paragraph 27 of this Agreement if the total cost to correct the conditions stated in the report(s) is less than $_____ ($0 if not specified) (the "Deductible Amount"). Otherwise, all provisions of paragraph 10, Option 2, shall apply, except that Seller will be deemed to have satisfied the terms of Buyer's Proposal if Seller agrees to perform corrections or offer credits such that the cumulative cost of any uncorrected or uncredited condition(s) is equal to the Deductible Amount.

7:17 Sample Form– Real Estate Purchase Agreement Page 4

2. WOOD INFESTATION INSPECTION CONTINGENCY

___ WAIVED. Buyer has the option to have the Property inspected for wood infestation by an inspector certified as a wood-destroying pests pesticide applicator. BUYER WAIVES THIS OPTOIN and agrees to the RELEASE in paragraph 27 of this Agreement.

___ ELECTED. Contingency Period ___ days (15 if not specified) from the Execution Date of this Agreement.

(A) Within the Contingency Period, Buyer, at Buyer's expense, may obtain a written "Wood Destroying Insect Infestation Inspection Report" from an inspector certified as a wood-destroying pests pesticide applicator and will deliver it an all supporting documents and drawings provided by the inspector to Seller. The report is to be made satisfactory to and in compliance with applicable laws, mortgage lender requirements, and/or Federal Insuring and Guaranteeing Agency requirements, if any. The inspection is to be limited to all readily visible and accessible areas of all structures on the Property except fences and the following structures, which will not be inspected:

_____

(B) If the inspection reveals active infestation(s), Buyer, at Buyer's expense, may within the Contingency Period, obtain a proposal from a wood-destroying pests pesticide applicator to treat the Property.

(C) If the inspection reveals damage from active or previous infestation(s), Buyer, at Buyer's expense, may within the Contingency Period, obtain a written report from a professional contractor, home inspector, or structural engineer that is limited to structural damage to the Property caused by wood-destroying organisms and a Proposal to repair and/or treat the Property.

(D) If Buyer is not satisfied with the condition of the Property as stated in the written inspection report(s), Buyer will proceed under one of the following Options as listed in paragraph 10 within the Contingency Period:

___ Option 1
___ Option 2

3. STATUS OF RADON

(A) Seller has no knowledge concerning the presence or absence of radon unless checked below:

___ 1. Seller has knowledge that the Property was tested on the dates, by the methods (e.g., charcoal canister, alpha track, etc.), and with the results of the test indicated below:

DATE   TYPE OF TEST   RESULTS (picocuries/liter or working levels)

_____

___ 2. Seller has knowledge that the Property underwent radon reduction measures on the date(s) and by the method(s) indicated below:

DATE   RADON REDUCTION METHOD

_____

COPIES OF ALL AVAILABLE TEST REPORTS will be delivered to Buyer with this Agreement. SELLER DOES NOT WARRANT EITHER THE METHODS OR RESULTS OF THE TESTS.

(B) RADON INSPECTION CONTINGENCY

___ WAIVED. Buyer has the option to have the Property inspected for radon by a certified inspector. BUYER WAIVES THIS OPTION and agrees to the RELEASE in paragraph 27 of this Agreement.

___ ELECTED. Contingency Period: ___ Days (15 if not specified) from the Execution Date of this Agreement.

Within the Contingency Period, Buyer, at Buyer's expense, may obtain a radon test a radon test of the Property from a certified inspector. If Seller performs any radon remediation, Seller will provide Buyer a certification that the remediation was performed by a properly licensed and certified radon mitigation company.

1. If the written test report reveals the presence of radon below 0.02 working levels or 4 picoCuries/liter(4 pCi/L), Buyer accepts the Property and agrees to the RELEASE in paragraph 27 of this Agreement.

2. If the written test report reveals the presence of radon at or exceeding 0.02 working levels or 4 picoCuries/liter (4 pCi/L), Buyer will proceed under one of the following options as listed in paragraph 10 within the Contingency Period.

___ Option 1
___ Option 2

4. STAUTS OF WATER

(A) Seller represents that the Property is served by:

___ Public Water
___ On-site Water
___ Community Water
___ None

___ _____

(B) WATER SERVICE INSPECTION CONTINGENCY

___ WAIVED. Buyer has the option to have an inspection of the quality and or quantity of the water system for the Property. BUYER WAIVES THIS OPTION and agrees to the RELEASE in paragraph 27 of this Agreement.

___ ELECTED. Contingency Period ___ days (15 if not specified) from the Execution Date of this Agreement.

1. Within the Contingency Period, Buyer, at Buyer's expense, may obtain an inspection of the quality and/or quantity of the water system from a properly licensed or otherwise qualified water/well testing company.

2. If required by the inspection company, Seller, at Seller's expense, will locate and provide access to the on-site (or individual) water system. Seller also agrees to restore the Property, at Seller's expense, prior to settlement.

3. If Buyer is not satisfied with the condition of the water system as stated in the written inspection report(s), Buyer will proceed under one of the following options as listed in paragraph 10 within the Contingency Period:

___ Option 1
___ Option 2

7:18 Sample Form– Real Estate Purchase Agreement Page 6

(C) In the event any notices (including violations) and/or assessments are received after Seller has signed this Agreement and before settlement, Seller will provide a copy of the notices and/or assessments to Buyer and will notify Buyer in writing within ___ days after receiving the notices and/or assessments that seller will:

1. Fully comply with the notices and/or assessments at Seller's expense before settlement. If Seller fully complies with the notices and/or assessments, Buyer accepts the Property and agrees to the RELEASE in paragraph 27 of this Agreement OR

2. Not comply with the notices and/or assessments. If Seller chooses not to comply with the notices and/or assessments, or fails within the time given to notify Buyer whether Seller will comply, Buyer will notify Seller in writing within ___ days that Buyer will:

    a. Comply with the notices and/or assessments at Buyer's expense, accept the Property, and agree to the RELEASE in paragraph 27 of this Agreement OR

    b. Terminate this Agreement by written notice to Seller, with all deposit monies returned to Buyer according to the terms of paragraph 30 of this Agreement.

    If Buyer fails to respond within the time stated in paragraph 18 (C) (2) or fails to terminate this Agreement by written notice to the Seller within that time, Buyer will accept the Property and agree to the RELEASE in paragraph 27 of this Agreement.

(D) If required by law, within ___ DAYS From the Execution Date of this Agreement, but in no case later than 15 days prior to settlement, Seller will order at Seller's expense a certification from the appropriate municipal department(s) disclosing notice of any uncorrected violations of zoning, housing, building, safety, or fire ordinances and/or a certificate permitting occupancy of the Property. If Buyer receives notice of any required repairs/improvements, Buyer will promptly deliver a copy of the notice to the Seller.

1. Within ___ DAYS of receiving notice form the municipality that repairs/improvements are required, Seller will notify Buyer in writing that the Seller will:

    a. Make the required repairs/improvements to the satisfaction of the municipality. If Seller makes the require repairs/improvements, Buyer accepts the Property and agrees to the RELEASE in paragraph 27 of this Agreement OR

    b. Not make the required repairs/improvements. If Seller chooses not to make the required repairs/improvements, Buyer will notify Seller in writing within ___ DAYS that Buyer will:

        (1) Make the repairs/improvements at Buyer's expense, with permission and access to the Property given by Seller, which will not be unreasonably withheld, OR

        (2) Terminate this Agreement by written notice to Seller, with all deposit monies returned to Buyer according to the terms of paragraph 30 of this Agreement.

    If Buyer fails to respond within the time stated in paragraph 18 (D) (1) (b) or fails to terminate this Agreement by written notice to Seller within that time, Buyer will accept the Property and agree to the RELEASE in paragraph 27 of this Agreement, and Buyer accepts the responsibility to perform the repairs/improvements according to the terms of the notice provided by the municipality.

2. If Seller denies Buyer permission to make the required repairs/improvements, or does not provide Buyer access before settlement to make the required repairs/improvements, Buyer may, within ___ DAYS, terminate this Agreement by written notice to Seller, with all deposit monies returned to Buyer according to paragraph 30 of this Agreement

3. If repairs/improvements are required and Seller fails to provide a copy of the notice to Buyer as required in paragraph 18 (D), Seller will perform all repairs/improvements as required by the notice at Seller's expense. Paragraph 18(D)(3) will survive settlement.

19. TITLE, SURVEYS & COSTS

(A) The Property will be conveyed with good and marketable title as is insurable by a reputable title company at the regular rates, free and clear of all liens, encumbrances, and easements, EXCEPTING HOWEVER the following: existing deed restrictions; historic preservation restrictions or ordinances; building restrictions; ordinances; easements of roads; easements visible upon the ground; easements of record; and privileges or rights of public service companies, if any.

(B) Buyer will pay for the following: (1) Title search, title insurance and/or mechanics' lien insurance, or any fee for cancellation; (2) Flood insurance, fire insurance with extended coverage, mine subsidence insurance, or any fee for cancellation; (3) Appraisal fees and charges paid in advance to mortgage lender(s); (4) Buyer's customary settlement costs and accruals.

(C) Any survey or surveys required by the title insurance company or abstracting attorney for preparing an adequate legal description of the Property (or the correction thereof) will be obtained and paid for by Seller. Any survey or surveys desired by Buyer or required by the mortgage lender will be obtained and paid for by Buyer.

(D) If Seller is unable to give a good and marketable title and such as is insurable by a reputable title insurance company at the regular rates, as specified in paragraph 19 (A), Buyer will:

1. Accept the Property with such title as Seller can give, with no change to the purchase price, and agree to the RELEASE in paragraph 27 of this Agreement, OR

2. Terminate this Agreement by written notice to Seller, with all deposit monies to Buyer according to the terms of paragraph 30 of this Agreement. Upon termination, Seller will reimburse Buyer for any costs incurred by Buyer for any inspections or certifications obtained according to the terms of this Agreement, and for those items specified in paragraph 19 (B) items (1), (2), (3) and in paragraph 19 (C).

(E) The property is not a "recreational cabin" as defined in the Pennsylvania Construction Code Act unless otherwise stated here (see information regarding Recreational Cabins): _____

20. CONDOMINIUM/PLANNED COMMUNITY (HOMEOWNER ASSOCIATION) RESALE NOTICE

__ NOT APPLICABLE

__ APPLICABLE

---

19. TITLE, SURVEYS & COSTS

(A) The Property will be conveyed with good and marketable title as is insurable by a reputable title company at the regular rates, free and clear of all liens, encumbrances, and easements, EXCEPTING HOWEVER the following: existing deed restrictions; historic preservation restrictions or ordinances; building restrictions; ordinances; easements of roads; easements visible upon the ground; easements of record; and privileges or rights of public service companies, if any.

(B) Buyer will pay for the following: (1) Title search, title insurance and/or mechanics' lien insurance, or any fee for cancellation; (2) Flood insurance, fire insurance with extended coverage, mine subsidence insurance, or any fee for cancellation; (3) Appraisal fees and charges paid in advance to mortgage lender(s); (4) Buyer's customary settlement costs and accruals.

(C) Any survey or surveys required by the title insurance company or abstracting attorney for preparing an adequate legal description of the Property (or the correction thereof) will be obtained and paid for by Seller. Any survey or surveys desired by Buyer or required by the mortgage lender will be obtained and paid for by Buyer.

(D) If Seller is unable to give a good and marketable title and such as is insurable by a reputable title insurance company at the regular rates, as specified in paragraph 19 (A), Buyer will:

1. Accept the Property with such title as Seller can give, with no change to the purchase price, and agree to the RELEASE in paragraph 27 of this Agreement, OR

2. Terminate this Agreement by written notice to Seller, with all deposit monies to Buyer according to the terms of paragraph 30 of this Agreement. Upon termination, Seller will reimburse Buyer for any costs incurred by Buyer for any inspections or certifications obtained according to the terms of this Agreement, and for those items specified in paragraph 19 (B) items (1), (2), (3) and in paragraph 19 (C).

(E) The property is not a "recreational cabin" as defined in the Pennsylvania Construction Code Act unless otherwise stated here (see information regarding Recreational Cabins): _____

7:20 Sample Form Extraction – Real Estate Purchase Agreement Page 7

Specific terms relating to

- The marketability of the title

- The ability to insure the title

- Restrictions specific to the property

- Easements, rights and privileges pertaining to the property

- The costs pertaining to the searching and insuring the title

- Survey completion and costs

may be incorporated into the sales agreement. If any item cannot be met according to the contract, the options available to the parties should be outlined.

These terms should be verified, specifically those relating to the party who will bear the costs associated with each of these contingency clauses. If any question exists pertaining to which party will pay for the costs associated with any clause, you should contact the buyer, seller or real estate agent to obtain a formalized agreement between the parties prior to completing the financial calculations of the transaction. The payment of these items could affect the loan terms, approval, and cash required from the borrower to complete the process.

Details regarding possession of the property as well as any lease assignments relating to the property should be incorporated into the sales agreement. Many standard agreements contain a clause that provides default instructions for a transaction. Any alteration to this clause would appear in an addendum to the contract. You should confirm the specific negotiations pertaining to possession. If possession is to occur at some point in the future or is based upon an unusual negotiation, you should confirm that these occupancy options meet with the approval guidelines of the loan. Approval is often based on the occupancy plans that the borrower has for the property with owner-occupied property being approved for a higher loan to value than non-owner occupied property. Any change to the planned or agreed upon occupancy of the property could create a delay during the underwriting processes or even result in a change to the loan to value approval status of the borrower.

Details regarding the earnest money deposit, the application of the deposit toward costs, and the specifics of how or when the buyer may regain or loose rights to the earnest money deposit should be outlined within the contract.

Standard contracts typically contain a specific clause dealing with the earnest money deposit, but these standard clauses can be altered through additions to the contract or by addendums to the sales agreement. Non-standard contracts should specify the pertinent handling of earnest money funds.

The handling of the earnest money deposit and method of applying this deposit will be important to the loan structure process, the sourcing of down payment money, and the calculation of the cash the borrower will need to bring to the closing table.

Other conditions or contingencies may be written into the sales agreement. Any item that is of concern or interest to either party may become part of the agreement for transfer. You should review the entire contract, addendums and other paperwork remitted to your office to gain a better understanding of the unique details in each transaction. As you can see, the specifics of the transaction will alter the methodology, details, and handling of the loan package and gaining a complete understanding of each potential alteration will benefit you by making closings a smoother process for all parties.

1. **This Agreement,** dated _____ , is between

SELLER(S): _____

_____ _____

_____ , called Seller, and

BUYER(S): _____

_____ , called Buyer.

CHAPTER

8

APPRAISALS

A comprehensive understanding of appraisals is another area in which you must obtain knowledge. Much of your training focuses on the borrower situation and approval guidelines.

An important factor that everyone involved in the transaction must consider is that the property is as important as the borrower in the loan process.

The underwriter will base the borrower approval upon the factors that influence the likelihood that the borrower will pay the mortgage debt as agreed. These likelihood calculations are based upon historical data dictating the actions of past borrowers and are simply predictions of the performance of your borrower, not guarantees of their performance.

In the event that the borrower defaults on their mortgage loan, the property will then become the medium that the lender holding the loan will employ to regain their capital investment.

It is critical that the property condition and value has the ability to meet the needs of the lender if a default should occur. One method that the lender will use to determine the capability of the property to provide this security is through the appraisal.

The borrower is responsible for repaying the loan. The property acts as collateral, in the event the borrower does not fulfill this obligation.

The Underwriting team will scrutinize property appraisals and other property related information. In an effort to facilitate smoother loan processes and stronger loan packages, you should understand the appraisal process, the components of an appraisal, and areas within the appraisal that present red flags to Underwriters.

A Red flag is any information that indicates an issue exists that will lower the security of a loan package.

Appraisers are important elements in a variety of components of the lending process. The valuation and accuracy of an appraisal must be dependable. Appraisals will be used for

- Sales Price Negotiation

- Loan-to-Value Assessment

- Collateral Security

- Homeowner's Insurance Policies

- Title Insurance Policies

- Borrower Equity

- Determining necessary repairs to the property

- Private Mortgage Insurance Premiums

- Equity assessment

This is not to be considered an all-inclusive list. The listing is a basic assessment of the appraisal uses. Appraisals may affect other facets of the mortgage and home-buying process.

Many lenders have approved appraisers that they prefer to have conduct the appraisal on any property being considered for a loan. The approval of an appraiser is based on the historical ability of that appraiser to provide appraisals that reflect the fair value of the property and do not contain exceptions to the preferred appraisal guidelines of the lender.

The most common appraisal form that you will counter is the *Uniform Residential Appraisal Report* or URAR.

UNIFORM RESIDENTIAL APPRAISAL REPORT

The purpose of this summary appraisal report is to provide with an accurate, and adequately supported opinion of market value of the subject property

Property Address		City	State	Zip Code

Borrower _____ Owner of Public Record _____ County

Legal Description

Assessor's Parcel # _____ Tax Year _____ R.E. Taxes $ _____

Neighborhood Name _____ Map Reference _____ Census Tract

Occupant __ Owner __ Tenant __ Vacant   Special Assessments $ _____   __ PUD HOA $ _____ __ per year __ per month

Property Rights Appraised __ Fee Simple __ Leasehold __ Other (describe)

Assignment Type __ Purchase Transaction __ Refinance Transaction __ Other (describe)

Lender Client _____ Address

Is the subject property currently offered for sale or has it been offered for sale in the twelve months prior to the effective date of this appraisal __ yes __ no

Report data source(s) used offering prices(s), and date(s)

I __ did __ did not analyze the contract for sale for the subject purchase transaction. Explain the results of the analysis of the contract for sale or why analysis was not performed.

Contract Price $ _____ Date of Contract _____ Is the property seller the owner of public record __ Yes __ No Data Source(s)

Is there any financial assistance (loan charges, sale concessions, gift or down payment assistance, etc.) to be paid by any party on behalf of the borrower? __ Yes __ No If yes, report the total dollar amount and describe the items to be paid.

Note: Race and racial composition of the neighborhood are not appraisal factors

Neighborhood Characteristics			One-Unit Housing Trends				One-Unit Housing	Present Land Use %	
Location Urban	Suburban	Rural	Property Values Increasing	Stable	Declining		PRICE AGE	One-Unit	%
Built-Up Over 75%	25-75%	Under 25%	Demand Supply Shortage	In Balance	Over Supply		$ (000) (yrs)	2-4 Unit	%
Growth Rapid	Stable	Slow	Marketing Time Under 2 mth	3-6 mths	Over 6 mths		Low	Multi-Family	%
Neighborhood Boundaries							High	Commercial	%
							Pred.	Other	%

Neighborhood Description

Market Conditions (including support for the above conclusions)

Dimension	Area	Shape	View

Specific Zoning Classification _____ Zoning Description

Zoning Compliance __ Legal __ Legal Nonconforming (Grandfathered use) __ No Zoning __ Illegal (describe)

Is the highest and best use of the subject property as improved (or as proposed per plans and specifications) the present use? __ Yes __ No If No, describe

Utilities Public Other (describe) _____ Public Other (describe) _____ Off-site Improvements – Type Public Private

Electricity		Water			Street		
Gas		Sanitary Sewer			Alley		

FEMA Special Hazard Area __ Yes __ No FEMAL Flood Zone _____ Fema Map # _____ FEMA Map Date

Are the utilities and off-site improvements typical for the market area __ Yes __ No If No, describe

Are there any adverse site conditions or extreme factors (easements, encroachments, environmental conditions and uses, etc.)? __ Yes __ No If Yes, describe

General Description	Foundation	Exterior Description materials/condition	Interior materials/condition
Units __ One __ One w Accessory Unit	Concrete Slab __ Crawl Space	Foundation Walls	Floors
# of Stories	Full Basement __ Partial Basement	Exterior Walls	Walls
Type __ Det __ Att __ S-Dec / End Unit	Basement Area _____ sq ft	Roof Surface	Trim/Finish
__ Existing __ Proposed __ Under Cons	Basement Finish _____ %	Gutters & Downspouts	Bath Floor
Design (Style)	Outside Entry/ Exist __ Sump Pump	Window Type	Bath Wainscot
Year Built	Evidence of __ Infestation	Storm Sash / Insulated	Car Storage __ None
Effective Age (Yrs)	__ Dampness __ Settlement	Screens	Driveway __ # of Cars
Attic __ None	Heating __ FWA __ HWBB __ Radiant	Amenities __ Woodstove(s)	Driveway Surface
__ Drop Stair __ Stairs	__ Other __ Fuel	__ Fireplaces # __ Fence	__ Garage __ # of Cars
__ Floor __ Scuttle	Cooling __ Central Air Conditioning	__ Patio/Deck __ Porch	__ Carport __ # of Cars
__ Finished __ Heated	__ Individual __ Other	__ Pool __ Other	__ Att __ Det __ Built-in

Appliances __ Refrigerator __ Range/Oven __ Dishwasher __ Disposal __ Microwave __ Washer/Dryer __ Other (describe)

Finished area above grade contains: _____ Rooms _____ Bedrooms _____ Bath(s) _____ Square Feet of Gross Living Area Above Grade

Additional Features (special energy efficient items, etc.)

Describe the conditions of the property (including needed repairs, deterioration, renovations, remodeling, etc.)

Are there any physical deficiencies or adverse conditions that affect the livability, soundness, or structural integrity of the property? __ Yes __ No If Yes, describe

8:1 URAR – Sample Form – HUD Release

KENNEY

Subject

Property Address		City	State	Zip Code
Borrower	Owner of Public Record		County	
Legal Description				
Assessor's Parcel #		Tax Year	R.E. Taxes $	
Neighborhood Name		Map Reference	Census Tract	
Occupant __ Owner __ Tenant __ Vacant	Special Assessments $		__ PUD HOA $	__ per year __ per month
Property Rights Appraised __ Fee Simple __ Leasehold __ Other (describe)				
Assignment Type __ Purchase Transaction __ Refinance Transaction __ Other (describe)				

8:2 Extraction URAR – Sample Form – HUD Release

The upper portion of the URAR contains identifying data, general details of the property being assessed, and information relating to the individuals involved in the transaction.

You should compare the details of this section to the application details from your files. If any discrepancy between the appraisal report and your file details exists, you should ensure that the error or variation is corrected before submitting the appraisal to the underwriting team. You should compare the

- Property Address

- Borrower Name

- Legal Description

entries to the 1003. These entries should match the application data exactly.

- Owner of Public Record

- Assessor's Parcel Number
  Tax Year
  Real Estate Tax Amount

- Neighborhood Name
  Map Reference
  Census Tract

should match the sales agreement entries. If a discrepancy exists, you must have the incorrect document corrected. Some of these details will be used to create the loan closing documents and having correct details ensures that all of the paperwork is correct and helps to stabilize the lender's security in the property.

The details relating to the occupancy refer to the present occupancy status of the property.

- Occupancy of the Property
  Owner
  Tenant
  Vacant

The area relating to special assessments will be important to the loan.

- Special Assessments
  PUD
  HOA
  Terms

You should ensure that any special assessments noted by the appraiser that are recurring costs are entered into the 1003. These assessments will become a factor in the borrower's DTI ratio. If the appraiser notes special assessments that you have not included on the 1003, these could become a red flag issue and underwriting will require that the application be modified and the DTI Ratio be recalculated. At times, special assessments could result in a loan approval being changed to a denial or the terms of the loan approval being modified so that the borrower's DTI Ratio falls within the guidelines.

The appraiser will define the rights being appraised. This section of the URAR refers to the rights that are available for transfer by the current owner of the property.
Property Rights Appraised

    Fee Simple
    Leasehold
    Other

The rights being transferred through the transaction may alter the security of the loan. It is important that you verify that these rights match the information remitted on the loan application.

The appraiser will note the type of transaction being conducted.

- Assignment Type
  Purchase Transaction
  Refinance Transaction
  Other

You should review each entry within this section and confirm that these entries match the information submitted on the loan application and sales agreement.

If you note an error in a document, you must determine which document contains the error. If it is simple typing error or name entry method, the error can be easily corrected by the individual responsible for creating the document. If it is a more serious error, such as one relating to special assessments, you should re-assess the loan application and ensure that the borrowers are still able to qualify for the present loan program. Once you have recalculated the loan specifics and corrected the application package details, you must submit the loan package to the underwriter so that they may issue a new approval that includes the corrected items.

CONTRACT

I __ did __ did not analyze the contract for sale for the subject purchase transaction. Explain the results of the analysis of the contract for sale or why analysis was not performed.
Contract Price $ Date of Contract   Is the property seller the owner of public record __ Yes __ No Data Source(s)
Is there any financial assistance (loan charges, sale concessions, gift or down payment assistance, etc.) to be paid by any party on behalf of the borrower? __ Yes __ No If yes, report the total dollar amount and describe the items to be paid.

8:3 Extraction URAR – Sample Form – HUD Release

Data pertaining to any sales contract or other contract that is a part of the transaction will be included within this section.

You will wish to supply a copy of the contract to the appraiser at the time of the appraisal request.

Upon receipt of the completed appraisal, you should review the inclusions within this section to confirm that they match the details of the transaction you used to structure the application.

The appraiser will note whether the details of the contract were or were not reviewed during the completion of the appraisal.

- Contract Price

- Date of Contract

- Confirmation of Seller

- Financial Assistance
  Seller Concessions
  Gift Funds
  Down payment Assistance

You should review the financial details that the appraiser enters into the appraisal report including details relating to seller concessions, down payment assistance, and gift funds. The appraiser will take these details from the sales agreement. You should ensure that these inclusions match those that you incorporated into your 1003.

Neighborhood

Note: Race and racial composition of the neighborhood are not appraisal factors									
Neighborhood Characteristics				One-Unit Housing Trends				One-Unit Housing	Present Land Use %
Location	Urban	Suburban	Rural	Property Values	Increasing	Stable	Declining	PRICE AGE	One-Unit %
Built-Up	Over 75%	25-75%	Under 25%	Demand Supply	Shortage	In Balance	Over Supply	$ (000) (yrs)	2-4 Unit %
Growth	Rapid	Stable	Slow	Marketing Time	Under 2 mth	3-6 mths	Over 6 mths	Low	Multi-Family %
Neighborhood Boundaries								High	Commercial %
								Pred.	Other %
Neighborhood Description									

8:4 Extraction URAR – Sample Form – HUD Release

Neighborhood Information

Details concerning the neighborhood of the property will be considered during the appraisal process.

Each line of the neighborhood assessment should be completed by the appraiser. There should be no blank lines or unchecked boxes. If an area is incomplete, you should contact the appraiser and request that they make the appropriate notations on the report before you submit the package to underwriting for review.

Neighborhood Red Flags

Assessments within the neighborhood section present vital information that may effect the loan terms and approval.

Any variance from a positive answer or an uncommon answer will be scrutinized by the underwriter as these entries may affect the ability of the property to serve as security in the event of a borrower default. If any item entered into the neighborhood assessment is negative in nature, you should discuss these variances with the Appraiser to determine if the information is correct.

Example: A property whose neighborhood is considered Rural may require additional comparable properties to substantiate the valuation of the property.

These additional comparables help to offset the distance factor inherent to most underwriting guidelines relating to appraisers.

Most underwriting guidelines require that the appraiser use sales from comparable properties that are within a certain, pre-set proximity to the subject property. Rural areas often exceed these limitations due to the oversize land owned by each property owner.

Red Flag Action

If a need exists for additional comparables on the appraisal, it is a more effective and a faster process to request the appraiser provide these immediately rather than waiting for the Underwriter to generate a stipulation for the additional comparable property.

Market Characteristics and Conditions

Market Conditions (including support for the above conclusions)

8:5 Extraction URAR – Sample Form – HUD Release

The appraiser will provide an assessment of market comparison and market conditions. You should review the appraiser's comments. Any comment that could be considered a negative factor may affect the loan approval. If the appraiser states that the market for property similar to the subject property is below average, the security inherent in the property may be lessened. This could result in a change in the loan approval or even a denial of the loan to the borrower for this specific property. The borrower may need to choose another home to purchase or renegotiate the purchase agreement the seller in order to meet the new conditions imposed by underwriting for that particular property.

SITE

Dimension	Area	Shape	View
Specific Zoning Classification	Zoning Description		
Zoning Compliance	Legal	Legal Nonconforming (Grandfathered use)	No Zoning	Illegal (describe)
Is the highest and best use of the subject property as improved (or as proposed per plans and specifications) the present use? __ Yes __ No If No, describe			
Utilities	Public	Other (describe)	Public	Other (describe)	Off-site Improvements – Type	Public	Private
Electricity	Water		Street	
Gas	Sanitary Sewer		Alley	
FEMA Special Hazard Area __ Yes __ No FEMAL Flood Zone	Fema Map #	FEMA Map Date	
Are the utilities and off-site improvements typical for the market area __ Yes __ No If No, describe			
Are there any adverse site conditions or extreme factors (easements, encroachments, environmental conditions and uses, etc.)? __ Yes __ No If Yes, describe			

8:6 Extraction URAR – Sample Form – HUD Release

The site segment of the appraisal describes the parcel on which the subject property is built and any issue regarding site usage that are apparent.

Any issues with the use of the land including easements, encroachment, boundary line issues, or other factors affecting the land should be reviewed and addressed. Issues affecting the use of the land may need to be corrected before the closing of the loan. Underwriting guidelines will dictate what generates a red flag stipulation regarding site and site usage.

The buyer and the seller may need to negotiate an addendum to the sales agreement relating to the correction of any site usage issues and who will pay for the correction of these issues.

The loan closing may be delayed while a site usage issue is corrected.

Improvements

General Description	Foundation	Exterior Description materials/condition	Interior materials/condition
Units ___ One ___ One w Accessory Unit	Concrete Slab ___ Crawl Space	Foundation Walls	Floors
# of Stories	Full Basement ___ Partial Basement	Exterior Walls	Walls
Type ___ Det ___ Att ___ S-Dec / End Unit	Basement Area ___ sq ft	Roof Surface	Trim/Finish
___ Existing ___ Proposed ___ Under Cons	Basement Finish ___ %	Gutters & Downspouts	Bath Floor
Design (Style)	Outside Entry/ Exist ___ Sump Pump	Window Type	Bath Wainscot
Year Built	Evidence of ___ Infestation	Storm Sash / Insulated	Car Storage ___ None
Effective Age (Yrs)	___ Dampness ___ Settlement	Screens	___ Driveway ___ # of Cars
Attic ___ None	Heating ___ FWA ___ HWBB ___ Radiant	Amenities ___ Woodstove(s)	Driveway Surface
___ Drop Stair ___ Stairs	___ Other ___ Fuel	___ Fireplaces # ___ Fence	___ Garage ___ # of Cars
___ Floor ___ Scuttle	Cooling ___ Central Air Conditioning	___ Patio/Deck ___ Porch	___ Carport ___ # of Cars
___ Finished ___ Heated	___ Individual ___ Other	___ Pool ___ Other	___ Att ___ Det ___ Built-in
Appliances ___ Refrigerator ___ Range/Oven	Dishwasher ___ Disposal ___ Microwave	Washer/Dryer ___ Other (describe)	
Finished area above grade contains:	Rooms ___ Bedrooms ___	Bath(s) ___	Square Feet of Gross Living Area Above Grade
Additional Features (special energy efficient items, etc.)			
Describe the conditions of the property (including needed repairs, deterioration, renovations, remodeling, etc.)			
Are there any physical deficiencies or adverse conditions that affect the livability, soundness, or structural integrity of the property? ___ Yes ___ No If Yes, describe			

8:7 Extraction URAR – Sample Form – HUD Release

Many of the red flags that occur with an appraisal review will occur in the area of the appraisal that relates to the improvements. The term improvement refers to the actual building of the property. All portions of the subject property should obtain at least a rating of average.

If any area relating to the property receives a rating of less than average, the seller and the buyer will need to determine the steps that will be taken to improve the rating or condition of the property.

The appraiser will check the boxes that relate to the property.

# of Units These will include the number of units contained within the subject property. You should ensure that the number of units reflected on the appraisal is the same as the number of units indicated on the 1003.

# of Stories The number of stories included in the property will affect the desirability of the property. The comparables used for the valuation portion of the appraisal should be of a similar number of stories.

Status The appraiser will note the status of the property including whether the improvements are existing, under construction or planned improvements. The status of the property should match the loan type that you are requesting.

        Example: Proposed Improvements   =   Construction Loan

Design The design of the property will affect the desirability of the property. The comparables used for the valuation portion of the appraisal should be of a similar design and appeal.

Year Built and
Effective Age The year that the property was built and the effective age of the property will affect the value. The year built is the actual age. Improvements, renovations, and updating are

factored into the effective age. A home may be a number of decades old and have a much younger effective age if the property has been renovated to bring it into line with newer construction.

Attic
The inclusion or exclusion of an attic may affect both the desirability and the value of a property. Square foot value is typically assessed to those areas that are heated and cooled. These areas are considered to be living square feet. If the attic is used as living square feet, it will be factored as part of the dollar per square foot valuation process. If the attic is used for storage and does not qualify as living square footage, it will still be a factor during underwriting, but more often as a determination that the property of similar design and appeal as the comparables used during the valuation processes.

Foundation
The type of foundation, including the type of basement that they property contains will effect both the desirability and the value of the property. Similar to an attic, a finished basement with a heat source may be considered as living square footage and factored as part of the dollar per square foot valuation. A basement used as storage will be apply as a determination that the subject property is of a similar design and appeal as the comparables used during the valuation process.

Issues
The appraiser will note any issues that are apparent in the basement area of the property. Any issues, including dampness, infestation, or settlement of the property may need to be addressed before the loan can proceed to closing. These issues may put the value and condition of the property at risk if left unaddressed. The job of the underwriter relating to the property is to gain the strongest collateral position possible. If an issue is left unaddressed, the property may continue to deteriorate and result in a loss of value over time.

Heating / Cooling
The type of heating and cooling contained within the subject property may affect the value and appeal of the property. The comparables used for valuation should contain a similar type of heating and cooling sources as the subject property.

Exterior/ Interior
The interior and exterior of the property should be in good condition. The underwriter will confirm that there is not a large discrepancy between the materials of the subject property and the materials of the comparable properties, but will be most interested in the appraiser notes relating to condition. The condition rating set by the appraiser should be at least average. Any condition rating below average may need to be addressed before the loan can proceed to closing.

Amenities
will add value to the property. The appraiser will note any special features or amenities relevant to the subject property. The underwriter will look at the information entered under the comparable property to see if they have any of the same amenities. If the subject property has either a great many or far fewer amenities and features than the

comparables, the underwriter may request an explanation from the appraiser or may determine that an alteration in value from that shown on the appraisal is in order.

Appliances   The inclusion of appliances in the transfer of real estate is not a factor unless the value of the appliances equals a substantial amount of the overall value of a property or if the comparables do include a much greater number or quality of appliances in the transfer.

Square Feet   The appraiser will enter the total square feet of the property and the number of rooms encompassed by this square footage. He will also note the number of these rooms that are bedrooms and bathroom space.

The appraiser will make adjustments during the valuation processes for the differences in square footage between the subject property and the comparable property. The appraiser will also make adjustments based on the use of the square footage.

Comment   The URAR form provides the appraiser with an area to provide opinion about the property. This option section has places available to comment on

- Additional features of the property

- Condition of the property including items that
  o   presently require repairs
  o   are in a state of deterioration
  o   are undergoing renovations
  o   have other apparent issues that the appraiser feels may affect the value of the property

- Deficiencies that affect the livability, soundness or structural integrity of the property

- Neighborhood in comparison to the subject property

The appraiser will enter any comments that they feel are important to the ability of the subject property to maintain its present value. If any item is defined within the comments area that creates a potential for a loss in value, the underwriter will typically require that the issue be cured, or corrected, before the transaction can proceed to closing.

You will want to review each entry within the Improvements Comment section and ensure you understand the problems that may arise. You will also wish to inform any applicable parties to the transaction about the comments.

We recommend contacting your appraiser if you note a discrepancy, error, or issue on the appraisal report. This recommendation does not indicate that you should influence the appraiser's decision and comments in any manner.

The purpose of the contact is to confirm the information in the URAR is correct according to the appraiser's record.

The only alterations you should request to a completed appraisal are alterations arising because of an error or omission.

You should never attempt to influence or alter the opinion of the appraiser.

UNIFORM RESIDENTIAL APPRAISAL REPORT

There are	comparable properties currently offered for sale in the subject neighborhood ranging in price from $		to $			
There are	comparable sales in the subject neighborhood within the past twelve months ranging in sales price from $		to $			

FEATURE	SUBJECT	COMPARABLE SALE #1		COMPARABLE SALE #2		COMPARABLE SALE #3	
Address							
Proximity to Subject							
Sale Price	$	$		$		$	
Sale Price/Gross Liv Area	$ sq ft	$ sq ft		$ sq ft		$ sq ft	
Data Source(s)							
Verification Source(s)							
VALUE ADJUSTMENTS	DESCRIPTION	DESCRIPTION	Adjustment	DESCRIPTION	Adjustment	DESCRIPTION	Adjustment
Sales or Financing Concessions							
Date of Sale / Time							
Location							
Leasehold/Fee Simple							
Site							
View							
Design (Style)							
Quality of Construction							
Actual Age							
Condition							
Above Grade Room Count	Total	Bdrms	Baths	Total	Bedrms	Baths	Total	Brms	Baths		Total	Brms	Baths	
Gross Living Area	sq ft	sq ft		sq ft		sq ft	
Basement & Finished Rooms Below Grade							
Functional Utility							
Heating / Cooling							
Energy Efficient							
Garage / Carport							
Porch/Patio/Deck							
Net Adjustment		+ ＿ -	$	+ ＿ -	$	+ ＿ -	$
Adjusted Sales Price of Comps		Net Adj % / Gross Adj %	$	Net Adj % / Gross Adj %	$	Net Adj % / Gross Adj %	$

I ___ did ___ did not research the sale or transfer history of the subject property and comparable sales. If not, explain

My research ___ did ___ did not reveal any prior sales or transfers of the subject property for the three years prior to the effective date of this appraisal.
Data source(s)

My research ___ did ___ did not reveal any prior sales or transfers of the comparables sales for the year prior to the date of sale of the comparable sale.
Data source(s)

Report the results of the research and analysis of the prior sale or transfer history of the subject property and comparable sales (report additional on pg 3)

ITEM	SUBJECT	COMPARABLE SALE #1	COMPARABLE SALE #2	COMPARABLE SALE #3
Date of Prior Sale/Transfer				
Price of Prior Sale/Transfer				
Data Source(s)				
Effective Date of Data Source(s)				

Analysis of prior sale or transfer history of the subject property and comparable sales

Summary of Sales Comparison Approach

Indicated Value by Sales Comparison Approach $

Indicated Value by: Sales Comparison Approach $ Cost Approach (if developed) $ Income Approach (if developed)$

8:8 Extraction URAR – Sample Form – HUD Release

FEATURE	SUBJECT	COMPARABLE SALE #1		COMPARABLE SALE #2		COMPARABLE SALE #3
Address						
Proximity to Subject						
Sale Price	$	$		$		$
Sale Price/Gross Liv Area	$ sq ft	$ sq ft		$ sq ft		$ sq ft
Data Source(s)						
Verification Source(s)						
VALUE ADJUSTMENTS	DESCRIPTION	DESCRIPTION	Adjustment	DESCRIPTION	Adjustment	DESCRIPTION
Sales or Financing Concessions						
Date of Sale / Time						
Location						
Leasehold/Fee Simple						
Site						
View						
Design (Style)						
Quality of Construction						
Actual Age						
Condition						
Above Grade Room Count	Total Bdrms Baths	Total Bedrms Baths		Total Brms Baths		Total Brms Baths
Gross Living Area	sq ft	sq ft		sq ft		sq ft
Basement & Finished Rooms Below Grade						
Functional Utility						
Heating / Cooling						
Energy Efficient						
Garage / Carport						
Porch/Patio/Deck						
Net Adjustment		+ -	$	+ -	$	+ -
Adjusted Sales Price of Comps		Net Adj % Gross Adj %	$	Net Adj % Gross Adj %	$	Net Adj % Gross Adj %

8:9 Extraction URAR – Sample Form – HUD Release

Page two of the URAR will contain the valuation and cost analysis the appraiser completes when assessing the value of the property. The cost analysis may take two forms either the Cost Approach or the Sales Comparison Approach.

You will see the sales comparison approach used more frequently within your files than the cost approach.

The sales comparison data assesses the characteristics and condition of the subject property as compared to other, similar properties sold within a given time period and in the same area as the subject property. Underwriting guidelines will have standards that must be met with regard to the comparable property that may be used. The property should be

- Similar in design and appeal as the subject property

- Similar in size and condition as the subject property

- Similar in features and amenities as the subject property

- Similar in site design, use, and view as the subject property

- Within a defined distance of the subject property

    Example: Within the same neighborhood

- Sold within a pre-set time limit of the date of the appraiser

If a comparable property included on the appraisal does not meet one of these qualifications, the appraiser will need to explain the reason that the comparable was selected as a data source.

Example: Rural property often exceeds the distance requirement as the mass of land encompassed by rural property often makes it difficult to locate many pieces of sold property within the same neighborhood and within the sales time limit.

At times, underwriting may require additional actions if the comparables used by the appraiser do not meet the standards set within the guidelines of the loan program. Common stipulations that relate to an unacceptable data source inclusion would be to request two additional comparables be incorporated into the appraisal or that an appraisal field review be conducted to verify the value and other information included within the original appraisal.

The subject property will be compared to each of the comparables selected by the appraiser.

Proximity   The distance between the properties being compared effects the value.

The appraiser should locate similar properties sold within a reasonable time that are close in location to the subject property.

Property values vary greatly from one neighborhood to the next. It is important that property comparisons use properties that are located in similarly valued areas.

A comparable property that exceeds reasonable proximity guidelines as set by underwriting for your loan program will require an explanation by the appraiser.

Additional comparables may be needed to validate the value indicated within the appraisal. Some loan programs will dictate that comparables that do not meet the neighborhood requirement will require a reduction in the LTV approval for the loan or a decrease in the value indicated by the appraisal.

Sales Price   The sales price of the comparables is the starting basis that will be used to determine the value of your subject property.

The factors listed below sales price will increase or decrease the value of the subject property in comparison with other closed sales in the area.

Any area of the subject property that is lacking as compared to the comparison properties will result in a decrease to the sales price baseline of the comparable.

Any area of the subject property that is a positive as compared to the comparison properties will result in an increase to the sales price baseline of the comparable.

Sales Price /
Gross Living A dollar figure will be determined for the cost per square foot of the comparable property.

This figure is determined by dividing the total sales price by the total square foot of each property.

Data Sources The appraiser will note the source from which they obtained each entry included in the appraisal.

The comparable property sales price will be adjusted based on comparison factors between the subject property and the comparable property. Each of these adjustment items will result in a change in the price valuation.

Concessions Any concession relating to the transfer of the comparison property will be included as part of the appraisal. These concessions may alter the transaction through an increase in overall value.

The appraiser will also review the sales agreement relating the subject property to determine if it contains any negotiations relating to seller or finance concessions.

Date of Sale A date that is too far removed (past) will need to be addressed.

This is a red flag issue.

The loan guidelines for the loan program being obtained will dictate how far in the past a sale may have occurred and still be considered viable for comparison purposes. All comparison property sales should occur within a reasonable time to ensure the correct market conditions are being addressed in regards to value.

At times, the appraiser may exceed the time limitations set by underwriting. This exception could occur for a variety of reasons including a slow market in which very few homes have transferred or a neighborhood that contains an exceptionally high number of long-term residences and few property transfers.

The appraiser should include an explanation regarding any property sale used for comparison purposes that exceeds the sale date requirements. The underwriter may require other actions to offset the exception in sale date including additional comparables, an appraisal field review, an LTV changes, a property value alteration, or other action.

Location   An assessment of average or above is desired with regard to property location.

Any assessment below average will need to be addressed.

This may be a red flag.

Any variance between the property assessment level and the assessment of the comparison property may result in an alteration to value.

Estate Type   The type of estate of the subject property should match the type of estate listed on the 1003. Any differences between the documents will need to be addressed. Most loan programs require that the fee simple estate be transferred because of the sale. Any limitations or changes to the estate type may affect the value and desirability of the property.

The estate transferred on each of the comparable properties should be the same as the type of estate being transferred in the subject property.

A variance between the estate types of the properties may result in an alteration to the value.

Site Size   The sites should be similar in size. A large difference between the land included with the transfer of the subject property and a comparable property will need to be addressed.

A variance between the site sizes of the properties will result in an alteration to the value. Most program guidelines have specific parameters regarding the percentage of the overall property value allocated to the land and the percentage allocated to improvements, setting very specific limits on the amount of the overall value that may be allocated to the land transferred in the sale.

This issue typically arises in the transfer of rural property.

If the land value of the subject property is excessive, the underwriter may reduce the value by the amount allocated to the land that is in excess of the loan program guidelines.

If there is a large discrepancy between the site size of a comparable and the subject property, the appraiser will need to include an explanation as to why this comparable was chosen as a data source. The underwriter may dictate additional actions required on the appraisal or changes to the loan program because of the variation in site size.

View

The sites should be of similar rating concerning view assessment.

A difference in the assessment of the view level between the properties may result in an alteration in the value of the subject property.

An assessment that indicates a below average rating of the view of the subject property will need to be explained by the appraiser and may result in stipulations or value changes by the underwriter.

Design / Style

The properties should be of similar design and appeal levels. A difference in the design and style of the properties will require an explanation by the appraiser. The appraiser will need to define the reason that they chose a comparable property of a different design or style than the subject.

If the subject property obtains a below average design and appeal assessment this may be a red flag to the underwriter. Any item that receives a below average rating may require actions on the part of the buyer or seller to correct the issue, additional stipulations, or an alteration to the value assessed to the property.

Quality of Construction

The properties should be of similar quality. Any difference in the quality levels of the property will need to be explained by the appraiser.

A difference in the quality of construction may result in an alteration in the value allowed by underwriting.

An assessment that the subject property is of below average construction quality may result in underwriting refusing financing on this property, a stipulation that specific repairs be completed to correct the item that is considered to be below average, a change in the value assessment allowed on the property or another action.

Age of Property

The properties used for comparison purposes should be similar to the age of the subject property. The age of a property affects its value and the appraiser will need to define the reason that the comparables used as data sources are of a different age basis than the subject property.

Room Count /Square Ft

The room counts and square footage of the properties should be similar.

A difference in the room count between the subject property and the comparable property will result in a change to the value assessment assigned by the appraiser.

Underwriting may require additional actions or explanations relating to the differences in property room count.

The dollar value per square foot calculations will be completed by the appraiser. These act as a baseline for the other value calculations. A large discrepancy in square footage between the subject property and the comparison property will alter the value assessed by the appraiser.

Basement

The size and use of the basement of the subject property and comparable properties should be similar. If the basement of the subject property is finished, the basement area of the comparable properties should also be finished.

A variance between the properties will result in an alteration in value.

Functional Utility

The functional utility of all of the properties should be similar. A difference in the functional utility of the subject property from the comparables will require an explanation by the appraiser.

A difference in the quality of construction may result in an alteration in the value allowed by underwriting.

An assessment that the subject property is of below average construction quality may result in underwriting refusing financing on this property, a stipulation that specific repairs be completed to correct the item that is considered to be below average, a change in the value assessment allowed on the property or another action.

The subject property should obtain an assessment of at least average.

An assessment below average will need to be addressed.

This is a red flag.

Heating / Cooling

The heating and cooling systems of the properties will need to be similar.

A difference between the types or inclusion of heating or cooling systems may result in an alteration in value. The type of heating and cooling systems may not be a red flag depending on the region and the commonality of the various heating and cooling systems in use. The addition or exclusion of a cooling system or the age of the heating and cooling system may be a factor.

Energy Efficient

The properties should be of similar levels of energy efficiency.

A large discrepancy in the energy efficiency levels of the properties may result in an alteration in value. The subject property must obtain a rating of at least average. A rating of below average will need to be addressed.

This may be a red flag.

Some programs may require alterations to the property to obtain an assessment of at least average in relationship to energy efficiency.

Some loan program guidelines consider a high level of energy efficiency to be a compensating factor.

Garage / Carport

The inclusion of a garage or carport should be similar between all properties. The appraiser will assess a value to the garage or carport. The comparison section of the appraisal should reflect the alteration in value that results from the inclusion or lack of a garage or carport in one of the properties.

If either the subject property or one of the comparables has or lacks a garage or carport and the other property does not, you should confirm that the value adjustments have been entered into the appropriate field by the appraiser. If there is no value adjustment relating to the inclusion or lack of a garage or carport, you should question the appraiser regarding the lack of an adjustment.

The appraisal may need to be modified to include this value change.

Porch / Patio / Deck

The inclusion of a porch, patio, or deck should be similar between all properties. The appraiser will assess a value to the porch, patio, or deck. The comparison section of the appraisal should reflect the alteration in value that results from the inclusion or lack of a porch, patio, or deck in one of the properties.

If either the subject property or one of the comparables has or lacks a porch, patio, or garage and the other property does not, you should confirm that the value adjustments have been entered into the appropriate field by the appraiser.

If there is no value adjustment relating to the inclusion or lack of a porch, patio, or carport, you should question the appraiser regarding the lack of an adjustment.

The appraisal may need to be modified to include this value change.

An alteration to this inclusion will result in an alteration in the value.

ITEM	SUBJECT	COMPARABLE SALE #1	COMPARABLE SALE #2	COMPARABLE SALE #3
I __did__ did not research the sale or transfer history of the subject property and comparable sales. If not, explain				
My research __did__ did not reveal any prior sales or transfers of the subject property for the three years prior to the effective date of this appraisal.				
Data source(s)				
My research __did__ did not reveal any prior sales or transfers of the comparables sales for the year prior to the date of sale of the comparable sale.				
Data source(s)				
Report the results of the research and analysis of the prior sale or transfer history of the subject property and comparable sales (report additional on pg 3)				
Date of Prior Sale/Transfer				
Price of Prior Sale/Transfer				
Data Source(s)				
Effective Date of Data Source(s)				
Analysis of prior sale or transfer history of the subject property and comparable sales				
Summary of Sales Comparison Approach				
Indicated Value by Sales Comparison Approach $				

8:10 Extraction URAR – Sample Form – HUD Release

Adjustments and Sales Price

The appraiser will enter details relating to the subject property and each comparable selected as a data source for the determination of value. The upper portion will contain details relating to the sale or transfer of each property, including the date of the sale or transfer. The date entered into the date field must be within the time term established by the underwriter. If the sale date of a comparable property exceeds the limitations set by underwriting.

A date that is too far removed (past) will need to be addressed.

This is a red flag issue.

The loan guidelines for the loan program being obtained will dictate how far in the past a sale may have occurred and still be considered viable for comparison purposes. All comparison property sales should occur within a reasonable time to ensure the correct market conditions are being addressed in regards to value.

At times, the appraiser may exceed the time limitations set by underwriting. This exception could occur for a variety of reasons including a slow market in which very few homes have transferred or a neighborhood that contains an exceptionally high number of long-term residences and few property transfers.

The appraiser should include an explanation regarding any property sale used for comparison purposes that exceeds the sale date requirements. The underwriter may require other actions to offset the exception in sale date including additional comparables, an appraisal field review, an LTV changes, a property value alteration, or other action.

Net Adjustments The net adjustments section of the appraisal is the area that the appraiser will use to enter the value calculation factors that will help to determine the final value assessed to the subject property.

Each item that the appraiser assesses for comparison between the properties will be assigned a value.

Any item that was lacking in the subject property but present in the comparison property will result in a reduction from the sales price of the comparable.

Any item that was lacking in the comparable but present in the subject will result in an increase to the sales price of the comparable.

Adjusted Sales Price These value adjustments will be added to or subtracted from the sales price of the comparable.

Example:

Sales Price	199,900
Garage	+ 1,500
Adjusted Sales Price	201,400

The total dollar figure resulting from these adjustments is the figure the appraiser believes the subject property would have sold for if given the same buyer, the same time, and the same conditions.

This is the comparison approach to property valuation.

Signature The signature of the appraiser indicates he has completed the appraiser and certifies that the market value of the property has been duly determined per appraiser guidelines.

Analysis and Indicated Value

The appraiser will place the value figure he has obtained through comparison, adjustments, and market research on the appraisal page.

This is the final appraised value of the property.

PAGE 3 - Additional Comments

The third page of the appraisal has space for comments of the appraiser.

Any issue noted in the first pages of the appraisal should be addressed in this area.

You should review all of the comments to ensure that you have located each potential red flag contained within the appraisal.

You should ensure the appraiser has addressed each issue that you have noted during your review of the appraisal inclusions.

Indicated Value by: Sales Comparison Approach $	Cost Approach (if developed) $	Income Approach (if developed)$

8:11 Extraction URAR – Sample Form – HUD Release

COST APPROACH TO VALUE

The cost approach is used to determine value based upon the replacement cost of the subject property. The cost approach is not usually used for a mortgage loan.

INCOME APPROACH TO VALUE

The income approach to value will often be used for rental or other income producing property. The income approach uses many of the same data indicators as the core appraisal but adds the factor of income to the final value of the property.

PUD PROJECT INFORMATION

If the transaction is being based upon a Planned Unit Development, the PUD section of the appraisal will play a role in the final value determination of the property. You should review this section for any additional red flags that may become apparent if your transaction involves a PUD.

FIELD REVIEWS

Any discrepancy, red flag, or issue on the appraisal may result in a requirement for a field review appraisal. The purpose of a field review is to confirm the opinion of the original appraiser as to condition, value, location and other factors concerning the subject property.

- Underwriting guidelines will stipulate what conditions create the need for a field review.

- Underwriting guidelines will define who is responsible for the cost for a field review.

- The underwriting department will typically request the field review appraisal directly form the appraiser and you will usually not be given the opportunity to review the inclusions of the field review before the underwriter has received a copy.

You will usually be aware of the need for a field review and the results of the field review, but will not be an integral part of the field review processes.

We recommend contacting your appraiser if you note a discrepancy, error, or issue on the appraisal report. This recommendation does not indicate that you should influence the appraiser's decision and comments in any manner.

The purpose of the contact is to confirm the information in the URAR is correct according to the appraiser's record.

The only alterations you should request to a completed appraisal are alterations arising because of an error or omission.

You should never attempt to influence or alter the opinion of the appraiser.

RIGHT TO RECEIVE A COPY OF THE APPRAISAL

When an appraisal has been conducted as a part of the transaction, the borrower has a right to obtain a copy of the appraisal.

- The appraisal will often be delivered directly to the lender during the course of the loan process.

- You should provide instructions to the buyer on how to obtain a copy of the appraisal if they desire one at or before the settlement meeting.

- These instructions must be signed and witnessed during the closing process.

UNIFORM RESIDENTIAL APPRAISAL REPORT

You are advised that you have the right, under the Equal Credit Opportunity Act, to obtain a copy of your Uniform Residential Appraisal Report.

If you wish a copy, please write us at the address shown below. We must hear from you no later than 90 days after we notify you about the action taken on your credit application or you withdraw your application.

Please send your written request to:

In your letter, give the following information:

Loan or application number (if known)

Date of application

Name(s) of loan applicant(s)

Property address

Current mailing address

A copy of your Uniform Residential Appraisal Report shall be mailed to you within 30 days after receipt of your request.

8:12 Extraction URAR – Sample Form – HUD Release

CHAPTER

9

THE GUIDELINE MATRIX

A guideline matrix is a chart that dictates the approval requirements, underwriting basis, and specific approval terms of each loan product that you might use for a borrower. You should view the matrix as a snapshot of the full underwriting guidelines that will be applied to the loan packages that you submit for approval.

The ability to review the matrix and determine where an application package will fall within the matrix will enable you to determine what loan programs might suit the needs of your borrower. The matrix will include data that enables you to assess the documentation that will be requested with the loan package, and begin the process of structuring the loan immediately upon the review of all of the application documentation.

- Each lender your work with will have a variety of loan products available.

- Each product will come with its own set of rules or guidelines that must be met in order to secure that loan for your borrowers.

It is impossible to convey to you the importance of learning the guidelines for each loan program that you have available. The more familiar with the loan guidelines you become, the more capable you will be at placing your borrowers in the appropriate program.

It is our goal to teach you the basics of Mortgage Origination and Loan Submission and to make you a Specialist at these tasks.

It must be your continued goal to review the loan programs available for your use. You must become familiar with the specifics of each program that you may use for your borrower. Your employer should have manuals detailing specific guidelines for each program available. If these are not available at your branch office, you will want to request a guideline manual from the Underwriting Department or have your manager do so.

Learning loan guidelines is imperative to your continued success within the mortgage industry.

Each loan program will have a product matrix available. These matrixes are a snapshot of the minimum requirements that are necessary to place a loan in a particular approval tier or level.

Approval guidelines should not be confused with proper documentation. Most approval guidelines are based on your borrower credit and debt ratios. Earlier we asked you to complete two practice forms. These forms were:

Credit Scoring

Debt-to-Income Ratio

You should locate these two forms and use them for this section of the course. If you have not yet completed the practice lessons, you will need to do so now. The practice materials we will review in placing and pricing the loan require these forms. The completed forms will contain valuable information you will need when determining loan placement and adherence to minimum level criteria.

SAMPLE PRODUCT MATRIX

Credit Grade	Credit Score	Mortgage History	Consumer History	Bankruptcy / Foreclosure	Maximum Debt Ratio	Maximum LTV	Maximum CLTV
A	660+	0x30	1x30	3/3	41%	97%	97%
A-	620-669	1x30	2x30	3/3	45%	95%	97%
B	590-619	2x30	1x60	2/2	47%	90%	95%
B-	560-589	1x60	2x60	2/2	50%	85%	95%
C	540-559	2x60	1x90	1/1	50%	80%	90%
C-	520-539	1x90	2x90	1/1	55%	75%	90%
D	490-519	2x90	3x90	>1year	55%	70%	85%
Contact U/W	>490	>2x90	>3x90	>1 year	55%	Contact U/W	Contact UW

Figure 9:1 Sample Guideline Matrix

Matrix Limitations/Key

The sample matrix applies to a non-conforming loan product. The sample matrix includes the minimum guideline requirements for each level. The minimum guidelines indicated by this particular matrix are included below. You should review these minimum requirements and limitations and compare the entries to the example matrix. This practice will assist you in gaining an understanding of how you will locate the limitations and requirements for each matrix that you will use.

- Maximum mortgage and consumer late payments are rated using the worst rating in history.

- All late payments lower than the worst rating mortgage and consumer history late payments may usually be discounted.

  Example: a 1x60 negates the use of all 30-day late payments.

- Mortgage and Consumer late payments are calculated over the preceding 12-month or 24-month period only.

- Credit scores requirements may be waived if adequate compensating factors exist in the credit profile.

- Foreclosure and Bankruptcy dates indicate the date of completion or discharge only.

- Maximum debt ratio limitations may be exceeded if adequate compensating factors exist in the credit profile

- Collection accounts under $2500 may be left unpaid for approval levels of B- or lower. Approval status of B or above must pay all open collections.

- Charge off accounts and all judgment accounts must be paid in full before closing for all approvals above C-. Approvals below C- must be reviewed by underwriting.

- Medical collections may be left unpaid for all approvals of B or below.

- Medical collections must be paid in full for approvals of A or A-.

- All approval levels require a minimum of three open lines of consumer credit.

- Mortgage/Rental history must be verified through a third party source.

This matrix is for example purposes only. Each loan program will have specific guidelines and approval levels. You should refer to your guideline manual for the approval guidelines of a particular loan program.

GRADING

Each loan program will have a product matrix available. These matrixes are a snapshot of the minimum requirements that are necessary to place a loan in a particular approval tier or level for a specific loan program.

Example:	Borrower	1st Matrix Level Approval Rate
Credit Score	589	B- (on tier possible bump)
Mortgage History	0x30	A
Consumer History	1x60	B
Bankruptcy	None	A
Foreclosure	None	A
Debt Ratio	43%	A-

Using this borrower example criterion and the data included within the sample product matrix, the borrower would qualify for an approval rating of B or a B-. B is the better approval rating and will provide the borrower with a more desirable LTV, CLTV, and interest rate pricing. Therefore, you desire a B for your borrower.

In order to qualify as a B rating compensating factors must used to improve the base approval of the borrower. The credit score in the example places the borrower within the B- tier, but all of the other factors are within the A or B approval level. A common compensating factor baseline request is that the credit score falls within a few points of the next highest approval tier.

The cover sheet you submit with the loan application for this borrower would indicate all compensating factors regarding your borrower and state the request for an underwriting exception with regard to the credit score.

In this scenario, we will assume the underwriter approved the credit grade exception request based on the compensating factors within the borrower's profile.

The B credit grade approval level carries the following details:

- LTV   90%

- CLTV   95%

- All collection accounts must be paid in full before closing.

- All charge off and judgment accounts must be paid in full before closing.

- Medical collections may remain unpaid.

We have placed the borrower within a B credit grade approval level. As a B credit grade approval, the borrower is qualified for an LTV of 90%, a CLTV of 95%.

If the basic criteria of the approval tiers suits the needs of the borrower, your next step is to price the loan to determine the interest rate level and to confirm that the debt ratio of the borrower meets the program guidelines.

The DTI ratio may change after you complete the pricing process due to the actual rate the borrower can receive. The debt ratio may continue to change as interest rate offerings fluctuate. Once the borrower locks in the rate using the rate lock / float option form, you can finalize the DTI ratio calculations.

Some underwriting criteria allow for exceptions to the debt ratio levels if there are adequate compensating factors in the borrower's profile to substantiate the exception.

Our example borrower has obtained an exception to the credit score requirement so compensating factors would need to carry a high impact with the underwriter to obtain a second exception.

If the new housing expense exceeds ratio limitations and you cannot obtain an exception, there would be alternative options available to you:

- Reduce the maximum sales price and loan amount your borrower may obtain.

- Reduce the points wrapped into the interest rate and accept a lower commission or obtain payment for your services on the front-end.

- Pay off consumer debt in an attempt to reduce debt load.

    *   Caution The action of paying off debt may reduce the credit score.

- Obtain seller assistance toward closing costs or additional borrower funds so that there is money available to buy down the interest rate to a level that generates a payment that fits within the debt ratio guidelines.

- Search for a different program whose approval tier gives a higher DTI ratio limit. This program change may enable the borrower to approve at the levels needed to close the loan under the present circumstances.

It is important to note that each approval grade provides a maximum LTV and CLTV. When you review the section relating to pricing the loan, you will note that a lower LTV compared to the maximum possible under a credit grade, the lower the interest rate will become. Even if your borrowers only require an LTV of 80%, you will still wish to locate the highest-grade approval possible for the borrower's profile because the grade approval will affect all elements of the loan process, not just the maximum LTV and CLTV.

This is a sample of a credit grading process. Each loan program will have different guidelines and factors that may affect the process. Each borrower will have a variety of factors that effect the approval options. You should review the guideline matrix for each program that you may use for a borrower to determine other variables that may affect the grading and approval practices of your office.

CONVENTIONAL LOAN UNDERWRITING GUIDELINES

Category		MANUAL UNDERWRITING	AUTOMATED UNDERWRITING
ELIGIBILITY	Programs	30-Year Fixed, 40-Year Fixed, 35-Year Interest Only	
	Loan Purpose	Purchase Transactions Only	
	Occupancy Status	Owner-Occupied Primary Residence Only	
	LTV / CLTV Limits	Maximum LTV 100%, Maximum CLTV 107% (90% Maximum LTV/CLTV on Manufactured Housing on 30 and 40-year only. Manufactured housing is NOT permitted on interest only	
	Minimum Contribution	None Required	
CREDIT	Minimum Credit Score	620 (regardless of automated underwriting findings)	
	Alternative Credit	Permitted. Minimum of four sources with a twelve month satisfactory payment record. One of the sources must be a twelve month VOR.	
	BK / NOD / Foreclosure	Minimum 3 years since discharge/sale date and evidence of reestablished credit required.	
	Collections	If individual account balance is less than $250 or the total of all such accounts is $1000 or less not required to pay at closing.	Determined by automated approval
	Student Loan	Must not be in default. Deferred allowed as long as payment calculated in debt ratios.	
RATIOS & INCOME	Back End Ratio	45% (35-Year Interest Only qualified as 35-Year fully amortized)	55% regardless of underwriting findings
	Temporary Buy downs	Temporary buy downs allowed on 30-Year & 40-Year Fixed Rate loans only. No buy downs permitted on Interest Only. LTV > 95% qualify at note rate. LTV < or = 95% qualify at buy down + 1	Determined by automated approval
	Non-Occupancy Co-Signor		Permitted on 30-Year & 40-Year Fixed rate loans only with LTV , or = 90%. Occupant borrower(s) total debt ratio max 55%, combined max 45%
	Boarder Income	None Permitted	
	PT / OT / 2nd Job / Bonus Income	Permitted with a minimum 12 month history	Determined by automated approval
PROPERTY	Eligible Property Types	Single family (no in laws suites/ granny flats) 5 acres maximum. Condominiums must meet FNMA Condominium Project Acceptance Policy or be FHA Approved PUD. Manufactured Housing – limited to 90% LTV/CLTV with 10% down payment from borrower's own funds on 30 and 40-year	
	Appraisals	One of the following appraisal forms is required: Uniform Residential Appraisal Report (URAR), Frannie Mae/Freddie Mac for 1004 (Single Family / PUD), Form 1004C (Manufactured Home Appraisal Report), Form 1073 (Individual Condominium Appraisal Report)	
FUNDS TO CLOSE	Minimum Down Payment	No minimum down payment required except for manufactured home loans which require 10% borrowers own funds	
	Cash Reserves	1 month	Determined by automated approval
	Gift Funds	Permitted. No Maximum. May be used to supplement cash reserves.	
	Seller Contribution	Contributions by any interested party towards recurring and/or non-recurring closing costs are limited to: 3% of the purchase price if LTV is > 90%, 6% of the purchase price if LTV is < or = 90%. Any contribution exceeding these limits requires a downward adjustment to the sales price to reflect the amount that exceeds the limits	
MORTGAGE IN-SURANCE	Monthly Mortgage Insurance	Required on all loans with an LTV > 80%	
	Mortgage Insurance Rates	(see table below)	

Mortgage Insurance Rates:

30-Year Fixed / 40-Year Fixed / 35-Year IOP (non-conforming loan)			35-Year IOP (conforming loan)		
LTV	Coverage	Pricing	LTV	Coverage	Pricing
95.01-100	35%	85	97.01-100	20%	59
90.01-95	35%	75	95.01-97	18%	50
85.01-90	35%	55	90.01-95	16%	46
80.01-95	35%	41	85.01-90	12%	34
			80.01-95	6%	23

9:2 Sample Guideline Matrix

PRICING THE LOAN

Loan program pricing is the process of determining the interest rate that the lender will apply to the borrower's new loan. Rate factors, including approval tiers, maximum limitations, and wrapped points will influence the interest rate that you can offer to the borrower.

After you have chosen a loan program for your borrower, you will need to price the loan based on the current rate sheet for that particular program.

You will want to be certain you are using the most up to date rate sheet to avoid errors in pricing.

- Before beginning the pricing process, you should review the rate sheet to determine if there are any restrictions to the pricing.

  Restrictions will include any internal requirement and applicable laws regarding loan pricing for the loan program you have chosen for the borrower.

  Example: Loans under $50,000 may not contain a pre-payment penalty.

You will want to ensure that you comply with all of the applicable restrictions on the rate sheet.

- The second item to review will be the qualifying guidelines on the rate sheet.

  These guidelines should match the product matrix you used to determine the approval level of your borrower.

  It is important that you confirm the matrix guidelines match the approval guidelines that you applied when placing the borrower within a credit tier. Loan programs are changed frequently and you must ensure that you are using the most up-to-date details when pricing the loan.

  You should note that some rate sheets may not contain guideline qualification information.

- You should familiarize yourself with the format of the rate sheet. Every lender has a variation on the rate sheet format that they like to use.

  The rate sheets will contain the same basic information. The layout used will be different.

- Locate the column on the rate sheet that contains the preferred loan terms for your borrower.

  Example: 30 year fixed

  Example: 3/1 ARM

- Once you have located the correct column, you will locate the row that is applicable to the borrower credit approval rating.

  A, A-, B or another credit approval designation depending on the lender to whom you are submitting the loan package

- Within the credit level designation, you will find various LTV's. You should locate the LTV that your borrower requires.

- You will scroll over within the LTV row to the column that indicates the pricing that you must obtain to make the loan figures work.

  Example: if you must price at par and will obtain payment up front, you will use the rate designated under the PAR column.

  Example   If you must wrap 1 point into the rate, you will use <1.00>

- Locate the corresponding interest rate.

You will offer this rate for your borrower.

You should enter this rate into all applicable documents and recalculate the loan payments.

It is important that you confirm the payment is entered correctly on the loan application documents. A small change in the monthly payment can alter the entire loan approval.

RATE SHEET

Grade	LTV	3/1 ARM			Margin	30 Year Fixed			15 Year Fixed		
		Par	<1.00>	<2.00>		Par	<1.00>	<2.00>	Par	<1.00>	<2.00>
A 660+	97%	8.000	8.500	9.000	4.125	8.500	9.000	9.500	8.000	8.500	9.000
Mtg 0X30	95%	7.875	8.375	8.875	3.875	8.125	8.625	9.125	7.875	8.375	8.875
Con 1X30	90%	7.625	8.125	8.625	3.375	8.000	8.500	9.000	7.625	8.125	8.625
3/3	85%	7.250	7.875	8.375	3.250	7.875	8.125	8.625	7.375	7.875	8.375
41%	80%	7.000	7.500	8.000	3.125	7.750	8.250	8.750	7.000	7.500	8.000
	75%	6.750	7.250	7.775	3.000	7.625	8.125	8.625	6.750	7.250	7.775
A- 620-669	95%	8.500	9.000	9.500	3.875	9.750	10.250	10.750	8.500	9.000	9.500
Mtg 1X30	90%	8.125	8.625	9.125	3.375	9.500	10.000	10.500	8.125	8.625	9.125
Con 2X30	85%	8.000	8.500	9.000	3.250	9.125	9.625	10.125	8.000	8.500	9.000
3/3	80%	7.875	8.125	8.625	3.125	8.875	9.375	9.875	7.875	8.125	8.625
45%	75%	7.750	8.250	8.750	3.000	8.375	8.875	9.375	7.750	8.250	8.750
	70%	7.625	8.125	8.625	2.875				7.625	8.125	8.625
B 590-619	90%	9.750	10.250	10.750	4.125	10.250	10.750	11.250	9.750	10.250	10.750
Mtg 2X30	85%	9.500	10.000	10.500	3.875	9.625	10.125	10.625	9.500	10.000	10.500
Con 1X60	80%	9.125	9.625	10.125	3.375	9.375	9.875	10.375	9.125	9.625	10.125
2/2	75%	8.875	9.375	9.875	3.250	9.250	9.750	10.250	8.875	9.375	9.875
47%	70%	8.375	8.875	9.375	3.125	8.875	9.250	9.750	8.375	8.875	9.375
B- 560-589	85%	10.250	10.750	11.250	5.250	10.875	11.375	11.875	10.250	10.750	11.250
Mtg 1X60	80%	9.625	10.125	10.625	5.125	10.250	10.750	11.250	9.625	10.125	10.625
Con 2X60	75%	9.375	9.875	10.375	5.000	9.625	10.125	10.625	9.375	9.875	10.375
2/2	70%	9.250	9.750	10.250	4.875	9.375	9.875	10.375	9.250	9.750	10.250
50%											
C 540-559	80%	10.875	11.375	11.875	6.250	11.625	12.125	13.125	10.875	11.375	11.875
Mtg 2X60	75%	10.250	10.750	11.250	6.000	10.875	11.375	12.375	10.250	10.750	11.250
Con 1X90	70%	9.625	10.125	10.625	5.875	10.250	10.750	11.750	9.625	10.125	10.625
1/1	65%	9.375	9.875	10.375	5.625	9.750	10.125	11.250	9.375	9.875	10.375
50%											
C- 520-539	75%	11.625	12.125	13.125	7.500	12.375	12.875	13.250	11.625	12.125	13.125
Mtg 1X90	70%	10.875	11.375	12.375	6.875	11.750	12.250	12.750	10.875	11.375	12.375
Con 2X90	65%	10.250	10.750	11.750	6.250	11.125	11.625	12.125	10.250	10.750	11.750
1/1											
55%											
D 490-519	70%	12.375	12.875	13.250	7.875	12.875	13.250	13.875	12.375	12.875	13.250
Mtg 2X90	65%	11.750	12.250	12.750	7.325	12.250	12.750	13.125	11.750	12.250	12.750
Con 2X90											
>1 Year											
55%											

Pricing assumes 3-year prepayment penalty.
Add .250 to rate for 1-year prepayment penalty.
Add .500 to rate for 0-year prepayment penalty.
No prepayment penalty may be charged on loans >50K.
Loans under 30K require a .500 rate adjustment.

10:1 Sample Rate Sheet

Pre-pricing Quick List

- Qualifying level of your borrower

- LTV required by your borrower

- CLTV required by your borrower

- ARM or Fixed priced loan program

- Prepayment penalty option

- How you are getting paid. Will you receive up front fees or must you wrap points?

To determine your borrower's approval level, you will want to refer to the credit scoring forms you completed earlier.

You will also need to verify the DTI Ratios to be certain they fall within the guidelines of the level where you wish to place your borrowers.

Note that each level has different LTV options.

- In general, the lower the LTV as compared to the maximum allowed the lower the interest rate.

The higher the credit-grade status of your borrowers the better interest rate they can expect.

- Keep in mind that using the maximum available options for the borrower's Credit Grade typically will increase the interest rate.

You must know the options that the borrower has chosen for the loan. If the borrower has not chosen term and penalty options, you might price all of the variables and provide your borrower with a range of program offerings at the approval meeting. ARM vs. Fixed Rate programs and the use of Prepayment Penalties are explained on the following pages.

Determine commission payment options before pricing the loan.

PRICING THE LOAN
Quick Guide

Credit Grade		You will need to refer to your credit worksheet to determine the credit grade for which your borrower's will qualify. Upon reviewing your Product Matrix and Guidelines, you should have developed you own system for charting the credit grade of your borrower's package under the various programs you are considering.	Each program will have a different set of terminology for their credit grades. Many will put the basic minim requirements for each grade level on the rate sheet so that you can double-check the approval tier as you price the loan.
	Credit Score	You will want to verify that the credit score you have determined as applicable for the program meets the minimum requirements for the grade level that you are pricing.	Keep in mind that different lender's will dictate the score that will apply to the loan program. Some lenders require the use of the middle credit score ranked by numbers and some will require the use of the most regionally accurate score for the borrower's location.
	Mortgage History	The rate sheet or guideline matrix will define the number and the time allowed for that grade with regard to mortgage late payments.	If the mortgage history is not on the credit report, you will need to provide documentation proving the mortgage or rental history status over the applicable period the chosen loan program.
	BK/FC	All credit grades require that a bankruptcy or foreclosure be 'seasoned" for a period. This refers to the date of discharge.	If the date is not apparent on the credit report, you will need to provide documentation proving the discharge date.
	Consumer Credit	As with mortgage history most Credit Grades will require that, the consumer history meets certain minimums requirements with regard to the number and term of any late payments evident on the history.	Some Credit Grade sheets will remove consumer history as a criterion. These lenders rely on credit scores to reflect the consumer history.
	Debt Ratio	Many rate sheets provide you with the maximum debt ratio allowed under that grade. If your borrower's ratio exceeds the requirements of the loan program, they will be dropped to the next lowest credit grade whose minimum requirements they do meet.	Bear in mind that the Debt Ratios must include the new housing payment and any subordinate financing payments the borrower plans to incur because of the purchase. Also, bear in mind that the Underwriting Team will typically pull another credit report just before closing. Any additional debt your borrower's incur between these credit reports will be factored into the debt ratio. Counsel your borrowers not to make credit purchases even if the credit is available to them until the new mortgage loan is closed.
LTV (Loan To Value)		This section lists the maximum loan to value options available for each credit grade	You will note that there are listings below the maximum LTV available to the borrower. In most cases, the lower the actual LTV as compared to the maximum LTV allowed the lower the interest rate offered.
ARM/FIXED		The next columns show the program term options.	You should discuss the term options with the borrower and assist them in choosing the amortization term and

KENNEY

		The term that your borrower chooses for the amortization of the loan will affect the interest rate offered to them by the lender.	method that best suits their needs and plans. You should not simply choose a term to achieve the best interest rate. The amortization term and method must be chosen to meet the needs of the borrower.
	PAR	Directly below the term option you will see the pricing details available the loan program. PAR, <1.00>, <2.00> and <3.00> To price at par means that there are no points included in the interest rate and you must obtain your commission points as an up-front payment at the closing. You will include these up front points in the good faith estimate and on the HUD Settlement Statement.	To price at <1.00> means that you are receiving 1% of the loan amount as back end commission. <2.00> means 2% commission points and <3.00> means 3% of the loan amount as back end commission. This is known as wrapping points or being paid on the back-end.
	Margin	Beside the Par section, you will see the word Margin. This only appears on the ARM options. The margin refers to the rate of adjustment that may occur after the fixed portion of the loan program expires.	It is essential that you explain the rate adjustment term and margin to the borrower before placing them in an adjustable rate program. ARM's can be useful tools if the borrower's plans match the adjustment term but should be used with caution. The borrower must be able to meet the terms of the newly adjusted loan. If you place a borrower in an ARM program and the DTI Ratio cannot support the adjusted monthly payment or the borrower cannot refinance or sell the home, the borrower's payment stability may be at risk.
Pricing		You will now incorporate all of the applicable pricing options to arrive at an interest rate quote. • find the correct credit grade • determine the desired loan to value • follow the column over to the correct loan term option and pricing (back end points)	The rate shown is the interest rate you will quote to your borrowers.
Examples		Borrower A is rated a credit grade A and requires a 95% LTV. You need to incorporate 2 points into the rate. The borrower is able to take a 3/1 ARM with a 3-year prepayment penalty	Rate Quote: 8.875
		If Borrower A is willing to pay all points up front, you can drop his interest rate accordingly.	Rate Quote: 7.875
		If Borrower A were able to secure gift funds from a family member in the amount of 10% of the sales price, your LTV would drop to 85% LTV. All other items remain the same as in example one.	Rate Quote: 8.375

194

A rate sheet will often have a variables box somewhere on the page. The variable box allows you to alter the rate by choosing additional options.

Example: if you chose a 1-year prepayment penalty with the loan examples above, you would add .250 to the rate quote.

If you choose no prepayment penalty, with the examples above, you might be required to increase the rate quote by .500.

Variables are very important to the pricing process because it is up to you to sell the borrower on the interest rate. It would also be up to you to explain why the rate changed if you missed a variable that was going to cause a rate increase.

We have included some sample credit reports in the Chapter Career Building Tools. We recommend you use the samples and forms included to practice preliminary product approvals and rate quotes.

ARM or Fixed Rate Options

You will typically have both ARM and Fixed Rate offerings available for your borrower. The decision to use an ARM or fixed rate program is one that you and the borrower must carefully consider.

Both program types carry potential benefits as well as potential drawbacks. You should review the borrower's present situation, plans, and the market conditions in order to educate your borrower and assist them in making the best possible decision.

ADJUSTABLE RATE PROGRAM

An adjustable rate mortgage is a mortgage program that carries a variable interest rate that can change over the life of the loan. The rate applied to the principal borrowed under an adjustable rate mortgage may go up or down depending on the status of the index to which it is linked.

Adjustable-rate mortgage programs are created with a pre-set margin. The margin or adjustment base is set on a major mortgage index such as the Libor. An adjustable rate mortgage program has the ability to affect the borrower's monthly payments through the application of the new interest rate that occurs at each adjustment period. This adjusting rate could place some borrowers at risk if economic conditions dictate that the rate goes up and the borrower's debt to income ratio is unable to bear the new monthly mortgage payment applied because of the increased interest rate.

An adjustable rate mortgage program can be customized around your borrower's homeownership plans, credit rehabilitation program, or the market prediction of rate activity.

- The credit rehabilitation program is the program you develop as a service to your borrower in an effort to secure future purchase and refinance loans from that borrower. This program offers them methods of rebuilding and repairing their credit in time to refinance before the rate adjustment occurs. You will want to familiarize yourself with conventional minimum guidelines before offering rehabilitation advice.

- When market fluctuations are expected to occur and the borrower plans to refinance the mortgage at the time of these occurrences, an ARM will allow a lower interest during the payment term. The ARM should be set to expire at or about the time of market condition changes.

- If the borrower intends to move or sell the home within a specified number of years, an adjustable rate program may help to decrease the costs of homeownership during the years that the borrower remains in the mortgage.

   Example: A borrower who works for a national corporation or serves in the military may be aware of future transfer plans. An adjustable rate loan program may be a good choice if the transfer plans are solid and the program can be customized around this expected move date.

In many cases, the adjustable rate programs will offer a rate discount to the borrower well below the basic fixed rate program offerings.

Many adjustable rate programs offer a 2, 3, even 5-year fixed rate term before the first adjustment.

Because of the rate adjustment period, you may also have the opportunity to write a prepayment penalty into the loan package.

A pre-payment penalty option provides the benefit of lowering the interest rate even further.

You should carefully consider the risk of incorporating a pre-payment penalty or adjustable rate into any borrower's loan program.

- An adjustable rate carries the risk that the payment may adjust by a large margin if the borrower is unable to refinance or sell the home before the adjustment period.

- A pre-payment penalty inhibits the refinance or sale activity of the borrower until the pre-payment penalty expires. If the borrower chooses to refinance the loan or sell the home before the date of the expiration, a fee or penalty will be imposed.

If your borrower desires an ARM and Pre-Payment penalty loan, you must assist the borrower in customizing the prepayment period to expire in time for the refinance but before the rate adjustment.

If a borrower's primary dwelling is going to be secured by an Adjustable Rate or Variable Rate loan, The Truth-in-Lending Act requires that additional disclosures be provided to the borrower.

When working with a borrower that is obtaining an adjustable rate mortgage, you must provide the borrower with educational notices and disclosures that assist them in understanding the loan program that they are obtaining.

- The Consumer Handbook on Adjustable Rate Mortgages

- A disclosure for each variable rate program offered to the borrower.

The disclosures must contain all the necessary information required by Regulation Z.

The Truth-in-Lending Act also requires loan servicers to provide disclosures to consumers each month an adjustment to the interest rate occurs.

ADJUSTABLE RATE MORTGAGE DISCLOSURE STATEMENT

IMPORTANT MORTGAGE LOAN INFORMATION
PLEASE READ CAREFULLY

PROGRAM NAME: _____

You have expressed an interest in applying for an Adjustable Rate Mortgage loan (ARM). This disclosure contains information regarding the differences between this ARM and other mortgage loans. This disclosure describes the features of the specific ARM that you are considering. Upon request, we will provide you with information about any other Adjustable Rate Mortgage programs we have available.

ADJUSTABLE RATE MORTGAGE LOAN: This loan is an Adjustable Rate Mortgage loan. The interest rate may change based upon movements of a specific interest rate index. Changes in the interest rate will be reflected by increases or decreases in the amount of your payments. The date or dates on which changes can occur will be specified in the ARM loan documents. This ARM is based on the terms and conditions of the program in which you have expressed an interest. We have based this disclosure on recent interest rates, index and margin values, and fees.

THIS DISCLOSURE: This disclosure is not a contract or loan commitment. The matters discussed in this disclosure are subject to change by us at any time without notice. DETERMINING THE INTEREST RATE: Your interest rate will be determined by means of an index that is subject to change

Your interest rate is based on the Index value plus a margin. A change in the index generally will result in a change in the interest rate. If the Index rate change since the previous adjustment is less than _____, the interest rate will not change. The amount that your interest rate change may also be affected by periodic interest rate change limitations and the lifetime interest rate limits set forth in your loan program.
Interest Rate Adjustments Your interest rate under this ARM can change every _____ years.
    Your interest rate cannot increase or decrease more than ____ percentage points at each adjustment.
    Your interest rate cannot increase or decrease more than ____percentage points over the term of your loan.
    Rate adjustments under this ARM will be reflected in higher or lower payments.

DETERMINING THE PAYMENTS: Your initial monthly payment of principal and interest will be determined based on the interest rate, loan term, and loan balance when your loan is closed. Your payment will be set to amortize the loan over a period of ___ payments.
Frequency of Payment Changes: Based on increases or decreases in the Index, payment amounts under this ARM loan can change every ____ years. Your monthly payment amount could change more frequently if there is a change in other loan factors not relating to the ARM. These factors may include taxes, assessments, insurance premiums, or other charges required when creating an escrow or impound account.

Limitations on Payment Changes: Your payment can change every ___ years based on changes in the interest rate, loan term, or loan balance.
Adjustment Notices: You will be notified if interest rate changes occur. If an interest rate change effects your monthly payment, you will be notified at least 25 calendar days before the changed payment is due. The notice will indicate the adjusted payment amount, interest rate, Index value, and the outstanding loan balance at that time.

** INSERT AN EXAMPLE AND INDEX TABLES AS THEY APPLY TO THE ARM UNDER DISCUSSION.
I/we acknowledge that we have received a copy of this disclosure:

10:2 ARM Disclosure Notice – HUD Release

What is a pre-payment penalty?

- A prepayment penalty is a monetary penalty that is assessed for the early payoff of a loan that contains a prepay clause. Most lenders offer 0, 2, 3, and 5-year prepayment penalties.

- These penalties offer the lender the security that the borrower will retain the loan for a certain period of time. This helps to secure a minimum financial return for the investor based on the expected interest payments over the pre-set term. If the borrower were to make an early payoff on the loan, the penalty is designed to offset the loss of interest suffered by the lender.

- Lenders will offer a reduction of initial interest rate in exchange for the prepayment clause because of the added longevity of loans on the books.

- Pre-payment penalties may not be a workable option for some borrowers. If you are working with a borrower who desires a pre-payment penalty or requires a lower interest rate than the base offering, you should ensure that the borrower's situation and plans can meet the requirements of the pre-payment penalty term.

Penalty Verbiage

If within the first (option #) of years full prepayment is made, the prepayment charge is an amount equal to the payment of six (6) months advance interest, at the interest rate provided under the note, on the amount prepaid which is in excess of twenty (20) percent of the original principal amount.

Some states have laws governing the use of prepayment penalties. You will want to familiarize yourself with your state law pertaining to the use of prepayment penalties.

PREPAYMENT NOTE ADDENDUM

This Prepayment Note Addendum is made this   day of   and is incorporated into and shall be deemed to amend and supplement the Note of the same date (the "Note") given by the undersigned (the "Borrower) to evidence the Borrower's indebtedness to

ADDITIONAL COVENANTS.   Notwithstanding anything to the contrary set forth in the Note or Security Instrument, Borrower and Lender further covenant and agree as follows:

1. Section 5 of the Adjustable Rate Note, is modified to provide for a prepayment charge upon Borrower's full prepayment. A "full prepayment" is the prepayment of all of the unpaid principal due under the Note. A prepayment of only part of the principal is known as a "partial prepayment".

Borrower can make a partial prepayment at anytime without paying nay charge. Borrower may make a full prepayment anytime subject to a prepayment charge as follows:

If within the first   months after the date Borrower executes the Note, Borrower makes a full prepayment (including prepayments occurring as a result of the acceleration of the maturity of the Note), Borrower must, as a condition precedent to a full prepayment, pay a prepayment charge on any amount prepaid in any 12 month period in excess of 20% of the unpaid balance. The prepayment charge will equal the interest that would accrue during a six-month period on the Excess Principal calculated at the rate of interest in effect under the terms of the Note at the time of the full prepayment.

2. All other provisions of the note are unchanged by this addendum and remain in full force and effect.

NOTICE TO BORROWER

Do not sign this loan agreement before you read it. This loan agreement provides for the payment of a penalty if you wish to repay the loan prior to the date provided for repayment in the loan agreement.

10:3 Example – Prepayment Rider

RATE LOCK OR FLOAT OPTION

The borrower must complete a rate lock or float option form. This form specifies the borrower's determination as to whether they wish to lock in the offered interest rate now or wait on the chance that the interest rate will change for the better during the loan processing stage.

The upper section of the form should provide identifying details relating to the borrower, the property, and the loan.

The form will have two areas that relate to the choices the borrower is making. The borrower should complete and sign the area that relates to their choice with regard to the offered interest rate.

If the borrower wishes to lock in the currently offered interest rate, they will complete the RATE LOCK section of the form. The rate lock section will show the offered rate, any points associated with the obtainment of this rate, and the number of days that the rate lock offer is applicable. The borrower will sign and date the form to illustrate their acceptance of the offered rate and terms.

If the borrower wishes to wait to lock the rate in the hopes that the market will improve thus improving the interest rate that they can obtain, the borrower will complete the DO NOT LOCK section of the form by signing and dating the applicable area.

The borrower should receive a copy of the completed rate lock form.

RATE LOCK

Loan Amount $\$$_____

Property Address _____

City, State, Zip   _____

This is to certify that I DO want to exercise my interest rate lock option at this time.

A.   My guaranteed interest rate will be _____%.

D.   The total points paid at settlement will not exceed _____. This total does not include settlement costs such as title insurance, homeowners insurance, transfer taxes, etc.

E.   This agreement will end _____ days from today. This date is called the ending date.

ACKNOWLEDGEMENT

_____   _____
Signed   Date

_____   _____
Signed   Date

This is to certify that I DO NOT want to exercise my interest rate lock option at this time.

A.   I understand that my lender cannot predict interest rate changes.

E.   If I want to obtain an interest rate commitment in the future, I may do so at any time up to ___ days before the closing of my mortgage loan.

F.   I understand that I must sign an interest rate lock-in agreement to obtain a guaranteed interest rate lock.

G.   I understand that it is my responsibility to advise the lender of my desire to obtain interest rate commitment.

ACKNOWLEDGEMENT

_____   _____

10:4 Sample Rate Lock / Float Option Form

CHAPTER

11

LOAN PROCESS

You will establish your own personal system for fulfilling all the myriad of tasks involved with a loan process from initial contact to closing the loan. The loan office where you work may have other specific methods they choose to use in the loan process. A large portion of your day will be spent moving the loan process toward a speedy closing. The more organized you become at incorporating all of the necessary tasks into your workflow the more vital to the office you will become.

To aid you in creating your own loan system, we have created a process overview that encompasses the required tasks in a timely manner.

Complete the Pre-Qualification Questionnaire
You will need to have the Pre-Qualification forms available at all times, preferably bound in a reference Binder.

Pull Credit
Pull the Credit report for both the borrower and the co borrower.

Review Credit Report
You will review the credit report and complete the credit history scoring key. You should note any additional

documentation requirements that the borrower may need to provide because of an entry on the credit report.

Qualify loan

You will gather all of the applicable forms necessary to begin qualifying the loan package, these include the

Pre-Qualification Questionnaire

Credit Report

D. T. I. Ratio Form

Credit History Form

Screen for possible programs

You should compare the borrower profile with the requirements of the different loan programs to choose a loan offering for the borrower. You will have the applicable lender matrix and guideline manuals available for your use.

Rate/Price Loan

Once you have chosen a loan program suitable for the borrower's goals and whose guidelines fit the profile of the borrower, you will determine a Rate and Price basis for the loan. You should gather all of the necessary documents, manuals, and forms required to complete the pricing tasks.

To price the loan, you will need all of the documents from the loan file, the Product Matrix for the chosen loan product, and the most up to date rate sheet for the loan program being considered.

Product Matrix
Rate Sheet
Worksheets

Set Appointment/
Request Documentation

Once you have completed the fundamental screening tasks on the loan file, you will typically return the package to the loan processor so that they may contact the borrower to set an appointment for the completion of the application and obtainment of file documents.

You will request documentation based on the guidelines of the loan program chosen for the borrower and on the borrower's specific situation.

You will nearly always request that the borrower bring

- 2 years W-2s,

- Year To Date pay stubs

  The borrower should bring pay stubs that cover the full 30 day period prior to the meeting.

- If the borrower rents from an individual rather than an entity, you should request 12 months proof of timely rental payments in the form of rent checks.

- Credit Documents

- Contested Items

- Divorce Decree etc

- Any additional items you feel may be requested by underwriting based on information on Pre-qualification Questionnaire and Credit report

Appointment

Once the preliminary file assessment, loan planning, and documentation list is complete, you will contact the borrower and set an Appointment for the application meeting.

You should ensure that the loan file contains all of the necessary data, disclosure forms, and application materials that are necessary for the meeting.

Once the application meeting is complete, you will review the file in preparation for submittal. You should review all of the documents contained in the loan file before submitting the package to underwriting.

If any discrepancies exist on the file, you will need to bring it to correct the file inclusions before the submittal.

Stack Loan Package

You will stack the submittal items according to the preferences of the particular lender chosen of the loan package. You will use the underwriting checklist or Submittal Summary Form to ensure that the documents are stacked correctly and that all of the necessary items are included.

If the borrower is completing the application by mail or telephone, you will mail the required signature documents and disclosures to the borrower.

You may be required to create a loan cover letter for the borrower. You should carefully review the loan file to ensure that you have an understanding of the plans and situation of the borrower. Remember, the initial submittal is the time to set the stage with underwriting. The cover letter should contain a brief summary of the planned loan, borrower qualifications and compensating factors, and missing documentation.

Submit Loan Package

You will submit the loan package according to the preferences of the lender. Some underwriting teams will accept fax transmittals while others require that you mail a hard copy of the package to their offices. You should ensure that you send all submittals in a timely manner.

Receive Loan Approval

After reviewing the loan file, underwriting will issue a decision. This decision can be denied, approved, or suspended.

- Denied means that aspects of the loan file do not meet the criteria for the loan program.

  The reason for the denial will be included with the denial notice.

  You should review the denial to determine if an action or additional documentation will correct the necessary aspects of the loan file.

  ➤ If the issue was a simple error or correctable file matter, you will correct the applicable information and contact the underwriter to notify them of the correction and re-submittal.

  ➤ If the issue is not a result of a simple error or correctable matter, you must issue a notice of denial to the borrower.

  You will save the file and all of the file contents in the location your office has designated for old loan file storage.

- If underwriting issues a **suspension**, they will provide you with details that define the reasons the file is suspended.

  A suspended file is missing some critical element that is necessary for underwriting to make a determination about the loan request.

  You should review the reason for the suspension, take the steps necessary to correct the file deficiency and then resubmit the package for review by underwriting.

- Each time you submit an initial loan package to the underwriting department, you are seeking an approval with stipulations.

  This stipulation list will become your primary focus over the coming days with regard to this loan file. You will gather the documentation items necessary to meet the stipulation list inclusions.

Upon receiving the notice of file approval with stipulations, you will review the approval and confirm that the terms meet the parameters of the loan the borrower is expecting.

You will then proceed with the documentation and file processing requirements.

Documentation Requests

The first resource for obtaining missing documentation or file information is often the borrower. You should call the borrower with a list of the required stipulations. During the conversation, you will want to confirm the commitment terms of the file with the borrower to ensure that they have a full understanding of the loan and to solidify their commitment to your loan program.

You should also mail a list of the necessary stipulations, commitment letter, and welcome letter to the borrower.

If a real estate agent is involved in the transaction, you should send a copy of the commitment letter to the Real Estate Agent. If the borrower is not yet working with an agent, you should consider the potential relationship building ability inherent in the outbound referral. A part of your job is to build referral and affinity relationships. Referring a borrower to a real estate agent is an excellent tool in building and solidifying the relationship you are building with that agent.

Documentation Orders
(Borrower)

After providing notice of the approval and stipulations to all of the parties; you will document the required details that relate to the borrower profile. For example, you will order a V. O. R. or V. O. M. to verify the status of the mortgage.

You should order any third party documentation requested on the stipulation list relating to the borrower to ensure that these items are available in the file to facilitate a speedy closing. You will order the property related stipulations after the borrower has chosen a home to purchase.

Each loan program will have different documentation requirements.

Receive sales agreement

When the borrower has located the home they wish to purchase and negotiated an agreement with the seller for that purchase, you will receive a copy of the sales agreement

You will restructure deal as needed to conform to the terms in the sales agreement.

Examples of items that may need restructured within the loan documents after your office receives the final sales agreement are

> Seller Concession
> Sales Price
> Source of Funds

Issue Additional Disclosures

The borrower may need to receive certain disclosures again after the final restructuring of the transaction. You will need to review the signed notices and disclosures and obtain the borrowers signature on any missing items.

Revise GFE/TIL

You will revise the Good Faith Estimate and Truth in Lending to conform to the final financial details dictated by the sales agreement. Upon completion of the restructured loan package, you will need to disclose the Good Faith Estimate and the Truth in Lending to the borrowers a second time. These revised documents will contain actual numbers rather than 'to be decided' information. This re-disclosure enables the borrower to see the best estimate of closing costs based on an actual property agreement.

Obtain missing documentation

At this time it is imperative that you secure any outstanding stipulations from the borrower or from third party sources.

Documentation Orders (Property)

You will Order the Title Search, Appraisal, and Inspections where applicable.
The type of inspections necessary will be dependent on the loan program and the negotiations within the sales agreement.

Title Request Form
Inspections (where applicable)
Appraisal Request Form
Other inspections or documents

You should ensure that you order all of the necessary paperwork, inspections, title work, and other documentation in a timely manner. Pay close attention to the section of the sales agreement that dictates the settlement date for the transaction.

Finalize Conditions

Once you have obtained all of the conditions listed on the stipulation list, you will submit the package to underwriting for a final review and approval.

You should stack this submission in the order that they appear on the stipulation list. In most cases, it is not a good idea to send each stipulation as it comes into the office. Most underwriting teams prefer that you submit all of the necessary stipulations in one packaged submittal. This enables them to have all of the necessary information to issue a loan approval. The exception is the appraisal.

You should submit the appraisal as soon as you receive it in your office. The underwriter may issue additional stipulation requirements because of the inclusions of the appraisal.

You should also review each stipulation that you receive to ensure that it does not contain any detail or issue that will create a delay in obtaining the approval. For example, if you receive the borrower's tax returns from the previous year and note a large discrepancy in income, you will wish to discuss the matter with the borrower and obtain the documentation necessary to address the discrepancy.

Perform Pre-Close

Once underwriting has issued the final loan commitment and the closing is scheduled, you should contact the borrower to perform a pre-close discussion.

If possible, arrange a time to meet with the borrower.

You will review the final terms of the loan with the borrower during the meeting. If the borrower has not chosen to lock the interest rate prior to this time, you will prepare a lock request.

It is a good idea to be certain the borrower understands every term on their finalized loan commitment. This helps to avoid turmoil at closing because of miscommunication or memory issues.

Closing

Most loan officers will attend their closings. Following closing it is a good idea to send a post-close package and referral request. As part of our marketing program, we have a whole system of post-close fliers and referral requests to use.

We recommend you send each borrower and the agents involved in the transaction certain items. These could include Thank You cards, Customer Surveys, Realtor Surveys, and Gift Certificates towards closing cost discounts that they may pass along to a future referral.

Chapter

12

FILE DOCUMENTATION

Your primary functions are to process borrower applications, obtain substantiating documentation proving all of the information on the loan application, and process the loan to a closing. To accomplish these tasks, you must gain a comprehensive understanding of the classification methodology applied to the various borrower situations by the mortgage industry.

Most borrowers are classified into two groups based upon the loan products for which they can qualify. These are

- A Paper, which is also called prime or conforming paper

- And B/C Paper sometimes called sub-prime or non-conforming paper.

The fundamental difference between a conforming and a non-conforming loan is that the standards set by Fannie Mae and Freddie Mac dictate the guidelines of a conforming. Fanny Mae and Freddie Mac are the two of the largest entities that purchase mortgage loans from lenders to package into securities and sell to investors within the secondary mortgage market. Because these two entities are the largest purchasers of mortgage portfolios, the guidelines that they establish are the industry standard with regard to borrower credit, income, down payment, debt ratio, and maximum loan amounts.

Any lending institution that intends to sell their packaged loans to an investor within the secondary mortgage market must consider these guidelines when providing mortgage funds to an applicant. If the application package does not meet the standards set forth by Fanny Mae and Freddie Mac, the likelihood of the lending institution being able to transfer the loan to an investor is diminished.

Within the category of conforming or conventional loans there is a sub-category termed Government Loans. Government loans sometimes enable a borrower whose situation or specifics falls outside of the standard conforming parameters to obtain a mortgage loan. The government will underwrite loans that fall within the category of Government loans. These loans will typically carry an insurance against default known as private mortgage insurance. This insurance enables borrowers whose credit, employment history, down payment amount, or other factors do not meet standard lending guidelines to obtain financing. These types of loans also carry very strict guidelines and parameters but the requirements are slightly lower in nature than those in the base conforming market.

The most common government loans are the F. H. A. and V.A. loans. Within these broad loan types are sub-types that offer different program specifics, approval parameters, and guidelines that will enable still more borrowers to qualify for mortgage financing.

The packages created by bundling groups of government underwritten loan products are often sold through Ginnie Mae. Ginnie Mae purchases mortgage loans from lenders to package into securities and sell to investors within the secondary mortgage market. Ginnie Mae loans are the most popular type of mortgage-backed securities because the U.S. government provides a guarantee of payment on the loan. These loans also usually provide higher returns than investment opportunities outside of the mortgage offerings.

Non-conforming loans are loans with a different set of criteria than the guidelines set forth by Fannie Mae and Freddie Mac. This criterion still considers all of the aspects of a borrowers file such as credit history, employment history, down payment, and debt to income ratios but sets the minimum levels for each item at a lower level than the conforming parameters. The types of borrowers who seek non-conforming loans include individuals whose situation is different from what is considered the norm. An example of a commonly encountered, non-conforming profile would be the self-employed borrower. Guidelines also exist that enable individuals with poor credit histories to obtain mortgage financing but these guidelines will require higher costs and fees, down payment amount, and other matters than the conforming loan products.

The fact that the non-conforming loan is structured under a set of guidelines that will fall below those sought by investors interested in the Fannie Mae, Freddy Mac and Ginnie Mae loan portfolios does not mean that these loans are not commonly transferred on the secondary mortgage market. The non-conforming loan will carry a higher interest rate and more costs than the conforming loan. This higher rate helps to offset the increased investment risk associated with the lower guideline standards of the non-conforming loan. Investing pools seeking to purchase the non-conforming loan portfolios will be those who can bear a higher level of risk in exchange for potentially higher returns.

Each of these general programs will have various approval levels and loan products. Each of these specific programs will have slightly different borrower qualifications and documentation requirements. We have been illustrating the basis for the loan programs and the general documentation necessary throughout the coursework. You should become familiar with the specifics of each loan program your office uses to obtain funding for borrowers and gain an understanding of the documentation requirements of each program. In general, you will need to gain the documentation necessary to prove the creditworthiness of the borrower and the value of the property that secures the loan. To do this, you will obtain documentation from many sources, compile all of the documentation into an understandable order, and remit all of the documentation to the underwriter assigned to the loan file.

After the initial meeting with the borrower, you will have a variety of documents to submit to the Underwriter. These are items such as the loan application, credit report, and all available substantiating documents provided by the borrower. The underwriter will review of the information and make sure that it conforms to the guidelines that the specific loan program requested has set forth. The underwriter will review the borrowers

- Income and Debt Ratios

- Employment History

- Credit History

- Savings / Source of Money for Down Payment

- The sales contract and the property appraisal if these are available at the time of the submittal.

Once the underwriter has reviewed the entire file, they will issue a written decision. This decision can take one of three forms.

Approved means that everything in the file meets the guidelines for the loan program.

Conditional or suspended meaning that Additional documentation is necessary to issue final determination on the file.

Denied meaning that aspects of the file do not conform to the guidelines

If the loan is approved, the underwriter will provide you with a written loan approval that defines any additional item or documents that the borrower may need to provide before the approval can be cleared for closing. These items are called "Conditions" or stipulations. A loan may be approved but still require updated "conditions" or items.

There are two types on conditions:

Prior to Loan Conditions are items that the underwriter must review and approve before the issuance of loan closing documents.

Prior to loan conditions must be given to the underwriter before the closing date can be scheduled.

Prior to Closing Conditions are items that must be the underwriter or loan closer must receive and review before they will release the funds necessary to close the loan.

Prior to closing conditions can be provided to the underwriter at any time up to the time of the closing meeting.

The loan processing of the file is the most time consuming aspect of the loan process.

The true definition of loan processing is the preparation of the loan file for presentation to the underwriting department.

If the borrower did not provide all of the original documents necessary to process the file at the initial application meeting, the processing stage is the time you will request these items again.

The processing stage is comprised of gathering all of the documents necessary to substantiate the creditworthiness of the borrower, value, and condition of the property, and ability of the seller to transfer the title to the property free and clear of any blemishes.

Some of the file documents required by underwriting must be verified by what is considered an uninterested third party. These verifications require that you contact a resource besides the borrower, seller, or real estate agent to obtain proof that the information contained in the borrower application and loan file is correct. You will use the borrower consent form and the forms created for the specific entity to which you are requesting information to obtain a statement verifying the specific detail.

Each aspect of the loan file must be fully documented in compliance with the underwriting guidelines applicable to the specific loan program. Ensuring that the correct and complete documentation is included in the loan file is your job.

You must properly document every loan package you submit to the Underwriting Department. Without the ability to review all proper documentation necessary, the Underwriting team cannot make a valid decision on your loan package. If the documentation is incomplete or missing, the underwriting department will request additional items or stipulations.

STACKING THE FILE

The loan process is much smoother if you provide all necessary documentation at the time of submission rather than submitting documentation based on a stipulation lists. We have been reviewing applicable documentation requirements throughout the coursework.

Each time you submit a stipulation the Underwriter in charge of that particular loan must re-review the entire package. This is a time consuming and lengthy method of gaining approvals. Many times, additional items will be required to clarify the stipulations you have just submitted. Most important –

sending packages in pieces is a very irritating practice that will not endear you to the underwriting team! By submitting packages piece meal, you create additional work for the underwriting team.

If you do not gather as many stipulations as possible at the initial application, you will gain a reputation of "stipping a loan to death". This reputation will cause referral partners and borrowers to doubt your professionalism and capabilities. It is also more time consuming to return to referral partners and borrowers for documentation necessary to close the loan.

Each time you submit a loan package there will be a transmittal summary or underwriting submission form your team prefers to have as a cover sheet. This sheet will usually contain a checklist of items the underwriting team requires to adequately review a loan package and make a decision for pre-approval. You will need to stack the items you are submitting in the order they appear on the submission form.

If there is no submission form, a best practice is to stack the items according to the usefulness and importance.

KENNEY

STACKING ORDER CHECKLIST

____ Loan Coversheet

____ Loan Submission Form

____ Stacking Order Checklist

____ Full 1008 or underwriting transmittal summary

____ Full, signed 1003 application

____ Purpose of Refinance Letter if applicable to the transaction

____ Credit Report

____ Credit Supplements if any are applicable to the loan file

____ Letter of explanation regarding any questionable or derogatory item on the credit report

____ A verification of mortgage or rent form or 12 months cancelled rent checks

____ All Bankruptcy Discharge Documentation if it is applicable to the transaction

____ A Divorce Decree if it is applicable to the transaction

____ A verification of deposit if checking or savings funds will be used toward the funds to close

____ A breakdown of the source of funds for closing

____ Gift letters signed by donors if they are applicable to the transaction

____ Verification of employment forms

____ Most Recent 30 Days Pay stubs

____ W-2's or full tax returns from preceding two years

____ Documentation of other income if it is applicable to the transaction

____ Sales Agreement including all pages and addendums

____ Rental or Lease Agreements if they are applicable to the transaction

____ Appraisal Report with original photographs

____ Preliminary Title Report

____ Title Commitment

____ Copy of any exiting note if the transaction is a refinance transaction

____ Escrow or funding instructions

____ Original Good Faith Estimate and Truth in Lending disclosures

____ ECOA, Fair Lending, and other Applicable Disclosures

____ Broker Agreements

____ And any other documentation specific to the loan file.

12:1 Sample Stacking Order Checklist

UNDERWRITING SUBMISSION FORM

FAX _____

Date: _____ Broker Name: _____

Broker Code: _____ Broker Contact: _____

Broker Phone: _____ Broker FAX: _____

If loan is locked – provide Loan Number: _____

Borrower's Name: _____

Co-Borrower's Name: _____

Purchase Price: $_____ LTV: _____% CLTV: _____%

Appraised Value: $_____ Loan Amount: $_____

LOAN PRODUCT	PURPOSE	OCCUPANCY	PROPERTY TYPE
__30 Yr Fixed	__ Purchase	__ Primary Residence	__ SFR
__15 Yr Fixed	__ Refi No Cash	__ Second Home	__ 2 Family
__ FHA/VA	__ Refi Cash out	__ Investment	__ 3-4 Family
__ FNMA Fallout			__ Condo/PUD
__ Lite Doc			
__ Other _____			

DOCUMENTATION
__ Signed 1003
__ Signed Good Faith
__ Pre-qualification 1003
__ Consent for Credit Check
__ Credit Report
__ VOR/VOM
__ W2/Tax Returns
__ Pay Stubs
__ Source of Funds
__ Other _____
_____

REQUEST INFORMATION: _____
_____
_____
_____
_____

12:2 Sample Underwriting Submission Form

KENNEY

Submission Sheet

DATE SUBMITTED: _____ ACCOUNT EXECUTIVE: _____

BROKER: _____

ADDRESS: _____

CONTACT: _____ PHONE: _____ FAX: _____

BORROWER/LOAN INFORMATION

BORROWER: _____ ***SSN:*** _____

CO-BORROWER: _____ SSN: _____

PROPERTY ADDRESS: _____

( ) Owner Occupied ( ) Purchase ( ) Full Doc ( ) SFR

( ) 2nd Home ( ) Refinance ( ) Lite Doc ( ) Townhouse

( ) Non-owner Occupied ( ) Stated Doc ( ) _____

LOAN AMOUNT: $_____ PROGRAM: _____

APPRAISED VALUE: $_____ RATE: _____ TERM: _____

SALES PRICE: $ _____ LTV: _____ CLTV: _____

BROKER'S FEES

ORIGINATION ____ % _____

REBATE ____ % _____

PROCESSING _____

APPRAISAL _____

CREDIT REPORT _____

_____ _____

_____ _____

FILE STACKING ORDER

__ SUBMISSION FORM   __ VOE'S

__ TYPED 1008   __ CURRENT PAYSTUBS

__ TYPED 1003   __ LAST 2 YEARS W-2'S/1099'S

__ HANDWRITTEN 1003   __ YTD PROFIT & LOSS STMT (SELF-EMP)

__ PURPOSE LETTER   __ LAST 2 YEARS 1040'2

__ CREDIT EXPLANATION   __ LAST 2 YEARS 1120/1065

__ CREDIT REPORT   __ APPRAISAL W/ ORIGINAL PHOTOS

__ VOM/12 MONTH RENT CKS   __ PRELIMINAY TITLE

__ BK SCHEDULE & DIS   __ COPY OF EXISTING NOTE

__ DIVORCE DECREE   __ EXECUTED SALES CONTRACT

__ VOD   __ BROKERS DISCLOSURES

ORIGINAL PACKAGE REQUIRED

12:3 Sample Underwriting Submission

INCOME

A borrower must have adequate income to cover the repayment of their mortgage. Before a borrower can be approved for a loan, the stability of income and the probability of the continuance of that income must be shown. All of the income that will be used to qualify the borrower must be proven through acceptable sources including the borrower's employment record. Most loan programs will require that the employer confirm that the borrower will likely continue to be employed.

The stability of income is usually proven through the employment history.

> ➢ A two-year employment history is needed.

> ➢ It is preferable that the history is in the same line of work.

> ➢ The actual history can be comprised of multiple jobs if necessary.

> ➢ Education may be included as part of the 2 year history if it was education for the same profession.

You will gain information that details the two-year employment history when you complete the pre-qualification questionnaire. The borrower will inform you of the type of employment or income they will be using to qualify for the loan. You will obtain documentation that proves this history.

Salary or W-2 Income

You must obtain documentation that shows proof that a two-year history of receiving this income exists and proof that this income is likely to continue.

The two-year history can be established by including the most recent 30-days pay stubs and the year-end Ww-2 for the prior two years.

Continuance of employment will be established using a V. O. E. form.

Overtime or Bonus Income

The borrower must show proof that a two-year history of receiving this income exists.

They must also show proof that this income is likely to continue.

The borrower will need to provide documentation, such as pay stubs for the most recent 30-day period of the present year and the final W-2 for the prior 2 years.

*   Each of these documents must show the inclusion of the overtime or bonus income.

The income will be factored as an average over the previous two years.

You will need to obtain a V. O. E. from the employer confirming the history and future probability of continuance for this income.

Part-time Income

If the borrower will use part-time income, such as income from a second job or seasonal employment, a two-year history of receiving this income must also be proven.

The documentation must show that the borrower has a 2-year history of receiving this income without interruption

The V. O. E. will be used to show proof that the part-time income has a high probability of continuing

If the income cannot be used as qualifying income because of an interruption in receipt of the income, a lack of a two-year history or the inability to confirm the likelihood of the continuance of this income, you will still wish to document it. It may be considered as a compensating factor.

Commission Income

Commission income is based on the average of the previous 2 years income.

The borrower must provide their full Federal Tax Returns, including all schedules, covering the past two years and you must obtain a year to date income statement from the employer.

Any un-reimbursed business expenses must be subtracted from the gross income in order to gain the usable income figures.

Retirement, Social Security Income, Public Assistance, or Disability Income

If the borrower is using retirement or social security income as part of their qualification package, verification from the source of the income must be obtained.

An award letter from the social security administration or a statement of retirement income will be used for documentation purposes.

If the income will discontinue within 3 years, the income cannot be used to qualify the borrower and used only as a compensating factor.

Alimony, Child Support, or
Income from Separate Maintenance This income is not required for qualification, but a borrower may choose to use this income if they wish.

To use this income, the borrower will need to supply a 12-month payment history from the ex-spouse or the courts showing timely payment will be required.

Evidence that such payment will continue for at least 3 years must be provided.

A copy of the

- divorce decree

- settlement agreement

- other legal documents illustrating

  ➢ amount of the income

  ➢ history of the income

  ➢ term for the continuance of this income

will be necessary.

Notes Receivable In order to use income from a note, the borrower must provide a copy of the endorsed and binding note.

The borrower must also provide proof that payments have been received for a minimum of 12 months.

* This proof can be in the form of bank statements or copies of the cancelled payment checks.

If the note expires within 3 years, it cannot be used for qualifying but may be considered as a compensating factor.

Interest and Dividends

Interest and dividend income may be used if documentation, such as tax returns or account statements, illustrates a 2-year history or receiving this income.

Rental Income

Rent received from investment properties owned by the borrower may be used if the receipt of these rents can be documented.

Income from roommates and boarders is not acceptable.

Rental income is calculated from the borrower's Schedule E of the 10 40.

Depreciation can be added back in to the total received.

You should note that while positive rental income is considered as gross income, negative rental income must be treated as a recurring liability.

Copies of the leases must be provided to prove this income.

Self-Employment Income

A borrower with 25% or more ownership interest in a business can be considered self-employed.

A borrower must have more than a one-year history for income to be considered.

A two-year full tax return will be required.

Bank Statements

Some loan programs will allow the borrower to use the deposits shown on 12-months or 24-months bank must be sent statements as proof of income.

In order to qualify for a bank statement program, the borrower's position must validate the probability that their business is cash based business.

The deposits showing on 12 consecutive months' bank statements will be totaled and divided by the 12 months to arrive at an average income.

Keep in mind that this is considered a light documentation loan and may be penalized with higher interest rates or a higher down payment requirement.

THIRD PARTY VERIFICATION

Many factors of the loan require verification of information. This verification must be obtained from a third party who has access to specific details concerning a borrower's profile.

It is important to understand a borrower's right to financial privacy. Details concerning Financial Privacy and Authorization to Release/Obtain Information forms in are included in ethics and disclosure chapter. If you are unsure of the process and requirements for the completion of these forms, you will need to review the pertinent section of Chapter for additional information.

The following pages provide you with example forms for specific situations.

- Verification of Employment (VOE)

- Verification of Deposit (VOD)

- Verification of Rent (VOR)

- Verification of Mortgage (VOM)

Each of these verification forms will provide specific information concerning your borrower's situation, past, present and future.

You should forward these verification forms to the appropriate company or agency for completion. The forms should be accompanied by a copy of the borrowers consent to release information.

VERIFICATION OF EMPLOYMENT (VOE)

In addition to verifying the income of the borrower through acceptable documentation, underwriting will often require verification of the borrower's employment and the probability of continued employment before the closing of the loan.

Verification forms must be sent to the employer to confirm all vital facts regarding employment, income, and continued employment.

A **Verification of Employment (VOE)** is a form sent to past and present employers for last two years to verify income and time on the job. Some employers have an automated 900 number for employment verification.

Receiving a verification of employment typically takes 1 to 2 weeks so you will wish to send your request early in the loan process.

REQUEST FOR VERIFICATION OF EMPLOYMENT

Privacy Act Notice: This information is to be used by the agency collecting it or its assignees in determining whether you qualify as a prospective mortgagor under its program. It will not be disclosed outside the agency except as required and permitted by law. You do not have to provide this information, but if you do not your application for approval as a prospective mortgagor or borrower may be delayed or rejected. The information requested in this form is authorized by Title 38, USC. Chapter 37 (if VA); by 12 USC, Section 1701 et. Seq (if HUD/FHA); by 42 USC, Section 1452b (if HUD/CPD); and Title 42 USC, 1471 et. Seq., or 7 USC. 1971 et. Deq. (if USDA/FmHA).

Instructions — Lender – Complete items 1 through 7. Have applicant complete item 8. Forward directly to employer named in item 1.
Employer – Please complete either Part II or Part III as applicable. Complete Part IV and return directly to lender named in item 2.
This form is to be transmitted directly to the lender and is not to be transmitted through the applicant or any other party.

Part I – Request

1. To (Name and address of employer)	2. From (Name and address of Lender)

I certify that this verification has been sent directly to the employer and ahs not passed through the hands of the applicant or any other interested party.

2. Signature of Lender	4. Title	4. Date	6. Lender's Number (Optional)

I have applied for a mortgage loan and stated that I am now or was formerly employed by you. My signature below authorizes verification of this information.

7. Name and Address of Applicant (include employee or badge number)	8. Signature of Applicant

Part II – Verification of Present Employment

9. Applicant's Date of Employment	10. Present Position	11. Probability of Continued Employment

12A. Current Gross Base Pay (enter Amount and Check Period) __ Annual __ Hourly __ Monthly __ Other (specify) $ _____ __ Weekly

13 For Military Personnel Only		14. If Overtime or Bonus is Applicable Is Its Continuance Likely? Overtime __ Yes __ No Bonus __ Yes __ No
Pay Grade		
Type	Monthly Amount	15. If paid hourly – average hours per week
Base Pay	$	

Type	Year to Date	Past Year 20_	Past Year 20_	Rations	$	15. If paid hourly – average hours per week
Base Pay	$	$	$	Flight or Hazard	$	16. Date of applicant's next pay increase
Overtime	$	$	$	Clothing	$	17. Projected amount of next pay increase
				Quarters	$	
Commissions	$	$	$	Pro Pay	$	18. Date of applicant's last pay increase
Bonus	$	$	$	Overseas or Combat	$	19. Amount of last pay increase
Total	$	$	$	Variable Housing Allowance	$	

20. Remarks (If employee was off work for any length of time, please indicate time period and reason)

Part III Verification of Previous Employment

21. Date Hired	23. Salary/Wage at Termination Per (Year) (Month) (Week)
22. Date Terminated	Base ____ Overtime ____ Commissions ____ Bonus ____
24. Reason for Leaving	25. Position Held

Part IV – Authorized Signature – Federal statutes provide severe penalties for any fraud, intentional misrepresentation, or criminal connivance or conspiracy purposed to influence the issuance of any guaranty or insurance by the VA Secretary, the U.S.D.A., FmHA/FHA Commissioner, or the HUD/CPD Assistant Secretary.

26. Signature of Employer	27. Title (please print or type)	28. Date
29. Print or type named signed in item 26	30. Phone No.	

12:4 Sample Form – Verification of Employment – HUD Release

You will complete sections 1 through 7 of the VOE request form.

➢ You will include the name of the employer and the applicable supervisor from whom the information is being requested.

➢ You should enter both your name and the company name as confirmation to the employer regarding the source of the request.

➢ Your full mailing address and any fax number that may be used for the return of the V. O. E. form should be included in the heading.

➢ You will sign the form as verification of the source of the request.

➢ Include your title and the date of the request.

➢ Section 7 allows you to include the information pertaining to the applicant so the employer has an easy reference when completing the form.

➢ The applicant should sign the form so that the employer knows that the release of the applicable employment data is authorized by the borrower.

* You may also attach the credit and information consent form that the borrower completed during the application process as additional verification that the borrower authorizes the release of the employment data.

The employer will complete PART 2 of the form and return it to your office.

When you receive the completed V. O. E., you should review all of the inclusions to ensure that they match the information contained within the borrower application.

If there is any discrepancy between the income information, employment data, or other inclusions of the forms, you should address this discrepancy and ensure that the incorrect information is corrected before submitting the verifications to underwriting for review.

MORTGAGE OR RENTAL HISTORY

The verification of mortgage or rental history is used to verify the payment history of the borrower relating to their previous housing obligations.

Mortgage or rental history is often used to project the probability of a borrower repaying their new mortgage in a timely manner. The theory behind this is that the manner that the borrower paid previous housing obligations reflects the seriousness with which they will approach the new housing payment obligations.

Mortgage histories are frequently included in a credit report.

If the mortgage or rental history is not included in the credit report, it must be verified in another manner.

V. O. M. stands for Verification of Mortgage

V. O. R. stands for Verification of Rent

These Verification forms are sent to a mortgage holder or a rental management company to verify the history of an account.

➢ Many lenders will not accept verification forms from a private party as these can easily be falsified. In that instance, you will need to acquire alternate documentation.

The borrower may supply copies of the most recent 12 months cancelled housing payment checks or money orders.

If these are not available,

The most recent 12 months bank statements can be obtained from either the borrower or the landlord showing 12 months concurrent withdrawals or deposits for the monthly housing payments.

More and more lenders are placing equal or greater weights on verification of rent or mortgages payments as on credit scores. It is a common belief that the history of payment of a mortgage or rent in the borrowers past reflects the probable payment performance in the borrower's future.

REQUEST FOR VERIFICATION OF RENT OR MORTGAGE

Privacy Act Notice: This information is to be used by the agency collecting it or its assignees in determining whether you qualify as a prospective mortgagor under its program. It will not be disclosed outside the agency except as required and permitted by law. You do not have to provide this information, but if you do not your application for approval as a prospective mortgagor or borrower may be delayed or rejected. The information requested in this form is authorized by Title 38, USC. Chapter 37 (if VA); by 12 USC, Section 1701 et. Seq (if HUD/FHA); by 42 USC, Section 1452b (if HUD/CPD); and Title 42 USC, 1471 et. Seq., or 7 USC. 1971 et. Deq. (if USDA/FmHA).

Instructions	Lender – Complete items 1 through 8. Have applicant complete item 9. Forward directly to landlord named in item 1. Landlord Creditor – Please complete Items 10 through 18 and return directly to lender named in item 2. This form is to be transmitted directly to the lender and is not to be transmitted through the applicant or any other party.

Part I – Request

1. To (Name and address of Landlord Creditor)	2. From (Name and address of Lender)

I certify that this verification has been sent directly to the landlord/creditor and ahs not passed through the hands of the applicant or any other interested party.

2. Signature of Lender	4. Title	4. Date	6. Lender's Number (Optional)

7. Information To Be Verified

Property Address	Account in the Name of __ Mortgage __ Rental __ Land Contract	Account Number

I have applied for a mortgage loan. My signature below authorizes verification of mortgage or rent information.

8. Name and Address of Applicant(s)	9. Signature of Applicant(s) X X

Part II – To Be Completed by the Landlord/Creditor

We have received an application for a loan from the above, to whom we understand you rent or have extended a loan. In addition to the information requested below, please furnish us with any information you might have that will assist us in processing the loan.

__ Rental Account	__ Mortgage Account	__ Land Contract
10. Tenant Rented from _____ to _____ Amount of rent $_____ per _____ Number of late payments _____ Is account satisfactory? __ Yes __ No	11. Date account opened _____ Original contract amount $_____ Current account balance $_____ Monthly Payment (P&I) $_____ Payment with T&I $_____ Is account current? __ Yes __ No Was loan assumed? __ Yes __ No Satisfactory account? __ Yes __ No	12. Interest Rate _____ % __ Fixed __ ARM __ FHA __ VA __ CONV __ Other Next pay date _____ No. of late payments _____ No. of late charges _____ Owner of First Mortgage _____

Payment History for the previous 12 months must be provided n order to comply with secondary mortgage market requirements.

13. Additional information which may be of assistance in determination of credit worthiness

14. Signature of Landlord/Creditor Representative	15. Title (please print or type)	Date
17. Please print or type name signed in Item 14		

12:5 Sample Form – Verification of Rent or Mortgage – HUD Release

The completion of the verification of rent or mortgage form is similar to the completion and remittal of the verification of employment.

> ➢ You will again enter the applicable information into section 1 and 2 of the form.

> ➢ You should sign and date the form and include your title to illustrate to the mortgage holder or landlord that you are an authorized representative of the lending institution and therefore privy to this data.

> ➢ You will enter the borrowers PRESENT or PAST housing address into the field property address.

    *   The address entered should be the one whose payment history you are verifying, not necessarily the borrower's present address. You should have the borrower sign the authorization so that the individual knows that they have approved the release of their personal history.

➤ The landlord or mortgage holder will complete part two of the form and return it to your office.

➤ Upon receipt of the completed document, you should verify that the payment history, payment amount, and term of occupancy equate to the information entered into the ten oh three.

    *   If there is any discrepancy between the information contained on the form and the information in the borrowers file, you should have the incorrect forms corrected before submitting the file to underwriting for review.

SOURCE OF FUNDS

You will need to verify the source of the funds that the borrower will use for the transaction. Oftentimes, the source of funds will actually be a combination of sources used to arrive at the total figure that the borrower will use to total the amount of money needed to pay the down payment, closing costs, and other costs associated with the transaction.

➤ Each approval will come with a Loan to Value shortened as L. T. V.

The LTV is the amount the lender is willing to finance as opposed to the overall cost of the property.

➤ Some loans will come with a C. L. T. V. meaning Combined Loan to Value.

The combined loan to value is the additional amount the borrower may finance through subordinate financing with the seller of the property or an outside lending source.

➤ The balance between the LTV or CLTV and the total price of the property including the sales price and all closings costs, must be sourced, often as the borrowers own funds.

Borrowers are often required to invest their own funds in the property to aid in securing the loan against default. Generally, the higher the credit risks the higher the percent of the borrowers required investment. The premise behind this requirement is that a borrower is less likely to default on a loan if they are losing their own personal funds through the default.

The borrower's cash investment in the property must be equal to the difference between the amount of the mortgage, excluding any up front fees, and the total costs to acquire the property. All funds must be verified through acceptable methods.

Savings and Checking   Some lending guidelines will require that the borrower have saved funds to close in a savings or checking account while others will accept that the borrower has saved the funds for close in cash.

> * You will want to confirm the specific holding requirements of the loan program you will be documenting.

Seasoning   Those lending programs that require the funds be kept in a savings or checking account may also require that the funds be seasoned.

The premise behind requiring seasoning of funds is that the time necessary to season funds helps to prove that the funds are the borrowers own money and not a result of a loan or gift from another entity or individual.

Seasoning means that the funds have been in the borrowers account a specific length of time. Often 90 days.

To prove seasoned funds, you will obtain a bank statement or a verification of deposit that covers the required seasoned term.

Certain loan programs do not require seasoned funds. These are often non-conventional programs.

> ➢ The underwriter will review the bank statements or verification of deposit form to insure that the funds have been in the borrower's possession for the required length of time.

> ➢ The underwriter will also use these statements to determine if the borrower is balancing and managing their bills properly.
>
> You will wish to review the bank statements before remittal.
>
> If the bank statement contains non-sufficient funds notations, the underwriter will require an explanation for the poor financial management and may place a hold on the approval.

> ➢ The underwriter may also use the bank statements to ensure that the debts illustrated on the credit report match up to the monthly payments shown on the statement.

They will review the deposits showing on the statements to determine if they are close to what the borrower is netting on their paycheck.

➤ If there are any large deposits, recurring debt not illustrated in the borrowers debt listing or other unusual entry on the bank statement, they will need to be explained.

* An occasional "N. S. F." may be cleared by underwriting if there is proper explanation as to why it occurred.

Cash saved at home

A borrower who has saved their money saved at home, can still purchase a home using this money.

The borrower must provide a written explanation of how the money was saved and the length of time taken to do so.

The lender will review the explanation to determine the creditability of these savings.

They will compare the statements to the borrowers

➤ Income

➤ Spending Habits

➤ History of using Financial Institutions for savings purposes

Many loan programs have limitations on the amount of cash saved at home, also termed mattress money that may be used for a transaction.

You will wish to check the specific underwriting guidelines for the specific program before allocating this mattress money to the transaction.

➤ If the amount of mattress money exceeds the limitations of the loan program, an alternate source of funds may be needed to gain underwriting approval for the transaction.

➤ If an alternate source of funds is not available, the funds may need to be deposited into a financial institution and the transaction placed on hold until the seasoning term requirements have been met.

The underwriter may request additional documentation relating to a mattress money transaction, including

- o additional bank statements

- o borrower statements

- o details regarding non-debt to income related expenses

- o other documentation specific to the situation

Gift Funds

Many loan programs will allow a homebuyer to receive all or some of the down payment for the purchase of a home as a "Gift".

A gift means that the borrower does not have to pay the funds received back. There are many acceptable sources of gift funds including.

- ➢ a relative

- ➢ the borrower's employer or labor union

- ➢ a charitable organization

- ➢ a governmental agency or public entity that has a program or established to provide homeownership assistance to low and moderate income families

NO REPAYMENT OF THIS GIFT MAY BE EXPECTED OR IMPLIED.

To use gift funds for the purchase a gift letter must be submitted to Underwriting.

This letter must be signed by both parties and state that there is no requirement to repay the funds received.

The gift letter must specify

- o the dollar amount given

- o be signed by the donor and the borrower

- o state that no repayment is required

o show the donor's name, address, telephone number, and relationship to the borrower

o It must also contain language asserting that the funds given to the homebuyer were not made available to the donor from any person or entity with an interest in the sale of the property including the seller, real estate agent, broker, builder, loan office, or any entity associated with any of these individuals or entities.

If the gift funds are already in the homebuyer's account

o You must document the transfer of the funds from the donor to the homebuyer by obtaining a copy of the canceled check or other withdrawal document showing that the withdrawal is from the donor's personal account along with the homebuyer's deposit slip or bank statement that shows the deposit.

If the gift funds are to be provided at closing
by certified check, the check must be from the donors account.

o You must obtain a bank statement showing the withdrawal from the donor's personal account as well as a copy of the certified check.

If the donor purchased a cashier's check, money order, official check or any other type of bank check as a means of transferring the gift funds, then the donor must provide a withdrawal document or canceled check for the gift showing the funds came from the donor's personal account.

If the donor borrowed the gift funds and, thus, cannot provide the documentation from his or her bank or other savings account, the donor must provide evidence that those funds were borrowed from an acceptable source.

o The donor cannot borrow the funds from a party to the transaction including the mortgage lender.

o "Cash on hand" is often not an acceptable source of the donor's gift funds.

Example: A retirement account would be an acceptable source of gift funds.

There may be limitations on the amount of closing funds that may be received as a gift.

You will want to check the specific guidelines for the loan program to confirm the gift fund limits and ensure that the source of funds necessary does not exceed these limits.

If the money that the borrower needs exceeds the gift fund maximum limits, you will need to assist the borrower in sourcing the necessary money from one of the approved source of funds items on the list.

Gift Equity

If the sale of a property is between immediate relatives, gift equity may be given as a seller concession toward the overall cost of the loan.

- Gift Equity is simply a reduction in the dollar amount the seller of the property expects to receive from the sale of the property.

- The reduction is given in the form of equity rather than a monetary gift or a subordinate loan.

The amount of equity that can be given as a gift between relatives is subject to maximum limitations and you will need to review the underwriting guidelines for the particular loan program to determine this maximum.

Gift Equity can only be given between immediate relative.

Earnest Money Deposit

Upon making an offer on a property, most Real Estate Agents require the buyer to remit an Earnest Money Deposit.

This deposit protects the agency and the seller in the event the buyer's change their minds and cancels the deal.

- Once an offer has been accepted, the property is removed from the market.

- If the buyer backs out of a deal once the property has been removed from the market, the earnest money deposit is retained between the sellers and the real estate agent.

- These funds are used as payment for the loss of time involved and any costs incurred.

If the transaction progresses as expected, the earnest money deposit is held in escrow, typically by the real estate agent and is used towards the borrower's funds necessary to close the deal.

In most cases, the source of the earnest money deposit will not need to be confirmed.

- o If the amount of earnest money exceeds 2% of the sales price or appears to be excessive based on the borrower's history of accumulating savings, the deposit amount, and the source of funds may require verification.

Otherwise, satisfactory documentation includes a copy of the borrower's cancelled check or verification from the bank.

Seller Concession

Most loan programs allow the seller to allocate a portion of their funds toward the payment of the borrower's non-recurring closing costs and possibly towards the borrower's necessary pre-paids.

- o This amount is vary by loan program but typically ranges from 3 to 6 percent of the sale price of the property.

Seller's concessions must be agreed upon in the Sales Agreement to count as source of funds.

You will document the seller concession by remitting the sales agreement to the underwriter.

You should also confirm that the seller concessions are allocated on the HUD 1 in the correct location.

Example: Some loan programs will not allow seller concession toward recurring closing costs and the closing department will reject the closing documents if the HUD 1 illustrates that the seller concession is being used to pay these bills.

Prepaid Charges

Any cost involved with the loan that the borrower has paid in advance of closing can be considered funds to close the loan.

Example: Many borrowers will pay the appraisal fee, application fee, or credit report fee at some time during the loan process.

You will document these payments through copies of the bill and corresponding checks.

These amounts may then be allocated as a source of funds to close the loan.

Prepaid charges will need to be documented in the form a copy of the check written to the lender or service provider.

401K or Retirement

Borrowers may draw or borrow from a 401K or Retirement Account and use the funds received toward the closing.

- If the borrower must borrow against an account, they must be able to qualify with the monthly repayment amount resulting from this advance.

- You will need to obtain a statement illustrating the monthly repayment amount required on the loan from the account.

- This amount must be factored as a recurring liability and the borrower must be able to meet the debt to income qualification requirements of the program.

Sales Proceeds

The sale of an asset is considered an acceptable source of funds for most programs.

The borrower must provide adequate documentation of the value of the item sold, the amount received from the sale, and proof that the sale occurred.

Documentation may include

- a copy of the bill of sale or the HUD-1 Settlement Statement if the property sold was real estate

- a copy of the check or verification of transfer of funds for the buyer to the borrower

- a copy of the borrower's deposit slip or bank statement showing the deposit of the funds

In some cases when the value of an item is in question, the borrower may need to prove that the sale price of the property was fair market value. This may be accomplished using appraisals, market condition proof, or other source of proof of value.

**Rent Credit and
Option Premium**

At times, you may be working on a transaction where the buyer has agreed to purchase the property from the seller under another transaction known as the lease option.

Under a lease option agreement, the buyer will typically give the seller a specific amount of money at the beginning of the transaction.

o   This money is termed an option payment.

It is similar to a down payment or earnest money deposit in that it is money credited by the seller to the buyer in the event the buyer chooses to purchase the property.

In exchange for the option premium, the seller agrees to sell the property to the buyer on or before a certain future date, at an agreed upon sum of money.

The buyer will occupy the property as a tenant until the purchase date.

If the buyer does not follow through with the purchase of the property, the seller retains the option premium in consideration of their removing the property from the sales market and holding any sale in abeyance for the buyer.

If the buyer follows through with the agreed upon purchase, the option premium is credited toward the purchase price and may be used as a source of funds.

o   You will document this source by remitting a copy of the original agreement between the buyer and the seller along with a copy of the check used to make the option payment.

Some lenders have set limitations on the amount of option payment that may be used toward a purchase.

If the option payment exceeds the limitations set by underwriting, a new agreement may be required that lowers the purchase price to enable a credit to the borrower for the excess amount paid.

○ Under a lease option, many sellers will agree to credit a portion of the borrower's current rental payment toward the purchase of the property the borrower.

The sellers will typically charge an amount for the monthly payment that is in excess of the fair market rent for similar property in the area.

This excess amount is typically considered an allowable source of funds for the purchase

○ The borrower will need to provide a copy of the rental/lease agreement showing the option to purchase with the clause stating how much of the rental payment is to be used toward the purchase.

○ You may also need to show proof that the rent payment is above the estimated fair market rent for other, similar properties in the area.

Fair market rent may be established by illustrating the rental income from similar rental properties of similar size and similar locations in the area.

○ Underwriting will often allow only those portions of the rental payment that exceed the fair market rent for the area to be credited as a source of funds for close regardless of the agreement between the buyer and the seller..

Example   If the borrower has rented a home with a fair market rent of $750 a month the borrower may only use monies from payments that total above $750 per month.

If the borrower pays $1,000 a month then $250 of each payment may be credited toward down payment funds.

If the borrower pays only $750 a month for this property then it is likely underwriting will allow none of the payment amount to be credited as down payment.

KENNEY

These are the most common source of funds acceptable to most Underwriting Teams. There are as many possibilities available as there will be borrowers in your office. Each situation is different and it is up to you to use your creativity in aiding your borrower in the sourcing of funds to close the loan.

Remember, any time you have a questionable source, run it past your Underwriting Team. They may have a method of documentation they will be willing to accept to consider this source as borrower funds toward closing.

Many of the sources of funds illustrated will require additional verification for documentation purposes. Some of this verification may be obtained from the borrower. Other verification documentation must be obtained from a third party source. The most common third party verification you will encounter is the Verifications of Deposit

The Verification of Deposit is a form sent to the borrower's banking institutions to verify average bank account balances for past 3 months.

Some banks will charge borrower a fee of up to $20 for this verification.

REQUEST FOR VERIFICATION OF DEPOSIT

Privacy Act Notice: This information is to be used by the agency collecting it or its assignees in determining whether you qualify as a prospective mortgagor under its program. It will not be disclosed outside the agency except as required and permitted by law. You do not have to provide this information, but if you do not your application for approval as a prospective mortgagor or borrower may be delayed or rejected. The information requested in this form is authorized by Title 38, USC. Chapter 37 (if VA); by 12 USC, Section 1701 et. Seq (if HUD/FHA); by 42 USC, Section 1452b (if HUD/CPD); and Title 42 USC, 1471 et. Seq., or 7 USC. 1971 et. Deq. (if USDA/FmHA).

Instructions — Lender – Complete items 1 through 8. Have applicant complete item 9. Forward directly to depository named in item 1.
Depository – Please complete Items 10 through 18 and return DIRECTLY to lender named in item 2.
This form is to be transmitted directly to the lender and is not to be transmitted through the applicant or any other party.

PART I - REQUEST

1. To (Name and address of depository)	2. From (Name and address of Lender)

I certify that this verification has been sent directly to the bank or depository and ahs not passed through the hands of the applicant or any other interested party.

2. Signature of Lender	4. Title	4. Date	6. Lender's Number (Optional)

7. Information To Be Verified

Type of Account	Account in Name of	Account Number	Balance
			$
			$
			$

To Depository: I/We have applied for a mortgage loan and stated in my financial statement that the balance on deposit with you is as shown above. You are authorized to verify this information and to supply the lender identified above with the information requested in Items 10 through 13. Your response is solely a matter of courtesy for which no responsibility is attached to your institution or any of your officers.

8. Name and Address of Applicant(s)	9. Signature of Applicant(s)

PART II – VERIFICATION OF DEPOSITORY To Be Completed By Depository

10. Deposit Accounts of Applicant(s)

Type of Account	Account in Name of	Account Number	Balance
			$
			$
			$

11. Loans Outstanding To Applicants

Loan Number	Date of Loan	Original Amount	Current Balance	Installments (Monthly/Quarterly)		Secured By	Number of Late Payments
		$	$	$	per		
		$	$	$	per		
		$	$	$	per		

12. Please include any additional information which may be of assistance in determination of credit worthiness. (Please include information on loans paid-in-full in Item 11

above)	

13. If the name(s) on the account(s) differ from those listed in Item 7, please supply the name(s) on the account(s) as reflected by your records.		

PART III – Authorized Signature – Federal statutes provide severe penalty for any fraud, intentional misrepresentation, or criminal connivance or conspiracy purposed to influence the issuance of any guaranty or insurance by the VA Secretary, the U.S.D.A., FmHA/FHA Commissioner, or the HUD/CPD Assistant Secretary.

14. Signature of Depository Representative	15. Title (please print or type)	16. Date
17. Please print or type name signed in item 14	18. Phone No.	

12:6 Sample Form – Verification of Deposit – HUD Release

Credit Report

You will order a preliminary credit report when the initial application is completed.

You may be required to order an updated credit report if the loan process takes longer than underwriting allocates for a credit report.

o Underwriting will set the standards for the age of the report.

o It is important to meet or exceed these standards and to caution the borrower not to take any action that may alter the credit report during the loan process.

o Any changes in the borrower's credit profile may create issues or changes to the loan approval status, causing delays in the closing of the loan.

Some underwriting teams require what is known as a tri-merge credit report or a full-factual credit report.

o A tri-merge report is one that uses the data from all three major credit report bureaus and blends it onto a single report.

o If the underwriting requests a full factual credit report, the credit bureau will verify all of the accounts and balances on the report prior to issuing the report to your office.

A full factual report typically takes 2 - 5 business days for completion.

Credit Supplements

You may need to acquire additional supplements regarding specific credit issues.

These supplements can be obtained from the credit bureau by completing and submitting the request.

Request forms can typically be found on the last page of the credit report.

These credit supplements will serve to verify or clarify a specific matter found on the credit report and can usually be obtained within 2 to 5 business days of the request.

Purchase Contract,
Addendums, Counter Offers You will need to obtain a copy of the Purchase Contract, Addendums to the Sales Agreement and documentation related to counter offers for purchase transactions.

These are the original contracts regarding the terms of the purchase of the property.

All of the completed and signed forms will be needed for the loan file.

You should obtain these forms before ordering the appraisal, as appraiser requires a copy of the contract to complete their functions.

The realtor estate agent will typically provide these documents to you as soon as an agreement has been reached between the buyer and the seller. T

The negotiation process between the buyer and seller typically takes between 2 and 10 days but may take longer depending on the complexity of the transaction.

Explanation Letters You may need to obtain Letters of Explanation from the borrower.

A letter of explanation is a letter written and signed by the borrower that explains any issues on the credit report, work history, bank account deposits, source of funds discrepancy, or other unusual matters relating to the file.

Appraisal The Appraisal will be ordered from an underwriting approved appraiser. The appraiser will

o   go to the property

o   measure square footage

o   verify required conditions

o   check other recent comparable home sales

o   determine value of the home

You will need to verify that the appraiser you choose to complete the appraisal process is one that is approved by underwriting.

You may also wish to discuss the appraiser you will use with your branch manager, as an appraiser is an affinity service provider who sometimes works with potential inbound referrals.

- o You or the branch may wish to build a better referral relationship with a specific appraiser.

Appraisals usually take 1 week to complete but may take longer depending on your market.

- o You will wish to request a timeline from the appraiser.

- o You must ensure that the seller or real estate agent is aware that the appraisal has been ordered so that they can make themselves available to provide the appraiser with entry into the property. .

When you request the completion of the appraisal, you should provide the appraiser with all of the details and documentation that they will need to speed their activity.

- o The appraiser can obtain this information from other sources, but you have it available and ensuring that the necessary details and documents are in the hands of the appraiser immediately upon receipt of the request helps to build stronger affinity service relationships and assists in speeding the appraisal completion time aiding you in processing faster closings.

You should fill in the appraisal request form completely.

- o The branch or appraiser may have a different form that they prefer using for the request.

o We have included a sample form to assist you in gaining an understanding of the actions that you must take when ordering an appraisal.

o You may use this form if your branch or appraiser does not have a preferred form available for your use.

Appraisal Request Form

DATE: _____   FROM: _____

TO: _____   FAX: _____

PURCHASE/REFINANCE/OTHER   FHA/VA/RURAL HOUSING/CONVENTIONAL

APPLICANT/BORROWERS: _____ PHONE: _____

REAL ESTATE AGENT: _____ PHONE: _____

CONTACT INFORMATION: _____

PROPERTY INFORMATION: _____

ESTIMATED VALUE   _____   SALES PRICE: _____

LENDER'S NAME: _____

PAYMENT OPTION: _____

ADDITIONAL COMMENTS: _____

ITEMS ATTACHED: ___ Sales Agreement Page 1
                  ___ Sales Agreement Page 2
                  ___ Original Purchase Document
                  ___ Previous Appraisal
                  ___ Other: _____

12:7 Sample Form – Appraisal Request Form

1. You should include all of the contact information that the appraiser may need including the telephone numbers for the individuals the appraiser may need to contact.

    These include the real estate agent, the seller, and the closing company.

2. You should send the appropriate pages of a Sales Agreement.

The appraiser will need to see the details included within page one of the sales agreement, and any addendums that relate to additional inclusions incorporated into the transfer.

You should note in the comments section of the appraisal request that page one of the sales agreement is attached.

3. If you remit the appraisal request by fax, you should place the confirmation page that shows the date and time that the request was sent in the file.

If you remit the appraisal request by mail or in person, you should include a copy of the dated request cover sheet in the file so that you have documentation of the actions taken on the file.

4. You should always note exactly how the appraisal bill is to be paid under the Bill Payment field of the request form. Common choices include

"Collect from Customer at door"

"Bill Office"

"Bill Customer"

"At closing"

You should remember that the ordering loan office is ultimately responsible for the payment of the appraisal bill. If the appraiser does not obtain the payment via another method, the appraiser sends the bill to your office. This is the reason that many lenders now require the appraisal fees to be paid in advance.

5. You should log the request date on the file tracking form.

Seventy-two hours after you have sent the request, you should contact the appraiser to determine the status of the appraisal.

   o If any issue exists that is prohibiting the appraiser from completing the appraisal, such as an inability to gain access to the property, you can address the matter and ensure that the appraisal is completed in time to complete the remaining tasks on the loan package.

   o It is your job to assist the appraiser in the process whenever possible.

6. If for some reason the appraisal is not complete after 72 hours, call appraiser every 24 hours until appraisal is complete.

   o If appraisal order is outstanding for more than one week, you need to begin searching for another appraiser partner.

This is an excellent example of the reason it is vital that your office develops a "relationship" with your affinity providers.

An appraisal that takes a week to complete can drastically slow your loan process.

Many lending professionals and real estate agents fail to remember the fact that the property is as important to the security of the loan being made as the borrower profile.

Ensuring that appraisals are remitted to underwriting promptly helps to speed the loan process, leads to better quality loan files, and enables your office to gain a reputation as the office that can get the job done smoothly, efficiently, and with fewer surprises.

Title Request Form

DATE: _____   FROM: _____

TO: _____   FAX: _____

Borrower Name: _____

Phone Number: _____ SS# _____ SS# _____

Mailing Address: _____

Property Address: _____

Proposed Lender: _____ Loan Amount: _____

Purchase ___ Refinance ___ 2nd Mortgage ___ Prepared by: _____

Current Owners: _____

Address: _____

Phone Number: _____ SS# _____ SS# _____

Estimated Close Date: _____

Purchase Price: $_____   Loan Amount: $_____

Attachments:

1003
Sales Agreement

_____

_____

12:8 Sample Form – Title Request Form

Preliminary Title Reports

come from the Title Company who will insure the title of the home.

They research the property, seller, and borrower for any legal items, liens, or loans that may affect title to the property.

The completion of the preliminary title report typically takes between 1 and 2 weeks but you will wish to confirm the time requirements with the title company your office chooses to complete the abstract of title.

The title or settlement company may be chosen by

o   the real estate agent

o   the borrower

o   the seller

o   or your office

You may wish to ask your branch manager if they have a title company preference.

A title company is an affinity service provider who sometimes refers potential borrowers to lending institutions.

Your branch manager may have a specific title company with whom they are trying to build or strengthen a relationship.

In many areas, the title company and closing company are blended into one office.

Requesting title to a property from the company that will close the transaction requires the submittal of all of the transaction details, transaction documents, and loan program instructions.

The submittal of all of the necessary details and documents ensures that the company has all of the information that they need to complete the necessary title and closing functions within the timeline set on the sales agreement.

TITLE REQUEST PROCESS

In general, you will want to use a closing company with whom you have a comfortable working relationship. You will want to check with your branch manager to determine if the branch has established affinity relationships already in place that can benefit you when ordering Title Work.

When ordering title and closing services, you should use a form that incorporates all of the necessary information and details related to the title and closing functions. Your branch or closing company may have preferred forms available for your use. We have included a sample form that you may use to request closing and title services.

1.   You should fill out Title Request form completely.

        Completing all entries will speed the process since the Title Company will not need to contact you for additional information.

2.   You should include all of the contact information and phone numbers for every individual concerned with the transaction. .You should include all of the contact details for

        o   Yourself

        o   The real estate agent

        o   The buyer

        o   The seller

        o   The closing department at the lenders offices

        o   Any inspection companies involved in the transaction

        o   Any other individual specific to the transaction

3.   When you send the title and closing request, you should also include the

        o   1003

        o   sales agreement

        o   any additional documentation specified by the closing company

        You should confirm the documents that the company commonly requires before submitting any request.

4.　　You should include any additional information such as the application of seller concessions that are specific to your transaction under the comments section of the request form.

Additional information included with the request should include any detail that is vital to the completion of the title work or closing.

You should always define any special loan characteristics that apply to your loan and define the closing costs concession and second mortgage information to ensure that the closing package is prepared correctly.

5.　　You should log the date that you sent the request on the file tracking form.

Logging activity ensures proper documentation of all actions on a file and enables you to conduct follow-up activity if a delay or another issue arises at a later point in the transaction.

6.　　Twenty-four hours after request has been sent you should receive a confirmation of the request from the company.

You should note this confirmation within the file tracking form and place the confirmation form in the file.

If you do not receive a confirmation, you should follow up with the closing company and note the follow up action and any information you receive from the company on the file tracking form.

7.　　One week to 10 days before closing, you should request the Title Commitment.

You may request the commitment verbally or with a fax request.

8.　　Upon receipt of the title commitment, you should contact the individual who will prepare the loan-closing package and confirm all of the transaction details. This confirmation helps to avoid calculations errors in the preparation of the closing documents. Some details to confirm include.

  o Sales Price

  o Loan Amount

  o Seller Concession

  o Estimated closing costs

  o Subordinate financing

9.   Within 48 hours, the Title Commitment should be provided to you for submittal to underwriting.

      When you receive the commitment, you should verify that there is a closing protection letter included.

10.   You will place a copy of the wiring instructions for the closing company with the commitment.

      If you use the same closing company for multiple transactions, they will typically provide you with a wiring instruction sheet that you can copy and attach to each file.

      If you do not have a wiring instruction sheet for the closing company, contact the company offices to obtain one and then keep it for future use.

11.   You will add the title commitment and wiring instructions to any remaining stipulations and submit the final file to underwriting for review.

12.   Underwriting should clear any final conditions on the file at this time. If any stipulations remain outstanding, you will need to obtain the necessary documents to clear them.

You should log all contacts and conversations on the file tracking form so that any individual who accesses the file can immediately see the status of the processing activity relating to the transaction. This log also assist you in remember the actions that you have taken on a file and the date of the activity if an issue arises that creates a loan process delay.

Homeowners Insurance   Your most important product is customer service. As an added service to customers, offices offer the service of obtaining Homeowner's Insurance quotes.

Many borrowers, especially the first time homebuyer, are uncertain of the process and information required to receive an Insurance quote and a binder. While this is not a typical part of your job, it is an added service that you can provide to the borrower that enhances their overall experience and satisfaction with your office.

Requesting an insurance quote for the borrower also enables you to build an additional affinity service relationship with the Insurance Agent.

Referring insurance quote requests to the Insurance Agent provides them with a possible source of business that they did not have previously. In providing this business source, you are setting the groundwork for a cross-referral program where they will refer borrowers to your office for their home lending needs.

It is important to remember to tell your borrower that you are performing this service on their behalf.

You MUST also tell the borrower that you are obtaining the quote for comparison purposes only and that they are under no obligation to use the service provider for their home insurance needs.

A sample of the Homeowner's Insurance requirements that might be set by underwriting is included to provide you with a better understanding of what homeowner's insurance stipulations may be required for the file.

A binder is required either before or at the closing.

Often the borrower will not have the time available to secure the entire homeowner's insurance policy. A binder showing proof that coverage has been obtained and a receipt showing proof the policy has been paid in full is sufficient to satisfy most underwriting requirements and enable the loan to proceed to closing.

Request for Homeowners Insurance Quote

Borrower : _____   Co-Borrower Name: _____

DOB: _____   DOB:_____

SSN: _____   SSN: _____

Mailing Address: _____

Home Phone: _____ Best Time to Call: _____

Property Address: _____

Value: _____ Sales Price: _____

Payment to be made: _____ Prior to Close   _____ At Close

Expected Close Date: _____   Binder Needed By: _____

Proposed Lender: _____

Additional Comments: _____

12:9 Sample Form – Homeowner's Insurance Quote Request

KENNEY

HAZARD INSURANCE REQUIREMENTS

Lender:

To: Escrow Officer

Date:
Escrow #:
Loan #:

Listed below are our Lenders policies, procedures and minimum requirements for Hazard Insurance, which must be provided covering the subject property. We will require that the insurance premium has been paid and date when renewal is due if property is a refinance.

1. Coverage required must be the lesser of the principal balance or the insurable value of the improvements. The coverage amount must fully compensate for any damage or loss on a replacement cost basis. If the loan program allows for potential negative amortization, the lender may require that the amount of coverage be increased to protect the amount of potential negative amortization.
2. The insurance company providing coverage must have an "A" rating or better in the latest edition of "Best's Insurance Guide", must be licensed in the State in which the property described above is located, and must be licensed to transact the lines of insurance required in the transaction.
3. Coverage shall provide at least Broad Form on one to four units, and at least "Vandalism and Malicious Mischief" over four units, with no deviation. Homeowner's policies must be equal to HO2 form.
4. Policies may contain deductibles on any peril as follows: Maximum deductible is the great of $1,000.00 or 1% of the coverage amount.
5. Policy must provide coverage for a term of at least one year. Premiums may be paid on an annual installment basis only if the policy provides the Lender will be notified in writing of cancellation 30 days prior to expiration of coverage, for any cause. Purchases: One year must be paid through escrow.
6. If an existing policy is provided and will expire within three months from recording, it must be renewed for the required term as noted above. These policies will be acceptable if they are current.
7. All forms and endorsements pertaining to the company requirements must appear on the Declaration page of the policy.
8. New policies must be accompanied by signed Broker of Record Authorization if borrower has recently changed insurance agents.
9. Verification of renewal of insurance policies must be in the Lenders office at least thirty days prior to the expiration date of the existing policy. If this requirement is not met, the LENDER OR ITS SUCCESSORS OR ASSIGNS MAY AT THEIR OPTION, BUT WITHOUT OBLIATION TO DO SO, PROVIDE COVERAGE TO REPLACE ANY EXPIRING POLIIES WHICH HAVE NOT BEEN PROPERLY RENEWED. The premium for such coverage will be remitted promptly by the undersigned, or Lender may charge borrower's account for the cost thereof.
10. Insurance agent's name, mailing address, and phone number must be on or attached to Binder/Policy.
11. Lender's Loss Payable Endorsement 438 BFU to be affixed in favor of:

12. Property address and insurance names to be designated as per ALTA Policy.
13. Our loan number must be shown on the policy and any subsequent endorsements.
14. Effective date of new policies, endorsements, and/or assignments shall be as of, or prior to, date of recording.
15. Please notify your agent to forward future premium notices directly to you.
16. If the security property is a condominium, larger than twenty units a fidelity bond in a minimum amount of at least equal to the sum of three months assessments on all units in the project for Directors and Officers is required. A copy of the master policy must be submitted to the Lender prior to funding.
17. The minimum amount of Flood Insurance required is the lesser of the outstanding principal balance of the loan, the full insurable value of the property, or the maximum amount of flood insurance available.

All policies, assignments, and or endorsements, for completion of our loan escrow are to be mailed to this lending office.

12:10 Sample Extraction – Lender's Insurance Requirements

Additional supporting documents
Additional paperwork may be needed on a case-by-case scenario.

The need for additional documents will vary by borrower's individual scenario and is one of the areas where you will await the stipulation list before requesting the documents.

As you gain in experience, you will become better able to anticipate what unusual documents underwriting may request, but for now, you will likely need to rely on the stipulation list.

Any Documents missing from initial loan application
You must also review the file package to ensure that you have requested and obtained any paperwork or documentation item that was missing from original loan application.

If the buyer or the seller is slow in providing the necessary documents, you may enlist the aid of the real estate agent in obtaining these items.

If an affinity service partner is slow in providing you with a necessary stipulation, you may need to discuss the services of the affinity service provider with your branch manager so that the speed of affinity services can be addressed and any issues resolved.

Escrow / Closing Instructions
Escrow or closing instructions are drawn up by the Escrow or settlement Company and they define the transaction and settlement details.

An Escrow or settlement company is an independent third party of the transaction that acts as the accountant. Some states call this the settlement company.

In California and some other states, a closing attorney or title company acts as the escrow or settlement agent.

The process of drawing up escrow instructions usually takes 2 to 7 days.

Since all of these documents are secured from various companies and individuals, this is most often, where there are delays. This portion of the loan process will normally take 1 to 3 weeks.

Developing relationships with your various affinity providers is essential in speeding this process. It is also very important to have an effective pipeline management system and loan process follow up system in place. This allows you to easily order items from service providers. This will also enable you to follow up on missing items with Real Estate Agents and borrowers efficiently.

A typical Real Estate Transaction involves the timely cooperation of many different parties. Due to the number of people involved, there can be problems.

Since no loan is closed until it is closed, this list of items is potential roadblocks. It is very important for you to bear in mind that you are ultimately responsible for organizing the loan process and ensuring that it moves along in a timely manner.

Some of the delays are easily avoided with an adequate loan process follow up and reminder system and others will require you to build strong relationships with affinity service providers.

The Real Estate Agents could create delays in the loan process and closing if they

- do not get all documents signed promptly

- Did not structure the transaction properly

- Did not pre-qualify the borrower for motivation

- Misunderstand the borrowers needs or your instructions due to a lack of real estate experience

- Won't return phone calls

- Transfer to another office

- Goes on vacation leaving no one to handle the file

- Has poor people skills with the borrower

- Gets the borrower upset over minor points

- Does not communicate with their borrower, your office, the appraiser or the settlement company

The Escrow or Closing Company may cause delays if they

- Fail to notify the real estate agent or lender of unsigned or un-returned documents so that they can contact the individual responsible for the document and cure the problem

- Fails to obtain information from beneficiaries, lien holders, title companies, insurance companies, or lenders in a timely manner

- Incorrectly prepares paperwork

- Is incorrect at interpreting aspects of the transaction

- Passes incorrect assumptions about the transaction to other parties

- Lets the principals of the transaction leave town without getting all necessary signatures

- Is too busy or overscheduled

- Loses the paperwork related to the transaction

- Does not pass on valuable information fast enough

- Does not coordinate well so that many items can be done simultaneously

- Do not find liens or problems until last minute

The Inspection Company or The Appraiser can cause delays if they

- Are overly picky during the inspection

- Infuriates the seller

- Makes mistakes when preparing the documents or completing the inspection

- Delays completing their report

The Seller may create delays if they

- Lose motivation for the sale

- Nets less money from sale than they originally believed that they would

- Cannot find another home to purchase

- Has an unexpected occurrence such as an illness or divorce

- Fails to disclose or does not know about defects in the property

- Receive a Home inspection that reveals defects that the seller is unwilling to repair

- Removes property from the premises that the buyer believed was included in the sale

- Is unable to clear up problems or liens against the property

- Did not own 100% of property as disclosed

- Thought that the obtainment of partners signatures were "no problem" but they were

- Leaves town without giving power of attorney to another individual who can finalize the transaction on their behalf

- Uses a notary that did not make a clear stamp when notarizing their signatures

- Delays the projected move-out date

By building strong affinity service provider relationships, providing clear instructions to each party involved in the transaction, and carefully coordinating and following up on each aspect of the loan process, you can minimize many of these delays. It is vital that you maintain a constant awareness of the status of each loan package so that you can ensure that each party completes all of the steps necessary to move the package to a smooth closing meeting.

Loan#	LENDER'S CLOSING INSTRUCTIONS		Date
Borrower		Property Address:	
Return Original Signed Documents to Lender:		Loan Terms	
		Loan Amount:	
		Interest Rate:	
		Term	
		Loan Type:	
		Loan Purpose:	
		___ 1st MTG or ___ 2nd MTG	
		Estimated Funding Date	
Settlement Agent		Title Company	
Phone:		Phone:	
Fax:		Fax:	
Email:		Email:	
Attn:		Attn:	
Closing #:		Order #:	

1.	LOAN DISBURSEMENTS							
	FEE	POC	BUYER	SELLER	LENDER	OTHER	HUD-1 PAYABLE TO	
	801 Origination Points							
	802 Lender Discount Pints							
	803 Lender Appraisal Fee to							
	804 Lender Credit Report to							
	805 Lender Inspection							
	806 Mortgage Insurance Ap Fee							
	807 Assumption Fee							

12:11 Example – Lender's Closing Instructions

808
809
810 Administration Fee to
811 Application Fee to
812 Processing Fee to
813 Wire Transfer Fee to
814 Underwriting Fee to
815 Flood Cert to
816 Tax Service to
817 Buydown Fee to
818
819
820
821
901 Prepaid Int (days @ /day)
902 PMI Premium
903 Property Insurance
904 Flood Insurance
905 VA Funding Fee
906
1001 Property Ins (pmts @ /mth)
1002 Mortgage Ins (pmts @ /mth)
1003 City Taxes (pmts @ /mth)
1004 County Tax (pmts @ /mth)
1005 Annual Asmnt (pmts @ /mth)
1006 Flood Ins (pmts @ /mth)
1007 School Taxes (pmts @ /mth)
1008 (pmts @ /mth)
1009 Aggregate Adjustment
1101 Settlement or Closing Fee
1102 Abstract or Title Search
1103 Title Examination
1104 Title Ins Binder
1105 Document Prep fee
1106 Notary Fee
1107 Attorney's Fee
1108 Title Insurance
1111
1112
1113
1201 Recording Fees
1202 City Taxes & Stamps
1203 State Taxes & Stamps
1204
1205
1301 Survey
1302 Pest Inspection
1303 Final Inspection to
1304
1305 Review Appraiser to
703 Commission Paid At Settlement
Totals

a)   Other than the fees listed, no other fees or charges may be charged without prior approval from Lender.
b)   Additional compensation of $ will be paid by Lender to   . This amount is not deducted from the principal balance of the loan. The compensation must show on HUD-1 as "Broker Fee paid by Lender POC"
c)   Unless notified otherwise by Lender, we will remit our wire to you in the amount of the loan, less fees paid to Lender. The "Broker Fee paid by Lender POC" will be included in the wire when applicable.

2.   PAYOFFS   COMPANY   ACCOUNT #   AMT. TO BE PAID

12:11 Example – Lender's Closing Instructions

3. REQUIREMENTS: The documents or requirements indicated below must be executed or satisfied. You are responsible to ensure that each borrower receives two signed, dated and fully completed copies of the NOTICE OF RIGHT TO CANCEL (if applicable) and one copy of the FEDERAL TRUTH-IN-LENDING DISCLOSURE STATEMENT.

__ Deed/Mortgage with applicable riders   __ Note with Applicable Addendums
__ Federal Truth-In-Lending Disclosure Statement   __ Original Application to be signed
__ Power of attorney (original)   __ Request for taxpayer's ID (IRS W-9)
__ Right to cancel notice   __ Typed application to be signed
__ Certified proof of funds to close   __ Itemization of amount financed
__ Tax Certification form   __ Grant/Warranty Deed
__
__
__

4. FUNDING CONDITIONS: The following approval conditions remain outstanding. Borrower is being allowed to sign documents subject to Lender's receipt and approval of these conditions. You are not authorized to disburse funds until Lender has approved the following:
HUD to be faxed to   for review and approval
Need certified copy of warranty deed (for CA grant deed) signed by seller(s)
Need copy of certified funds buyer bring for closing costs (CAN'T DISBURSE FUNDS WITHOUT IT)
Need evidence of hazard insurance, paid for one year
All taxes to be current at close
All signed docs to be returned to us immediately after signing in return fed-ex envelope provided

5. In connection with this loan, we enclose the necessary documents requiring signature and acknowledgement where applicable. All loan documents must be executed exactly as the names are shown below the signature lines. No alterations or erasures to these documents are permitted without our approval.
   a. A Specific Power of Attorney cannot execute documents, without prior approval from Lender. A General Power of Attorney will not be accepted. Examples of POA signatures
   John Jones by Nancy Jones as Attorney in fact. Initials should read as JJ by NJ as A.I.F.
   Nancy Jones as Attorney in fact for John Jones. Initials should read NJ as A.I.F. for JJ

6. In addition to the above, return the following:
   b. Original HUD-1 settlement statement with all payees as shown on these instructions. Sellers closing cost credits are limited to non-recurring costs only, and are further limited to 6% (3% for TX home equity) of sales price of the home. Credit can't exceed the actual non-recurring costs. Examples of recurring closing costs are: odd days interest, hazard, flood, windstorm insurance premiums, property taxes, HOA dues. Broker credits must also be included in this 6% credit figure.
   c. Certified copy of all checks for balance due at closing from borrower. Must be certified check, no cash deposits allowed unless approved by lender.
   d. 2 Certified copies of signed, notarized Deed of Trust/Mortgage and Riders
   e. Certified copy of second Deed of Trust/Mortgage and Note in the amount of $, interest rate %, monthly payment $ and term of
   f. Certified copy of any Grant/Warranty Deed from seller (seller to match Preliminary Title Report), inter-spousal transfer deeds or other quitclaims being executed for this transaction.
   g. Original copy of any and all duly executed Settlement Closing Instructions and amendments thereto, including correct lender, rate and terms.
   h. Copy of borrower's valid photo identification used at closing.

7. We require a standard ALTA Policy within 15 days from the funding of this loan.
SHORT FORM POLICES ARE NOT ALLOWED
Individual title reports required for first and second mortgages. The ALTA Policy must contain a Plat Map or survey Endorsements 100 and Form 8.1 as required without deletion, 116, 115, 116.2 (if subject property is a Condominium Estate), 115.2 (if the subject property is a Planned Unit Development), and Special Endorsements:
With liability in the amount of our loan(s) on the subject property, subject only to:
   a) General and special taxes and assessments not yet due (all such taxes and assessments, which are due as of the settlement date must be paid current at closing) and
   b) Items   as shown on the preliminary report of title No.   date

8. Secondary financing in the amount of $ (none if left blank) has been approved. The total consideration in this transaction except for our loan(s) proceeds and any permitted secondary financing, must be paid in cash. Do not record or disburse funds if you have knowledge or reason to suspect the borrower intends to obtain secondary financing to purchase the subject property other than as permitted herein.

Additionally, you are instructed not to record or disburse funds if you have knowledge or reason to suspect that the purchase price of the subject property is not $ or that any portion of the purchase price is being paid other than with certified funds without prior written authorization from us. No other subordinate financing is allowed without prior written approval from Lender.

9. It is strictly forbidden to allow a Broker, or Broker affiliate company to close our transaction.

12:11 Example – Lender's Closing Instructions

10.   All closing documents should be executed in BLUE INK.

11.   If State requirements exist, a Non borrower must execute a Deed of Trust/Mortgage, Riders, Federal Truth-In-Lending Disclosure Statement, Itemization of Amount Financed, Notice of Right to Cancel, Warranty and Compliance Agreement, Signature Affidavit and AKA Statement, and Correction Agreement Limited Power of Attorney. A valid photo I.D. must also be provided.

12.   ALL TRANSACTIONS: Prior to the disbursement of any funds the closing agent must fax to the Lender the documents listed below for their review and approval. Owner occupied refinance transactions may not be disbursed prior to the day following the Rescission expiration date provided to the borrowers on the notice of right to cancel.

   Signature page of: Note and Addendums, Deed of Trust/Mortgage and Riders
   Executed Grant/Warranty Deed witnessed and notarized, if applicable
   Copy of any certified check(s) for funds to close. Remitter must be the borrower's name and drawn on the borrower's bank
   Any specific closing conditions outlined above under FUNDING CONDITIONS
   Executed final HUD-1 statement
   Federal Truth-in-Lending Statement
   Notice of Right to Cancel, if applicable
   Power of Attorney, if applicable

13.   We reserve the right to withdraw these instructions and enclosures if this loan is not closed on or before
   if for any reason this loan does not close, return all documents, together with these instructions, to the Lender and notify Lender immediately. We will incur no expense in the closing of this transaction unless otherwise noted in these instructions.

12:11 Example – Lender's Closing Instructions

Once the Underwriting department has determined that all of the stipulations are acceptable and issued a satisfaction status, you will need to schedule the closing and request the closing documents.

The loan document process is the stage when the funding agent is preparing the loan documents. These loan documents are the legal binding documents to finalize the transaction.

They will include important items to be signed. Nearly every transaction will require the completion of the

Promissory Note   defining the amount borrowed, the interest rate charged, and the terms or repayment method applied to the loan, and the monthly payment amount.

Deed of Trust   that places the property as security to the loan and note

HUD 1   that provides an itemized breakdown of all fees incurred for obtaining the loan, all costs related to the transfer of the property and any other financial matter related to the sale.

NOTE

A promissory note is a contract between the borrower and the lender. Often simply referred to as a note, the document must contain certain key components to ensure it is legally binding and enforceable.

- The note must be in writing.

- The note must be between a borrower and a lender both of whom have the ability to enter into a legally binding contract.

- The note will state the borrowers promise to pay a certain sum of money and the terms under which those monies will be paid.

The borrower will sign the note document and the completed note is given to the lender.

Promissory notes need not be complicated but they must clearly outline the terms under which the loan is being granted. Terms could include:

- the principal amount of the mortgage

- the interest rate agreed upon

- the date payment is due

- the late charge, if any, incurred when a payment is paid beyond the due date

- the date that these late charges are assessed

- the length of time payments shall be made

- how the payments will be credited on the account

    Example: Payments will credit to interest and then to the principal

- any other details which have been negotiated between the buyer and the lender with regards to the repayment of the agreed to monies

Simply put a promissory note is the written promise to repay a debt and the outlining of the acceptable terms and method for payment.

A promissory note can be obtained from a variety of sources and the notes that you will review at the closings that you oversee may not appear the same as the note included for your review. Notes may contain a variety of contingencies based upon the agreed upon financing secured. Notes will be customized to suit the transaction being completed and as each transaction you close will be different, the notes will be different. The basic elements of the notes will be incorporated regardless of the other inclusions. You should familiarize yourself with the essential elements of the note and review the sample note that we have included for display purposes. The sample note is a highly customized note incorporating all of the financial negotiations outlined within the lender instruction display in this program.

The components of a promissory note allow certain rights to be legally enforced on the part of both the buyer and the lender. The promissory note will be custom designed incorporate all of the negotiated transaction specifics. The promissory notes that you will review in relationship to your closing will have standard features that are common regardless of transaction specifics. These features will include

- A statement that the document is a promissory note

- The location and the date of the notes signing, in other words the specifics of the settlement meeting.

  As with any contract, the location stated in the contract establishes which   state laws govern the execution of the document.

- A statement that the borrower has received something of value and promises to pay the debt as described in the note.

- The person who is to make the payments will be detailed.

- The company or person who is to receive payments will be clearly identified.

- The exact mailing address and/or location for delivery of payments will be shown.

- The exact debt amount agreed upon by the note will be detailed.

- The interest rate on the debt will be detailed.

- The date from which interest will be charged and payments shall begin will be shown.

- A specific detail pertaining to the amount of the payments to be made including a breakdown of application of the payments toward principal and interest will be entered.

- Any changes to the interest rate, such as ARM requirements will be stated and details explaining such changes will be entered.

- The prepayment penalty information will be incorporated.

  Prepayment of all or part of the loan funds prior to a specified date is sometimes penalized as part of the negotiation process. Prepayment penalty regulations vary by state and if a prepayment penalty is to be imposed on a loan, the applicable laws should be fully researched.

- The grace period, if any, which is allowed prior to the addition of a late-charge to the payment will be indicated.

- The note will often contain a specific clause that provides the lender with the right to accelerate the loan and demand immediate payment of all interest and principal owed if the borrower misses any individual payments.

- The wording of the note will typically cause the borrower to agree to pay any costs incurred by the lender if the borrower falls behind on the agreed to payments.

- If the promissory note is tied to a mortgage that secures it making this a mortgage loan, the mortgage details will be entered. Without this reference, the note would be a personal loan.

- A specific location will be available where the borrower will sign the note.

  The buyer is sometimes referred to as the note maker.

  If two or more persons sign the note, it is common to include a statement in the note that the borrowers are jointly and severally making the note.

  This means that the terms of the note and the obligations created are enforceable on the makers as a group or upon each note maker individually.

In addition to the basic note, the loan structure that you have created will sometimes require the integration addendums and riders to the note. Addendums will typically elaborate on the specific funding clauses contained within the note. These documents should be signed and witnessed in the same manner as the note. If addendums are to be incorporated into the closing package, the closing instruction sheet will indicate what documents must be signed and the closing package will include the applicable documents.

It is important that you remember that notes are customized to suit the transaction. Each transaction you oversee will vary in specifics and so each note may vary in entries. This variation from the norm will be dependent on the needs of the parties in the transaction and the structuring you completed on each loan.

MORTGAGE DOCUMENTS

Financing transactions that contain real estate are typically secured using a mortgage.

- A mortgage causes the note to be secured against real property rather than other property or as an unsecured personal loan.

Typically, a lender will utilize both a note and a mortgage in these types of financing situations.

- The note is the promise to repay the funds detailed in the manner detailed.

- A mortgage is a separate agreement from the note and provides the security or collateral of the real property involved in the transaction in the event of non-payment on the part of the buyer.

In addition to the legal form of a mortgage, two key components will often be incorporated into the document.

- the act of putting the property as collateral in return for the funds being provided will be detailed

- the conditions under which the borrower will maintain the collateral to protect the interest of the lender until the terms of the note are satisfied and all funds are paid will be outlined

The following page contains an example of a mortgage contract generated in keeping with the note examples provided earlier in the coursework. This example will illustrate all of the basic requirements needed to create a legally binding document.

Mortgage Key

A legal mortgage document may vary in appearance from the sample included for your review. As with all closing documents, the inclusions of the mortgage agreement will vary depending on the specific negotiations between the parties involved in the transaction. In general, you can expect to find the following specific items in a mortgage.

- the date of the making or signing of the mortgage agreement

- the names of the parties involved in the mortgage including both the borrower and the lender

    Mortgagor is the person who owes the mortgage or borrower

    Mortgagee is the person who is receiving the payments or the lender

- The debt for which the mortgage is being held as collateral is named.

- The borrower of the funds conveys the property being held as collateral to the lender.

- The mortgaged property is then described.

- The borrower states that the property being provided as collateral legally belongs to them and that the borrower will be responsible for defending ownership against all other claims of interest by other properties.

  The lender will want to verify this claim by the buyer through a title search.

- A defeasance clause will be incorporated.

  This clause outlines the provisions to nullify and make void the mortgage when the note has been paid in full.

- The borrower makes certain promises to the lender, which protect the collateral or property, which acts as security for the loan.

Covenant to Pay Taxes	**The borrower agrees to pay the property taxes** on the mortgaged property.
	This is an important factor for the lender because if the taxes are not paid they may create a lien on the property, which is superior to the lien held by the lender.
Covenant Against Removal	The borrower is prohibited from removing or demolishing any building or improvement on the property.
	Demolishing or removing improvements may reduce the value of the collateral offered to the lender against the note.
Covenant of Insurance	The borrower is required to carry adequate homeowners insurance to protect the lender interest in the collateral in the event of the damage or destruction of a part of the property.
Covenant of Good Repair	The borrower must keep the collateral in good condition.
	This is also sometimes referred to as the covenant of preservation and maintenance.

A clause providing the lender with the right to inspect the property to ensure it is being maintained in a manner, which protects the value of the collateral given to the lender, is often incorporated into the mortgage.

Acceleration clause   The acceleration clause permits the lender to demand all monies owed as payable immediately.

If the borrower cannot pay the money owed in full, a foreclosure proceeding is implemented and the property is sold with the lender receiving monies from the sale to pay the funds owed.

This clause is used if the borrower breaks any clause included in the agreement.

Alienation clause or
due-on-sale clause   This clause allows the lender to call the entire loan balance as due if the property is sold or conveyed by the borrower to another individual.

If any part of all of the property is taken by the act of eminent domain this clause provides the lender with the right to receive any money paid as part of the action to offset the balance of the loan owed.

- A section will be incorporated that states the borrower has created this mortgage. The signature of the borrower fulfills the same requirement.

- The borrower will acknowledge the mortgage by the signing of the document.

When a note or loan is paid in full, the lender will typically return the promissory note to the borrower. The lender will also provide the borrower with a satisfaction of mortgage document that states the promissory note has been paid in full. This allows the mortgage to be discharged from the public records.

The lender will typically also require that the borrower complete additional legal forms to help to confirm that the borrower understands the transaction, verify the borrower's statements during the loan process, and promote the security of the transaction.

ITEMIZATION OF AMOUNT FINANCED

Borrower   Creditor:

Loan Number: Date:

Property Address: Term:
                                              Rate:
                                              LTV:

Listed below is the ITEMIZATION OF AMOUNT FINANCED.

Existing Lien: $
Loan Amount $

ITEMIZATION OF PRPAID FINANCE CHARGES:

     -- Origination Points   to LENDER
     -- Lender Discount Points   to LENDER
     -- Administration Fee to LENDER
     -- Prepaid Interest for
     -- Settlement or Closing Fee to

           TOTAL PREPAID FINANCE CHARGE: $_____
           AMOUNT FINANCED: $

OTHER SETTLEMENT CHARGES:
       AMOUNTS PAID TO OTHERS ON YOUR
       BEHALF BY CREDITOR

     -- Lender Appraisal Fee to
     -- Abstract or Title Search to
     -- Notary Fee to
     -- Title Insurance to
     -- Recording Fee (Deed: $)

           TOTAL OTHER SETTLEMENT CHARGE: $_____

           LOAN PROCEEDS: $_____

FEES PAID BY LENDER

           TOTAL FEES PAID BY LENDER: $_____

I (We) hereby acknowledge that I (we) have received and read a completed copy of the HUD Special Information Booklet "Settlement Cost", unless the loan being applied is for refinancing the property.

If for any reason the loan I (we) have applied for does not close, and if permitted by applicable law, I (we) agree to reimburse the lender for any and all costs incurred to process my (our) application including, but not limited to: appraisal, survey, and title insurance.

12:12 Example – Itemization of Amount Financed

While some of the inclusions contained in the itemization of the amount financed may be the same as those appearing on the HUD 1 Settlement Statement or the instructions of costs from the lender, others will not be included on these documents.

The Itemization of Amount Financed is a different document and should not be used in the creation of or incorporated into the Settlement Statement. This document is intended as a legal disclosure document from the lender to the borrower of funds. This disclosure will include items paid by the lender on the borrower's behalf and then financed as a part of the transaction.

CORRECTION AGREEMENT
LIMITED POWER OF ATTORNEY

On   , the undersigned Borrower(s), for and in consideration of the approval, closing and funding of their mortgage loan (No.   ) hereby grant
as settlement agent and/or   as Lender limited power of attorney to correct and/or execute or initial all typographical or clerical errors discovered in any or all of the closing documentation required to be executed by the undersigned at settlement. In the even this limited power of attorney is exercised, the undersigned will be notified and receive a copy of the document executed or initialed on their behalf.

THIS LIMITED POWER OF ATTORNEY MAY NOT BE USED TO INCREASE THE INTERST RATE (NOR THE MARGIN OR INDEX FOR VARIABLE RATE LOANS) THE UNDERSIGNED IS PAYING, INCREASE THE TERM OF THE UDNERSIGNED'S LOAN, INCREASE THE UDNERSIGNED'S OUTSTANDING PRINCIPAL BALANCE OR INCREASE THE UNDERSIGNED'S MONTHLY PRINCIPAL AND INTEREST PAYMENTS. Any of these specified changes must be executed directly by the undersigned.

This Limited Power of Attorney shall automatically terminate 180 days from the closing date of the undersigned's mortgage loan.

12:13 Example Correction Agreement – Limited Power of Attorney

At times, after the closing is complete, a typographical or specific clerical error may be discovered in the fully executed documents. Rather than return to the signor and request a new signature, a limited power of attorney is often executed at the closing. This limited power of attorney provides for specific individuals to correct the typographical or clerical errors on behalf of the signor.

This authorization expressly states that the signor will receive a copy of all altered documentation.

The authorization also specifically excludes alterations to the index or margin of an adjustable rate loan, interest rate, term, principal balance, or principal and interest payment.

The limited power of attorney will also contain a specific end date for the authorizations granted.

Date:

Lender:

Borrower(s):

Loan Number:

Property Address:

WARRANTY AND COMPLIANCE AGREEMENT

In order to induce the lender to make the above loan and in consideration thereof, the undersigned borrower(s):

1.   Warrants and represents to the lender that all information it or its agents have provided to the lender, including without limitation all information contained in the loan application and all documents associated therewith, is true and accurate in all respects as of the date below. In making this statement, the borrower understands that (a) the lender has relied on the accuracy of such information in its decision to make the loan, and (b) if any such information is inaccurate, the lender or its assignee may foreclose or cancel the loan and pursue other legal remedies, including damages for fraud UNDER THE PROVISIONS OF THE DEED OF TRUST, ITEM 6.

2.   Agrees that if any document evidencing the loan does not correctly or accurately reflect the terms of loans offered by lender in the program under which the undersigned applied, including, but not lmited to, maturity date, interest rate, refinance options, etc., or is not on a form approved for such program as a result of a mistake or clerical error by lender, whether such mistake or error is mutual or unknown to the undersigned, the undersigned will:

        (a)   execute and/or initial modifications, amendments, or replacement documents as necessary to accurately and correctly reflect the terms of the loan or to ensure the loan is evidenced by the proper documentation; and

        (b)   take such other actions as the lender may reasonably request under the circumstances to   correct such mistake or clerical error.

In this connection, the undersigned acknowledges that the lender is a mortgage banker which only makes loans that meet criteria established and/or approved by secondary market investors to whom many of the loans it makes are ultimately sold. The undersigned further understands that the lender only offers loan programs which are approved by such investors or meet their established criteria, that any failure to perform the covenants and promises set forth in this agreement may render a loan unmarketable and thereby result in loss or damage to the lender, and that the undersigned's execution of this agreement and willingness to perform obligations assumed herein are material to the lender's decision to make the loan.

12:14 Example Warranty and Compliance Agreement

The borrower will be asked to confirm or warranty that all of the information provided during the loan application is correct. This document will specify that the borrower is guaranteeing that they have provided only accurate statements in association with the loan application and will state that the borrower agrees that penalties may be invoked if any information provided is found to be untrue.

The document will also detail for the borrower the steps that they must take if they find an error or discrepancy in the mortgage documents.

The lender may be subject to random file reviews or may have need to confirm the information contained within the buyer's application, loan package and tax documents at some time in the future. This could occur for a variety of reasons such as the packaging of loans to sell on the secondary mortgage market, standard lender reviews or servicing transfers. Regardless of the reason, many Lenders require documents in the file that allow them to access and verify certain borrower records.

**USE OF YOUR TELEPHONE,
FACSIMILE AND CELLULAR TELEPHONE NUMBERS**

Date:

Borrower(s):   Lender:

Property Address:

Please provide the following information:

Home Telephone Number	( ) _____	( ) _____
Work Telephone Number	( ) _____	( ) _____
Cellular Telephone Number	( ) _____	( ) _____
Facsimile Number	( ) _____	( ) _____
Email Address	_____	_____
Name of closest relative	_____	_____
Relative's Telephone	( ) _____	( ) _____

By signing below, Borrower agrees that the lender, lender's affiliates, the loan servicer and their respective successors and assigns (collectively "we" may contact you at the telephone numbers and email addresses listed above for any purpose related to the servicing and collection of any loan(s) or line of credit we have made to you. You agree that we may use automated dialing and announcing devices to make such calls and that we may contact you at any telephone, facsimile, cellular telephone number, or email address that we may subsequently obtain.

12:15 Example Use of Contact Information Form

When credit is provided, it is becoming a common practice for a lender to obtain all possible contact information for the borrower. They may also request the contact information of individuals who might assist in locating the borrower in the event an issue arises with the repayment of the borrower funds. Many individuals have multiple means of contact and all of them will be requested.

If the borrower's contact information is requested during the closing, specific authorizations as to how the lender may use that contact information will often be incorporated into the request.

Occupancy Declaration

An occupancy declaration is a statement by the borrower that defines the use they intend to make of the property.

When a mortgage lender provides a mortgage loan, one aspect that will affect the approval is the use that the borrower intends to make of the property.

It is commonly believed that a borrower will make payments against their primary residence better than they will against a second home, investment property or other form of residence. As such, the entry that you make on the application form pertaining to occupancy plans of the property will change many aspects of the loan including interest rate, percentage of the value they will lend against and documentation requirements based on the occupancy plans of the borrower.

During the loan application process, the borrower will have provided information pertaining to the intended occupancy status of the property being transferred.

It is a common practice to request that the borrower complete a statement that confirming these occupancy plans during the settlement meeting.

This occupancy declaration will be included in nearly every closing package and it is essential that you have confirmed the occupancy plans of the borrower prior to remitting the initial application to the underwriting department for review.

A closing could be stopped if the borrower arrives and refuses to sign an occupancy declaration.

If you have conducted an adequate interview and completed the application forms properly, this document will have a limited impact on your closing.

OCCUPANCY DECLARATION

Lender:

RE: LOAN NO:
         PROPERTY ADDRESS

The undersigned Borrower of the above described property does hereby declare, under penalty of perjury as follows:

1.   Borrower shall occupy, establish and use the Property as Borrower principal residence within sixty days after execution of the Security Instrument and shall continue to occupy the Property as Borrower's principal residence for at least one year after the date of occupancy unless Lender otherwise agrees in writing, which consent shall not be unreasonably withheld, or unless extenuating circumstances exist which are beyond the Borrower's control.

      You are hereby informed that the Lender from time to time makes spot checks for owner occupancy on properties upon which we have secured a mortgage.

      Between the first and thirteenth day, after close of escrow, occupancy may be checked more than once. If after this check Lender is to believe that you never intended to occupy the subject as your primary residence, we may choose to call your note due and payable or increase your note rate by 100 basis points, in accordance with the applicable sections itemized on your note and Security Instrument and allowable by law.

2.   Borrower shall be in default, if during the loan application process, gave materially false or inaccurate information or statements to Lender (or failed to provide Lender with any material information) in connection with the loan evidenced by the Note, including but not limited to, representations concerning Borrower's occupancy of the Property as a Principal residence.

3.   The Lender has the right to foreclose on the loan under the terms of the Security Instrument if items 1 or 2 above are violated.

4.   Should Borrower's intention change prior to close transaction, then it is agreed that Lender will immediately be notified of that fact.

5.   Borrower understands that without this declaration of intention, Lender may not make the loan in connection with the property.

12:16 Sample Occupancy Declaration

FEE DISCLOSURE

APPLICANT(S) NAME AND ADDRESS	MORTGAGE BANKER/BROKER NAME AND ADDRESS
PROPERTY ADDRESS	TYPE OF LOAN

Today you have submitted a mortgage loan application to the Mortgage Banker or Broker listed above. All fees paid by you are nonrefundable. State law (   ) requires that the following information be disclosed to you.

12:17 Sample Fee Disclosure

The Mortgage Banker or Broker is required to refund all fees paid by an applicant borrower, other than those fees paid by the Mortgage Banker or Broker to a third party, when a mortgage loan is not produced within the time specified by the Mortgage Banker or Broker at the rate, term and overall cost agreed to by the borrower.

However, this provision shall not apply when the failure to produce a loan is due solely to the borrower's negligence, borrower's refusal to accept and close on a loan commitment or borrower's refusal or inability to provide information necessary for processing the loan, including, but not limited to, employment verifications and verifications of deposit.

This disclosure does not constitute approval of your loan or a commitment to make a loan to you.

12:17 Sample Fee Disclosure Continued

Fee Disclosure   Many lenders now require that the payment for certain fees be given to the lender by the buyer. These funds are held by the lender to pay for services that will be ordered in relationship to documenting the loan.

Other fees may be paid directly to service providers during the transaction processing stage or paid out of the proceeds at the closing table.

FINAL ACTIONS

Rate Lock   If the interest rate has already been locked-in, the document person draws the loan documents.

If the interest rate has not been locked in, you should ensure that the form is completed at this time.

Document Prep   Once the loan documents are printed, they are then over-nighted to the Escrow Company or Settlement Company.

Schedule Meeting   The settlement agent then contacts the borrower with the final figures for the scheduled closing.

This process from document order to signing will normally take 2-5 days.

Settlement   After the loan documents have been prepared, signed, dated, notarized, and returned, they will go into funding.

Funding

Funding is the time when all of the signed documents are reviewed by the lender to insure that everything is signed correctly.

At this point, they will also do a final back-up quality control check of your borrower's credit and employment to insure nothing has changed since the loan was approved.

Once everything has been verified and checked, the lender will fund the loan.

The funding of the loan is the time when the monies borrowed are wired to the closing company, escrow office, or the closing attorney for disbursement.

o This is when the actual exchange of money is completed.

   This funding is usually completed through an electronic wire transfer.

o Some lenders do dry closings in which the funds are not sent until all the review activity is complete.

   In this case, the funding will usually take place 2 to 4 days after the loan documents have been returned to the lender by the closer.

o In other cases, lenders send the funds to the escrow or closing company before the settlement meeting. If the funds are available at the settlement meeting, the escrow or closing agent will cut the checks and have them available for dispersal at the settlement table.

Recording

The recording process is the time that the legal, binding loan documents that were signed and notarized are taken to the county recorder office for recording.

The actual recording is simply, the time when the documents are time and date stamped by the county recorder office, recognized, and filed as an official public document.

The recording process usually takes place 24 to 48 hours after the loan has been funded and the electronic wire confirmed.

In some places a "special recording" or a same day recording may occur.

At this point, the loan is finalized and closed.

Developing Relationships

A very important part of your career success will be developing relationships. The Chapter Career Building Tools and our Advanced Marketing Courses discuss developing rapport with affinity groups and borrowers. For now, you must focus your efforts upon some very important relationships.

Many loan officers neglect to foster positive service relationships. No matter how hard you work or how proficient you become, you will lose business unless you have a strong support network with affinity service providers.

The affinity service provider group includes anyone who must complete their tasks in a timely, professional manner in order for you to accomplish your goal – closing the loan.

Underwriters, Lending Closing Specialists, Title Company Staff and Closers, Appraiser, Inspection Personnel, the list is long and varied. Every one of these people is someone you must depend on to accomplish your ultimate goals.

Many loan officers choose to see this group as both unimportant and peripheral to the overall process or as simple service providers who are collecting a paycheck off of the loan officer's hard work. The truth is, unless you have the aid of these essential people you cannot accomplish your ultimate goals – closing loans quickly and smoothly.

An appraiser can shelve your order for days before he sets an appointment to view the subject property. A closing specialist can forego the extra effort it would take to make room in their very tight schedule to close your loan. An underwriter can scrutinize your loan 'to death' – the more time an underwriter spends reviewing a file the longer the required stipulation list can become.

We are not saying that these people are bad people. We are also not saying they will intentionally place blocks in the path of your loan progress. We are saying their attitude towards you dramatically affects their attitude toward your loan packages!

By treating these providers in a respectful, friendly, and considerate manner, you will begin to foster a positive relationship, build rapport, and create an overall good relationship. Look at these people as partners in the loan process, threat them as you should and you will quickly see the positive results of your attitude.

CHAPTER

13

CHARTING YOUR CAREER

The first decision you will make as a loan officer is whether you will choose to create your business within the structure of a traditional banking institution or within a mortgage brokerage. Included within this decision is whether you will base your office out of a home office or within the conventional environment of the mortgage bank or brokerage.

Once you have completed your training, obtaining a position as a loan officer is relatively easy.

You will want to create your resume, listing not only previous work and educational experience, but also any community activities or volunteer programs in which you have been involved. These activities show the hiring manager that you have contacts within your community. These contacts will prove invaluable when you begin marketing for direct borrowers. Any person in your community is a potential loan application as are any people with whom they come in contact.

Your interview package should also include any "brag book" materials you have available. The brag book should include items such as:

- The certificate of completion for this program

- Any positive items from previous customers – letters, thank you cards, even notes, showing you performed in an efficient and professional manner.

- Any awards or certificates received in the past.

- Numbers showing your performance in previous years no matter what the position held.

  Numbers are a very important item when interviewing with a Lending Manager.

  Lending is a numbers based business and most lenders are comfortable assessing a situation based on true numbers.

Later in the manual, we will give you ideas on how to accumulate items for your future brag book. The brag book will prove invaluable in any future interview-type situation as well as when meeting with potential borrowers.

Before setting your first interview, you should spend some time planning your career strategy as well as your initial marketing plan. You will need to revise both of these items once you have chosen the lender you will work with. Having preliminary versions of these items available at the time of interview allows the Lending Manager assess your potential as a loan officer. They will see how committed to your new career you have become and assess your knowledge of the position requirements and how realistic your goal planning will be.

Interview Questions

The last item you should have available for your interview process is a list of questions.

The term interview questions does not refer to questions such as "How much do I get paid?" or "What are the hours?" but rather refer to questions customized around the company with which your are hoping to work.

Spend some time doing specific research on the institution to gain some basic knowledge. It is impressive to a hiring manager to know that you are excited enough by their company to have taken the time to gather some basic knowledge before the first meeting.

Questions serve a purpose beyond showing preparation and interest. Many people fear the interview process. They become nervous and tongue-tied. This occurs with good reason. When you walk into an interview with basic industry knowledge but not a lot else, you are asking to be grilled by the Manager conducting the interview. All of the questions we suggest show an interest and knowledge of the industry as well as a certain level of drive on your part.

The series of questions you choose to use serve to remove some of the pressure from your shoulders by turning the process around somewhat.

The truth is there are many lenders out there and you want to be certain you accept a position with the correct one for you. You are interviewing the lender and the particular office for which you are applying. Obtaining a position in an office or with a lender is only valuable to you if you are able to achieve your goals in that environment.

Following are a series of questions you may use to pattern your interview technique:

1.   What is the exact description of the position for which I am being hired?

        This question allows you to obtain the basic outline of what is expected of you to ensure that the goals of the Lending Institution and the Branch Manager will be compatible with your expectations.

        There are various positions you may be offered. The two most common position titles are:

COMMON TITLES

A **Loan Originator** is someone who spends a great part of the workday on the streets soliciting borrower referrals from affinity groups. They bring these borrower referrals back to their office structure the loan package that meets the borrower's needs and document a package that will enable the lending institution to fund a solid loan. The act of being an originator means that your primary focus is to originate loans.

A **Loan Officer** is someone who spends a great deal of his or her time in the office, interviewing potential borrowers and structuring the available loan products to meet the needs and specific situation of the borrower. The primary goal of the loan officer is to ensure that each loan closed provides all of the parties involved with the best possible loan package.

A **Mortgage Broker** is someone who uses their vast knowledge of the mortgage industry to bring potential borrower packages to the right lending institution to obtain the loan program that meets the needs of both the borrower and lender. The broker acts as a liaison and brings the potential borrowers together with the right lender, loan program and loan parameters to ensure that the borrower achieves their dreams of homeownership.

A **Loan Processor** assists the borrower in obtaining all of the documents and services that are required to complete the loan process and purchase transaction.

Your training provides you with all of the knowledge and tools to obtain a position that provides a blend of the positions typically titled Originator or Officer.

You will desire a well-rounded position in which you spend:

A portion of your time originating loans

A portion meeting with borrowers and selling loan programs

A portion of your time structuring and processing loan programs

Specialty Programs   Some lenders hire loan officers to fill the position of Specific Loan Program Specialists.

These lenders designate different employees to complete different loan programs. The assumption is that if you specialize in a specific program you will be a more effective lender in that area of the market. This is a good idea in its way, but it does limit your borrower base.

Examples of specific program specialties would be Government, Conventional, Building Programs, and Sub-prime.

If the question of loan programs is not clarified through the answer to this question, you will want to ask specifically:

Is there a loan program specialty I will be required to perform or may I cross over multiple programs?

2.   What is the history of <u>Institution Name</u>?

Many Lending Institutions have undergone mergers and changes in the previous years. You should pay close attention to the history of the lender as it can tell you of some changes that may occur in your position after hire.

If a merger is planned, you will want to ensure that the new company's structure will suit your needs as much as the current company for which you are interviewing.

3.   Will I be working primarily from this office or will I be working in the field?

Some lending institutions assume you will perform many of your duties from home or in the affinity groups offices.

It is important to establish the working conditions to be sure you have the resources available that you will need.

Example: a home office, a laptop, and a mobile printer

4.   Do you do your applications on the computer or by hand?

This question allows you to determine the progressiveness of the institution.

Some institutions do everything by hand. While this is a workable option, those companies with more technology available for your use will tend to have more options available to ease your career path.

If you are not adept at working with computers, you may wish to target only those companies who do everything by hand.

5.   Why is this position available?

You need to determine if the company has a problem with employee retention or if it is hiring because of increased business.

Some institutions have an employee retention issue. Much of the institution's focus is on the customer with little left over for the satisfaction of the employees.

6.   How many programs do you have available?

A Loan Originator is only as effective as the programs he or she has available.

Whether working with a bank or a brokerage it is important to establish that the available repertoire of programs will meet all the communities lending needs.

You do not wish to have a high turn down ratio that causes borrowers to shop elsewhere.

7.   What is the promotion potential?

It is important to establish exactly where your career with this institution may take you.

If the institution is smaller, which is typical of a brokerage, there may be limited promotional opportunities available. Even if there is no promotion opportunity, the institution can still offer valuable benefits; however, you must be aware of the limitations of each institution as well as the benefits.

You will also want to add some questions specific to the interviewing company based upon your research of that institution.

These company specific questions can be simple questions that show knowledge of the institution not just the industry as a whole. This is flattering to the interviewer since it shows that you took the opportunity to research their company.

The point of the questions is not to simply gather information but to control some of the flow of the interview.

As a new originator, you may have some nervousness when interviewing to obtain your first position. Having the series of questions available for your use allows you to deflect some of the focus of the interview process onto the interviewer and away from you. This allows you to relax and carefully consider your answers to the interview questions, which will be sent your way.

Understanding and Negotiating Income

The final consideration when entering the Mortgage Lending Field is income.

Your income potential could vary greatly depending on where you choose to work and what types of lending you choose to perform.

Salary

You may be offered a position as a loan officer paid a salary.

The loan officer on a fixed salary is often the type who is office bound, processing applications that are originated by the institution for which you work.

This is an excellent opportunity to increase your comfort in using the skills you are learning.

The potential for high levels of income is limited if you obtain only a salary.

Draw vs. Commission

Loan Officers often obtain a position with a draw vs. commission style pay-structure.

A draw vs. commission structure guarantees a certain amount of income each month, similar to a salary.

The guarantee income is offset against the commission earnings on each loan package.

It is only after you have earned enough income to cover your draw that you are awarded additional commission funds.

Example: If you draw is fixed at $2,000 you are guaranteed to take home $2,000 each month even if you only earned $1,000 per month off of all loan income.

Each dollar earned above the fixed $2,000 draw is paid out to you in commission.

If you earned $3,000 in commission income in a given month, the first $2,000 would be paid as a portion of the guarantee and the $1,000 would be paid in addition to the guaranteed draw.
Most institutions have a running draw sheet that you must first meet before you are paid commissions.

If you have worked with the institution for 6 months at $2,000 draw a month, you would have taken home a guaranteed draw of $12,000. If, during that same 6 months you only earned $11,000 in commission income you would owe the institution the next $1,000 in commission income earned to offset your previously received draw.

Each loan and each lending institution will pay differently. Most managers will offer a contract detailing exactly how you will be paid.

The end of this Chapter details loan closing income and actual commission payroll examples.

Commission Structure

Commission structures are a variable item that you will want to review carefully and negotiate with your Branch before starting with that institution.

Some variables on the commission structure are:

- What fees and points count toward the commission pay division?

  As you will saw when reviewing the Good Faith Estimate and Pricing the Loan in earlier Chapters, there are a variety of points, fees and back-end points you may charge on a loan package.

It is important to determine exactly which items charged are going to count toward your pay structure. Sometimes, simply changing the name of a fee you charge may transfer it from a branch only payment to an Officer-Branch split payment.

Underwriting Fees are usually not split with the loan officer while a Processing Fee may be split based upon the negotiated percentage.

- Is the guarantee a draw or a fixed salary?

If a draw is there a certain time during training (typically three months), during which the draw is forgiven if I do not earn enough commission?

> It is a common practice offer a three-month period where the draw is in effect a fixed training salary. This means you do not have to add the payments to your accumulated earnings/offsets. You do not have to pay back a fixed training draw if you do not supersede the amount earned with commission income.

- What is the commission percentage?

The commission percentage is the percentage of all fees and costs charged on a loan package that the loan officer receives.

You can negotiate this percentage at the time of hire, at periodic performance reviews or at any other time that seems appropriate.

An increase in commission percentage is often a method used to reward an employee, in effect a raise.

The percentage paid to a particular loan officer can vary greatly between companies and even between employees within the same company. Careful attention should be paid to the percentage you receive.
The actual percentage a loan officer receives may not be as important as the loan income that counts toward that percentage.

Never lose sight of what makes up the "commission".

If ½ of the costs charged are part of the commission split then a 75% commission split is not as good of a deal, as a 50% commission split on ALL costs charged on the loan package.

Example: INSTITUTION A

If the negotiated commission split is 75% loan officer and 25% branch and the split is based on 50% of the fees earned on a package the income for the loan officer would be $1,162.50 for a loan earning $3100 in fees.

If a package earned a total income of		$3,100
50% of those costs were fees considered as part of the commission for the loan officer	x	.50
The commission split would be based on the new figure		$1,550
Taking the new figure that counts toward commissions		$1,550
Times the negotiated split of applicable loan income of 75% LO/25% Branch the Commission Income	x	.75
The loan officer would earn	=	$1,162.50

Example: INSTITUTION B

If the negotiated commission split is 50% loan officer and 50% branch and the split is based on all fees earned on a package the income for the loan officer would be $1,550 for a loan earning $3100 in fees.

If the same package earned a total income of		$3,100
ALL of those fees were considered as part of the commission for the loan officer	x	.100
The commission split would be based on the		$3,100
Taking the total loan income		$3,100
Times the negotiated split 50% LO/50% of all applicable Loan income	x	.50
The loan officer would earn	=	$1,550

As you can see from this example the Lending Institution B, paying the Loan Officer a lower percentage on a higher quantity of fees charged on the package is actually paying more money per loan to the loan officer than Lending Institution A who is paying the higher percentage split but paying it on a lower number of fees charged.

For each offer you consider, run some sample numbers to determine which offer is actually more beneficial to you in the end.

CHAPTER 14

PLANNING A
MARKETING STRATEGY

In the following pages, we will lead you in developing your first marketing plan.

The primary task, before you begin marketing for your first application, is developing a system for tracking the effect of your marketing efforts.

Early in your career, you will spend the balance of your time marketing. You will complete a variety of tasks such as making contacts, building relationships, and getting your name out to your target groups. The abundance of time available early in your career enables you to take the opportunity to experiment. You will be able to use a variety of marketing methods to determine what works best for you.

Each person's strengths and weaknesses are different and therefore each person's marketing plan should be different.

Sometime in the first 90 days as a loan officer, you will need to begin redirecting the bulk of your efforts to processing and closing loans. At that time, it will become very important to expend your marketing efforts in the areas that bring you the strongest return.

To determine where your valuable time and energies should be expended you will need solid market penetration figures. As time management becomes vital to your continued success, these figures will allow you to determine, based on solid tracking numbers, exactly what marketing efforts provide success for you!

During the training included in Chapter 2 Basic Mortgage Loan Officer Process Training, we recommended that you bind each month's original pre-qualification questionnaires in a master folder. If you have asked each borrower how they heard about you, these forms – readily available in your binder – will give you an excellent overview of what marketing efforts have yielded a return.

You may wish to develop a different system that works for you. An excellent computerized system is the ACT! Program. This program offers an enlarged database that you customize to include all pertinent information about a loan. These programs will also generate reports upon request. These reports can give you your market referral numbers at the touch of a button.

Experiment to find the tracking system that will work for best for you. Just be sure you HAVE a system. Whatever method of tracking you use, knowing what brings in the borrowers and what is a non-returning waste of your time, money and efforts is well worth the time involved in creating and utilizing the tracking plan.

Choosing Marketing Areas

There are seven beginning marketing options with proven results for a loan officer.

Advertising

Group Presentations

Flier/Mail Campaigns

Gift Campaign

Wine and Dine

Telemarketing

Networking

Your market plan may contain only a couple of these options or a combination of all of these options.

You will need to balance your strengths, budget, market conditions, and time to determine how you wish to work within your particular market.

Advertising

Most branches have an advertising budget available. You may be eligible for a certain allocation of that budget or you may need to share advertisement space with another loan officer. You may need to purchase a portion of your advertisements out of your own pocket. No matter who pays the bill it is important to spend you advertising budget carefully.

Your first goal is exposure. Unless your target market knows who you are, where you are and what you can do for them, they will never call!

Print Media and Radio Media are the two most common forms of advertising for a beginning loan officer.

Radio Advertisements are designed to promote name recognition while print advertisements are designed to convey information. As a beginning loan officer, you will probably want to focus on print. This allows you to leave the more costly radio advertising and name recognition creation to your branch location. They will build name recognition in the market place and you will build personal recognition.

Many newspapers offer a free "new in business" advertisement. This brief blurb tells the public that you are now in business. The advertisement should tell the public: who you are, your specialty, and your contact information. This is an excellent first step in getting your name out there. Best of all it is typically free.

Many branches, no matter their advertising budget are willing to place a "Welcome Aboard" advertisement notifying the public that they have a new loan officer available. Check with your branch manager to see if this is a common practice. If not, research pricing and write your own advertisement. Often, when approached with a completed package your manager will rubber-stamp his or her approval on the advertisement. Exposure for you is exposure for the branch!

A welcome aboard advertisement should look something like this:

<u>Company Name</u>
is proud to Welcome <u>Your Name</u>
a certified home mortgage loan officer.

Specializing in <u>Type of Loans</u>
home loans, <u>Your Name</u> is available for
FREE pre-qualifications!

Give <u>Your First Name</u> a call today and welcome him/her aboard!
<u>Telephone Number</u>

You will note the advertisement gives:

Your company (where you are)

Your name (who you are)

Your title (showing your capabilities)

Your specialty (notifying your target market that you are here FOR them)

A FREE offer (nothing will make your phone ring faster than the word FREE!)

An order to call today (people sometimes need permission to call and instructions on how and when to contact you to feel comfortable taking that first step.)

If you are able to place an advertisement specific to you, you will want to make every dollar count.

- Research ALL the print media in your area.

  Example: Primary newspapers, Real Estate Guides, Bargain Shopper Style Newspapers, and anything else specific to your region

- Determine the target market and circulation of the media you are considering. Also, determine how the circulation compares with your target market needs.

- Assess the cost of advertising. Assess where other lenders are finding success.

After you have these figures, arrange a meeting with your branch manager to determine exactly what the branch is willing to fund for you.

After you know what you can spend, make the final decision as to where you wish to place your advertising.

- Carefully weigh the cost of the advertisement against the circulation and market of each media source.

   You should quickly determine that one or two options outstrip the   competition.

- Now it is time to write your first advertisement.

   You will want your advertisement to be understandable, efficient, and direct.

   Bear in mind, when composing the advertisement, the majority of the population comprehends at no more than an 8th grade reading level.

A sample advertisement might be:

WHY ARE YOU RENTING?
Little or no down payment?
Less-than-perfect credit?
Cannot find the home of your dreams?

I can help!
Call your name at your company and telephone number
for your FREE pre-qualification and let me put you
in the home of your dreams!

- Notice the attention-getting header that targets a market in need of home loans.

- The questions that are actually the most common excuses for why people do not call a lender

- Followed by simply I CAN HELP - A strong statement

- Lastly, you are giving them permission to call and you are stressing the word FREE.

Many people cannot resist free especially when it is tied to something they truly want – the HOME OF THEIR DREAMS!

The advertisement is short (therefore less costly), concise and simple to understand. An advertisement, which contains all of the characteristics of the one above, should make your telephone begin to ring very quickly.

The last item you should consider before placing any advertisement is that there are laws regarding appropriate real estate related advertising. These laws limit the discrimination against individuals through advertising.

The Federal Fair Housing Act prohibits the use of discriminatory advertising or advertisements that state a preference for a particular type of person. You may not advertise in a manner meant to attract or deter a potential borrower based on race, color, religion, sex, handicap, familial status, or national origin.

HUD released a clarification of acceptable words and phrases, which can be used in real estate related advertisements. You must use caution when composing your advertising so as not to include any item that is discriminatory in nature. More information regarding acceptable advertising is included in the Advanced Mortgage Marketing Course or directly from HUD.

The nature of advertising allows you a broad spectrum in which to operate. It is important to remember that discrimination in real estate practice is illegal. Providing you are not targeting particular strata of society for either positive or negative effect, staying within the guidelines is relatively easy.

Federal Agencies evaluate their policies and programs on a regular basis to determine any modifications and executive orders that must be added as a protected class under the fair housing laws. You should review these policies and laws frequently to ensure your advertisements remain within the guidelines.

Group Presentations

Group presentations are an excellent method of conveying your information to a large group of people at the same time. Before you begin planning your carefully composed and rehearsed presentation, you will need to think about the following "tips":

- Think of a presentation as a performance.

  You might want to entertain, motivate, and inspire your audience all at the same time.

  Instead, you should carefully consider which your primary objective is and never lose focus.

- Grab your audience.

  Do not give the audience the opportunity to lose interest.

  Grab them from the beginning with a "hook".

  > A hook is a statement that conveys why they, not you, need know this information.

  > Everyone wants to know "what's in it for me".

- Engage your audience.

  Most presentations are boring.

  Keep the presentation moving along and engaging and your audience will be more responsive.

- Make eye contact with your audience – even before you begin to speak.

- Keep your presentations moving

  State your background.

  Hit them with the facts on what you do and what you can do for them.

  Finish.

  Most presentations fail because the speaker tries to include too much information.

- Use a strong speaking voice.

  Even if you feel uncomfortable, a strong tone will inspire confidence.

A mousy tone will cause your audience to lose interest.

- DO NOT wiggle rock or pace.

  Transfer excess energy to your voice, expression, and hands.

- Control your desire to rush.

  Slow down.

  Use pauses.

  Let the audience into your presentation.

- Do not walk in unprepared

  An interested audience will turn your presentation into a discussion.

  Know the answers to any question they may ask.

  If you do not know the answer, do not "fake it". It is always better to say, "I don't know the answer to that question at the present time... let me get back to you." Make sure you find the answer and get back to them – SOON!

- Change the tempo.

  Changes in tempo help an audience maintain interest.

  Emphasize what is important by saying it more slowly and more loudly.

  For points of lesser importance, speak more softly and more quickly.

- Do not forget to "close" your presentation.

  Review your important points and finish with a memorable closing line.

- Follow your close with a thanks and farewells.

  Leave behind a good feeling about you and your presentation.

  Resist the urge to stay and chat.

When creating your presentation it is important to establish the goals of your audience. You would not give the same presentation to a Real Estate Agent as you would at a first time Homebuyer's Seminar. The key to each presentation is what you can do FOR THEM.

You might target many groups for your first presentation. We will cover the two most common.

Real Estate Agencies: Each Real Estate Brokerage or Agency will typically have a weekly meeting.

These meetings are times for the sales staff to meet, discuss problems, goals, and important information. It is also the time most Agents expect presentations

You might consider teaming up with an established loan officer to give the presentation. Perhaps one who specializes in Government loans? The borrower base you are soliciting will be different from a Government specialist. This gives both of you the perfect opportunity to expand your reputation, as the loan officers who can and do handle any issue.

The turndowns of a government specialist may be your perfect borrower!

Real estate agents are commission based.

That means they are paid if the loan can close. Because of this they are very particular about who they use for their affinity service providers.

The Lender is an affinity service provider for the agent.

An agent must trust that you are able to take their buyer's and turn them into homeowners.

There may have been lenders in your region in the past that promised and did not deliver. There may have been predatory lenders who took advantage of the less-than-perfect credit homebuyers. Both of these may have left a bad feeling in your agent's office concerning new loan officers. It is your job to address these issues and overcome the objections.

Meet these problems head on – tell your agents about predatory lending laws. Tell them how you treat your borrowers with compassion. Most of all tell them you never promise what you cannot deliver and then make sure you do not. An important consideration that many loan officers fail to tell Agents is that you are paid the same way the Agent is paid. Tell the Agent that you are paid on commission the same as them. You are not paid if the loan does not close, so you plan to work extra hard on each package that comes your way!

Remember; offer the agent the reasons they will profit by placing buyer's in your capable hands!

Homebuyer's Seminar

Targeted at people who currently rent and have a true desire to purchase their first home. This is a ready-made group of driven pre-qualifications!

In the beginning, before you have established the trust of your affinity groups, it may be difficult for you to gain an invitation to become a part of their seminar. The simplest task is to stage your own seminar.

Staging your own seminar gives you the opportunity to invite the most successful affinity partners in your area to become a part of YOUR group rather than waiting, often in vain, to be invited to join their group.

You will first need to determine what information you wish to include in your seminar. Obviously, your loan products are the first priority. If you are specializing only in the B/C market, invite an A Paper Specialist to join your seminar. Specialists working only in the A markets are an excellent referral sources for the loan officer working only the B/C market because their turndowns are your borrowers!

Invite a Real Estate Agent to give the basics of finding and offering for a home.

Invite a closing company representative to explain what a closing or settlement is and what the homebuyers' can expect.

Invite an appraiser to explain the appraisal process.

Invite anyone who works with the same target market you do and has important information to convey that will be of interest to a first time homebuyer.

Inviting a team to each give a portion of the overall presentation accomplishes two essential tasks.

1. Inviting other people to join your presentation begins to create a relationship with each of these essential professionals. One of your

289

focus goals will be to establish relationships with these people in the coming months. This relationship may provide referral sources for you and, as mentioned earlier, affinity service providers play a huge role in your loan process.

2. Dividing the presentation also serves to remove some of the pressure from you. You will want to be assured that your presentation will take center stage, but by having these professionals discuss their role in the home buying process, you are allowing yourself to focus only on your portion of the process.

When structuring your portion of the presentation, remember to follow the presentation tips given earlier. Always give the prospective homebuyers the opportunity to pre-qualify.

Give the audience your pre-qualification questionnaire to complete right at the seminar. If you are lucky enough to have a laptop and printer, you can begin pulling credit and pre-qualifying right at the seminar. If you do not have that ability, collect the questionnaires and qualify them THAT day at your home or office.

Be sure to contact the prospects within 48 hours of the seminar before their interest has the opportunity to wane.

You can offer many more presentations. Begin by creating the presentation for one or both of these groups. If you are uncomfortable creating your own presentations, ask your branch manager what is available for use or purchase a ready-made presentation from a training company. We have an entire series available in our advanced marketing package.

Flier/Mail Campaigns

Direct print campaigns can be aimed toward affinity groups or your prospective borrowers. Either way, the goal of a direct print campaign is to have your name and information in front of the people that you are targeting.

Examples of affinity groups you may target include:

Divorce/Bankruptcy Attorneys

Financial Planners

Real Estate Agents

FSBO'S

Contractors

Prime Lenders

Anyone and everyone who has contact with the same group of borrowers you do are perfect for a direct media campaign.

When developing a flier/mail campaign you will want to construct direct, concise messages that will hold the attention of the target.

You will also want to vary your approach. Sending a letter every week for 10 weeks is not the correct way to approach a contact. Perhaps send a letter, followed by a postcard and then follow up with a personal visit to deliver a flier. Changing your method of approach reduces the possibility of boring your target. Before beginning a direct marketing campaign, make certain the contacts you plan to use are fresh and exciting. New loan officers sometimes purchase ready-made marketing flier programs. Many of these programs include only the same, stale fliers and letters used by hundreds of loan officers in previous years. Your market will not find these re-used marketing tools interesting. Make certain any marketing tool you use is the newest and is fresh within your market.

Each contact should convey a different message of interest to the target. Always stress what you can do to increase their business or reputation. Once you have established personal contact, give them an opportunity to refer to you. Perhaps drop off a fill in form that allows them to list any person they feel could benefit from your service. Be sure the target is very clear what you CAN do before asking to be allowed to get near their borrowers.

We recommend that you target one or two groups to start.

Develop your entire contact campaign before initiating the first contact. A recommended number of initial contacts are a minimum of one contact per week for six consecutive weeks.

Your ultimate goal with these contacts is to build to the point where you are comfortable requesting and they are comfortable referring joint borrowers.

Developing the Campaign

- Determine why your focus group would benefit by sending borrower's to you.

  Example: We will detail a Divorce Attorney as an example.

  Divorce settlements are often tricky when real property is involved.

Divorce tends to create financial strain causing blemishes on the credit report.

As part of the settlement agreement on party will often retain possession of the house and be required to give a cash amount toward built up equity value to the other party.

You can refinance home loans for those whose credit has sustained some dings in the recent past. This benefits the divorce attorney by smoothing the settlement process.

- Develop a program to convey those reasons to the target partner.

Develop your mail/flyer campaign based on the reasons you generated earlier.

Step 1: Begin with a letter of introduction, telling who you are, your specialty, and a few basic program guidelines targeted toward refinance. Close with an explanation of how this benefits his borrowers and reduces the length of divorce negotiations.

Step 2: The next contact might include a flyer emphasizing the points covered in your letter. Stop by his office to drop it off personally.

Step 3: If you get the opportunity to speak directly to the Attorney when delivering your flier, send a follow up thank you card. If not, send a postcard reminding the Attorney of the important points of your letter and flier.

Step 4: Your next contact should be a letter requesting a meeting to discuss which of his or her borrowers you will be able to help.

You will want to have a carefully prepared presentation available in case the Attorney is interested in meeting with you.

Step 5: Whether you arrange a face-to-face interview with the Attorney or not, re-cap the presentation in a simple booklet form and hand deliver it to the Attorney's office.

Step 6: Next, you will want to ask for referrals.

Make this easy for the Attorney.

Create a form for easy entry of borrower's names and telephone numbers.

Do not ask for every piece of information you will need to work with these borrowers. The basic contact information is all you should request to keep the process simple for your referring partner.

Another option is to drop off some "referral coupons" offering a discount on fees to any borrower bearing that coupon. It may be easier for the Attorney to hand out your coupons to his borrowers and let them contact you than it is for the Attorney to take the time to give you the information needed to contact his borrowers.

If, at this point, you have received referrals from your target be certain to keep them informed of the progress of the package. Even when you feel the information you have to convey is not vital to the referral source, they may feel differently.

Remember, each time you initiate a contact to convey progress; you are putting yourself in the forefront of the referral sources mind. In the forefront of their mind is exactly where you need to be if you expect continued referrals!

Again, if you are not comfortable developing your own series of print contacts there are many great systems available for purchase that incorporate some of the ideas above. Our system is patterned closely to the process we described and includes all of the mentioned affinity groups and more. Always be sure the system you are purchasing is newly generated so that you are not simply using old, out-dated fliers and letters that the referral partner has seen many times in the past.

Gift Campaign

Many loan officers prefer making calls bearing gifts.

You will be targeting the same affinity groups mentioned previously but you will be targeting them in person rather than by mail.

Each month of the year offers a variety of "special events" that lend themselves to cute and memorable gifts. These gifts do not need to be expensive – just unique.

We have developed weekly "hand out" gifts that cost less than $1.00 a piece. Most of our gifts are edible and sometimes we will even stage a contest, which runs over a series of weeks.

Each gift should come with a business card, a flier or catchy tag and a referral coupon.

An example of a cost-effective gift we use would be:

2nd Week in February – Valentine's Handout

- Take two red and white candy canes (purchased for .10 cents a box after the Christmas Season)

- Using a hot glue gun, glue the candy canes together to form a heart.

- Tie a bow around one side of the heart with a satin ribbon in either red or white or your company's color.

- Attach a business card to the bow.

- Leave these for each potential referral source with a flier underneath.

  They will have to remove your card in order to eat the candy.

  After going through that effort, they are likely to put your card in a prominent place on their desk.

This cute hand out costs approximately 3 cents to create and is memorable. You can use your creativity to design your own inexpensive and unique gifts, review crafting books and web sites for ideas, or purchase a pre-planned gift campaign.

Wine and Dine

Everyone loves to be treated to a lunch or special event. As a lender, people perceive you as having money. Let us face it – you sell money and therefore are inextricably linked to money in people's minds.

This is a more costly marketing technique that you will have to consider carefully to determine if the benefits outweigh the costs.

The primary benefit to taking a referral source to breakfast or lunch is that you will have a captive audience throughout the meal. This is a perfect opportunity to emphasize how you can improve their business. Be sure to do this in a non-aggressive manner. In some regions of the country, discussing business over a meal is considered inappropriate. You will want to assess the trends in your area and act accordingly.

An additional benefit is that once a person has eaten a meal with another they feel more connected. The more connected this affinity partner feels with you the more likely they are to remember you the next time they have a borrower who can use your help.

Telephone Marketing

Many states have now implemented a do not call list. You will want to confirm whether your state has such a list and if so gain access to guarantee that you are not marketing to people who have requested they be removed for all such lists.

If telephone marketing is available in your area, it is a great method of capitalizing on unused evening hours to create a larger borrower base.

Lists are readily available through marketing services that spend their efforts compiling target lists of prospects within your group. You can customize the list you request and buy as many or as few contacts as you wish. These lists, while better constructed than other options, are often rather costly. You will have to weigh the benefits verses the costs for yourself.

Another method of obtaining contact sheets for your area is the County Courthouse. Most courthouses provide, for a nominal fee, mortgages listed on their records. You can customize this list by lender, by year of closing, sometimes even by value of the mortgage.

Now is a great time to contact current homeowners because rates are still at an all-time low but are beginning to rise. Many homeowners will benefit by refinancing if they act quickly.

If you are working specifically within the sub-prime market, purchase those lists that contain mortgages funded by a finance company. Often the rates are extreme and the people who use finance companies did so because their credit was less-than-perfect.

Also, be sure to target mortgages written far enough in the past for some equity build-up to have occurred. You will want to have the option available of wrapping all costs up in the loan balance. This limits objections based on a lack of funds.

Complete telephone-marketing programs and scripts are available. We have scripts customized toward mortgage marketing as part of our advanced marketing programs.

Networking

Perhaps the easiest of all marketing methods is simple networking.

Every person you meet has a home. Whether they own or rent they still have home lending needs.

Every person you meet has an additional network of family and friends – all with home lending needs.

Whether at your church, grocery store, mechanics, or doctors office you meeting people who may need your help. Make an extra effort to initiate conversations wherever you go.

Remember tell people what you do – they cannot know you can be of service to them unless you tell them.

Always carry business cards.

Always have a pre-qualification questionnaire nearby! You will be amazed at how many people are willing to be pre-qualified and where!

Generate a Marketing Plan

Now that you have the information concerning initial marketing options, you may begin creating your marketing plan. In the appendix, we have included a sample month. You will need to purchase or create a schedule page that divides each day into hourly segments.

- First review the marketing options detailed in the preceding text.

- Determine which options you would like to put into effect first.

- Weigh each method and allocate the method a certain amount of time in your overall scheduling budget.

  Remember to allow time in your schedule for continued study of product matrix and guidelines.

- Begin filling in your schedule.

- Budget the appropriate amount of time for each task you wish to accomplish.

- Treat each task on your schedule as an appointment.

  Treat each marketing task as a place you must be and an activity you must perform regardless of weather conditions, other time pressures, or your nervousness on a given day.

- Now begin your career as a loan officer!

Sales Call Summary

Date: _____   Customer Name: _____

Time: _____   Purpose: _____

Outcome: _____

_____

Action Plan: _____

Date: _____   Customer Name: _____

Time: _____   Purpose: _____

Outcome: _____

_____

Action Plan: _____

Date: _____   Customer Name: _____

Time: _____   Purpose: _____

Outcome: _____

_____

Action Plan: _____

Date: _____   Customer Name: _____

Time: _____   Purpose: _____

Outcome: _____

_____

Action Plan: _____

Sample Training Plan/Marketing Strategy
Month 1

Overview training program	Materials Review – Assess current knowledge	Basic Study	Basic Study	Complete Exercises Credit
Phone Skills – Practice Pre-qualification Questionnaire	Study Marketing Techniques	Create Marketing Plan	Send Introduction to Newspaper	Create advertising campaign
Create Fliers, ads, mailers and other needed marketing tools.	Create Fliers, ads, mailers and other needed marketing tools.	Create Fliers, ads, mailers and other needed marketing tools.	Solidify marketing plan Develop operations system/ organize	Review all materials assessing for comprehension
Review specific product matrixes as suggested by Manager	Review specific product matrixes as suggested by Manager	Call on first face-to-face affinity group	Send Mailer to first by-mail affinity group	Place Advertising Plan month 2 marketing program

Managing your Pipeline

A pipeline is the number of active loan files you have open at any given time. The purpose of tracking a pipeline is to move loan packages through the steps required achieving a closed loan.

Many loan officers allow important leads and pre-qualifications to fall through the cracks, failing to follow up on possible sources of business.

Other loan officers forget important tasks that must be completed on a loan package and are in a rush to accomplish them at the last possible moments.

By keeping a weekly pipeline report, you will know at the beginning and end of each week exactly where each package on your desk is in the process. You will want to create a tracking form or system customized for your use. Your branch manager may require weekly reports on the status of all open loan files in your pipeline so that he or she will know where you most need their aid. If your branch has a pipeline reporting system, it is best to use that in the beginning. As you become more experienced, you will discover methods, which work best for you.

Because of properly managing your pipeline, you will know exactly what follow up or reminders are required on your loan packages. We have an intricate system of reminders available with our advanced marketing program but you are very capable of creating your own program.

The most important benefit of managing your pipeline properly is the ability to estimate your income.

You will be aware at all times of what loan packages are preparing to close and what packages you can expect to close in the following month.

Tracking and Contact Management

Tracking each action on each loan program is a vital activity. As mentioned earlier you may purchase a software system that will aid in this process, your loan application program may include a section to enter loan notes or you may choose to track all actions manually.

You will find completion of pipeline reports, estimation of income and remembering the details of a specific loan and what action you took and when you took them is much easier if you keep sufficient records.

It is important that you realize that today you may remember the details of each loan in your pipeline but as your pipeline grows in the coming months, you will find this more difficult.

A Loan Officer who is properly organized will be more successful for many reasons. The most obvious is that they will not allow loans to fall through the cracks for lack of attention.

Following is a simplistic file tracking form that can be attached to the front of each loan file for quick reference.

FILE TRACKING LOG

DATE	ACTION	BY

GLOSSARY OF MORTGAGE TERMS

1-year ARM: An adjustable-rate mortgage (ARM) that has an initial interest rate for one year, and thereafter has an adjustment interval of one year. The adjustment is based on comparison interest caps and the indexed rate

3/1 ARM: An adjustable-rate mortgage (ARM) that has an initial interest rate for three years, and thereafter has an adjustment interval of one year. The adjustment is based on comparison interest caps and the indexed rate.

5/1 ARM: An adjustable-rate mortgage (ARM) that has an initial interest rate for five years, and thereafter has an adjustment interval of one year. The adjustment is based on comparison interest caps and the indexed rate

7/1 ARM: An adjustable-rate mortgage (ARM) that has an initial interest rate for seven years, and thereafter has an adjustment interval of one year. The adjustment is based on comparison interest caps and the indexed rate

10/1 ARM: An adjustable-rate mortgage (ARM) that has an initial interest rate for ten years, and thereafter has an adjustment interval of one year. The adjustment is based on comparison interest caps and the indexed rate

Abstract of Title: A written history of all the transactions that bear on the title to a specific piece of land An abstract of title covers the time from when the property was first sold to the present. Used by the Title Company to produce a title binder

Acceleration Clause: The section of a mortgage document that allows the lender to speed up the payment date in the event of default, making the entire principal amount due

Acre: An area of land 43.560 square feet

Adjustable Rate Mortgage: Mortgage in which the rate of interest is adjusted based on a standard rate index. Most ARM's have caps on how much the interest rate may increase

Adjustment Interval: How often the loan's rate can be changed

Alternative Mortgage: 7/23 and 5/25 mortgages with a one-time rate adjustment after seven years and five years respectively Also known as a hybrid mortgage or a two-step mortgage

Amortization Schedule : A timetable for the gradual repayment of a mortgage loan An amortization schedule indicates the amount of each payment applied to interest and principal, and the remaining balance after each payment is made

Amortization Term: The amount of time required to amortize (repay) a mortgage loan. The amortization term is usually expressed in months. A 30-year fixed rate mortgage, for example, has an amortization term of 360 months

Annual Percentage Rate (APR): A standardized method of calculating the cost of a mortgage, stated as a yearly rate which includes such items as interest, mortgage insurance, and certain points or credit costs

Appraisal: A written report by a qualified appraiser estimating the value of the property

Appraised Value: An opinion of a property's fair market value, based on an appraiser's inspection and analysis of the property

Appraiser: A person qualified by education, training, and experience to estimate the value of real property

Appreciation: An increase in the value of a property due to changes in market conditions or improvements to the property

ARM: See Adjustable Rate Mortgage

Assessed Value: The value of a property as determined by a public tax assessor for the purpose of taxation

Assumable: A mortgage that a buyer can assume, or take over, from the seller of the property

Balloon Mortgage: A loan that has regular monthly payments, which amortize over a stated term but call for a final lump sum (balloon payment) at the end of a specified term, or maturity date such as 10 years

Basis Points: $1/100$th of 1 percent If an interest rate changes 50 basis points, for example, it has move ½ of 1 percent

Binder: See title binder

Biweekly Mortgage: A mortgage that schedules payments every two weeks instead of the standard monthly payment The 26 biweekly payments are each equal to one-half of the monthly payment. The result for the borrower is a substantial reduction in interest payments because the mortgage is paid off sooner. See also prepayment plan

Bridge loan: A loan that "bridges" the gap between the purchase of a new home and the sale of the borrower's current home. The borrower's current home is used as collateral and the money is used to close on the new home before the current home is sold. Some are structured so they completely pay off the old home's first mortgage at the bridge loan's closing. Others pile the new debt on top of the old. They usually run for a term of six months

Broker: See mortgage broker

Broker Premium: A premium paid to the mortgage broker as the "middleman" in the mortgage process between the lender and the borrower

Built-ins: Cabinets, ranges, ceiling fans and other items permanently attached to the structure, and which a buyer may assume will remain with the structure

Buy down: The process of trading money for a lower mortgage rate The borrower "buys down" the interest rate on a mortgage by paying discount points up front. It can also be a mortgage in which an initial lump sum payment is made to reduce a borrower's monthly payments during the first few years of a mortgage

Caps: The maximum amount the interest rate can change annually or cumulatively over the life of an adjustable rate mortgage. F or example, if the caps are 2 percent annual and 6 percent life of loan, a mortgage with a first-year rate of 10 percent could rise to no more than 12 percent the second year, and no more than 16 percent over the entire life of the loan

Certificate of Title: A statement provided by the Title Company or attorney stating that the title to the real estate is legally held by the current owner

Chattel: Personal property

Clear title: A title that is free of liens or legal questions as to ownership of a piece of property

Closing: The meeting at which the sale of a property is finalized The buyer signs the lender agreement for the mortgage and pays' closing costs and escrow amounts. The buyer and seller sign documents to transfer the ownership of the property. Also known as the settlement

Closing costs: Expenses incurred by buyers and sellers in transferring ownership of a property. Closing costs normally include an origination fee, an attorney's fee, taxes, escrow payments, and charges for title insurance. Lenders or Real Estate Agents provide estimates of closing costs to prospective homebuyers

Closing Statement: A financial disclosure accounting for all funds changing hands at the closing See also HUD-1 Statement

Cloud on title: Any fact or condition that could adversely affect the title

Commission: In real estate, the broker, or mortgage associates fee for assisting in the transaction Usually expressed as a percentage of the total paid by the buyer

Commitment: A formal offer by a lender stating the approved terms for lending money to a homebuyer

Common Area Assessment: A levy against individual unit owners in a condominium or planned unit development to pay for upkeep, repairs, and improvements to the property's common areas, such as corridors, elevators, parking lots, swimming pools and tennis courts

Comparables: Refers to "comparable properties" which are used for comparative purposes in the appraisal process. Comps are recently sold properties that are similar in size, location, and amenities to the home for sale. Comps help an appraiser determine the fair market value of a property

Condominium: A real estate project in which each unit owner has title to a unit of the project, and sometimes and undivided interest in the common areas

Conforming Loan: A loan that conforms to the standard rules for purchase by Freddie Mac or Fannie Mae

Contingency: A condition that must be met before a contract is legally binding. For example, homebuyers often include a contingency that specifies that the contract is not binding until after a satisfactory report from a home inspector

Contract: In real estate parlance, the contract is the legal document by which buyer and seller make offers and counteroffers. The real estate contract describes the property, includes or excludes items in the property, names the price, apportions the closing costs between the parties and sets forth a closing date. When a buyer and seller agree on the terms and sign the same document the property is said to be "under contract". More formally known as the agreement for the sale, purchase agreement, or earnest money contract

Conventional Mortgage: Usually refers to a fixed-rate, 30-year mortgage that is not insured by FHA, Farmers Home Administration, or Veterans Administration

Convertible Mortgage: An adjustable rate mortgage ARM that can be converted to a fixed mortgage under specific conditions

Cooperative: A type of multiple ownership in which the residents of a multiunit housing complex own shares in the cooperative corporation that owns the property, giving each resident the right to occupy a specific apartment or unit

Cost-of-funds: A yield index based upon the cost of funds to savings & loan institution in the San Francisco Federal Home Loan Bank District. It is one of the indexes commonly used to set the rate of adjustable rate mortgages

Covenant: A written restriction on the use of land, most commonly in use today in homeowners associations

Credit report: A report on a person's credit history prepared by a credit bureau and used by a lender in determining a loan applicant's record for paying debts in a timely manner

Debt-to-Income Ratio: The percentage of a person's monthly earnings used to pay off all debt obligations Lenders consider two ratios, constructed in slightly different ways. The first called the front-end ratio, the ratio of the monthly housing expenses – including principal, interest, property taxes, and insurance, (PITI) is compared to the borrower's gross, pretax monthly income. In the back-end ratio, a borrower's other debts such as auto loans and credit cards are figured in. Lenders usually consider both and set an acceptable ratio. Some lenders and some lending qualifying agencies only consider the back-end ratio

Deed: The legal document conveying title to the property

Depreciation: A decline in the value of a property as opposed to appreciation

Discount Points: A type of point (1 percent of the loan) paid by the borrower to reduce the interest rate

Down payment: The amount of a property's purchase price that the buyer pays in cash and does not finance with a mortgage

Earnest money: A deposit made by potential homebuyers during negotiations with the seller. The sum shows a seller that the buyer is serious about purchasing a property

Easement: The right of another to use a property The most common easements are for utility lines

80-10-10 Loan: A combination of an 80 percent loan-to-value first mortgage, a 10 percent down payment and a 10 percent home equity loan. This is also sometimes referred to as a CLTV (Combined Loan-to-Value)

Encumbrance: A lien, charge, or liability against a property

Equal Credit: A federal law that requires lenders and other creditors to make credit equally available with out discrimination based on race, color, religion, national origin, age, sex, marital status, or receipt of income from public assistance programs

Equity: The value of a homeowner's unencumbered interest in real estate Equity is the difference between the homes fair market value

and the unpaid balance of the mortgage and any outstanding liens
Equity increases as the mortgage is paid down or as the property
enjoys appreciation

Escrow Payment: The portion of a homeowner's monthly mortgage
payment that is held by the loan servicer to pay for taxes and insurance
Also known as reserves The loan servicer holds the escrow funds
separately from money meant to pay principal and interest

Fair Credit Reporting Act: A consumer protection law that regulates
the disclosure of consumer credit reports by credit reporting agencies
and establishes procedures for correcting mistakes on a person's credit
record

Fannie Mae: Nickname for Federal National Mortgage Association
It is a government-chartered non-bank financial services company and
the nation's largest source of financing for home mortgages It was
started to make sure mortgage money is available in all areas of the
country

FHA Mortgage: A mortgage insured by the Federal Housing
Administration

First mortgage: A mortgage that is the primary lien against a
property

Fixed-rate Mortgage: A mortgage in which the interest rate does not
change during the entire term of the loan, most often 15, or 30 years

Flood Insurance Insurance that compensates for the physical
property damage resulting from rising water It is required for
properties located in federally designated flood areas

Foreclosure: The legal process by which a homeowner in default on a
mortgage is deprived of interest in the property This usually involves a
forced sale of the property at public auction with the proceeds of the
sale being applied to the mortgage debt

Freddie Mac: Nickname for Federal Home Loan Mortgage Corp A
financial corporation chartered by the federal government to buy pools
of mortgages from lenders and sell securities backed by these
mortgages

Ginnie Mae: Nickname for the Government National Mortgage
Association

Good Faith Estimate: A written estimate of closing costs that the
lender must provide to prospective homebuyers within three days of
submitting a mortgage loan application

Government National Mortgage Association (Ginnie Mae) A
government-owned corporation within the US Department of
Housing and Urban Development (HUD) Created by Congress in
1968, GNMA has responsibility for the special assistance loan
program known as Ginnie Mae

Hazard Insurance: Insurance coverage that compensates for
physical damage to property from natural disasters such as fire and
other hazards Depending on where a piece of property is located,
lenders may also require flood insurance or policies covering
windstorms (hurricanes) or earthquakes

Home Inspection: An inspection by a building professional that
evaluates the structural and mechanical condition of a property

Homeowners Association: A nonprofit association that manages the
common areas of a condominium or PUD Unit owners pay the
association a fee to maintain areas owned jointly

Homeowner's Insurance: An insurance policy that combines personal
liability insurance and hazard insurance coverage for a residence and its
contents

Housing Expense: The percentage of gross monthly income that
goes toward paying a Ratio mortgage or rent on a home

HUD-1: The document with an itemized listing of closing costs
payable at the closing or settlement meeting when buying property
The closing costs can include a commission, loan fees, and points, and
sums set aside for escrow payments, taxes, and insurance It is signed
by both the buyer and the seller, who may be paying some of the
closing costs The statement form is published by HUD

Hybrid Mortgage: See alternative mortgage products.

Index: A published measure of the cost of money that lenders use to
calculate the rate on an ARM The most common indexes are the one-
year Treasury Constant Maturity Yield and the FHLB 11th District
Cost of Funds

Indexed Rate: The sum of the published index plus the margin For
example, if the index were 9 percent and the margin 2.75 percent, the
indexed rate would be 11.75 percent. Often, lenders charge less than
the indexed rate the first year of an ARM

Initial Interest Rate: Starting rate of an ARM

Interest Tax Deduction: Most mortgage holders can deduct all the
interest paid on the loan in filing income tax The deduction applies to
people with just on mortgage on a primary residence, as well as those
with a combination of loans. Within certain time limits set by the IRS,
points paid up front on a mortgage are usually deductible in the year
the house was purchased

Jumbo Mortgage: Mortgages larger than the limits set by Fannie Mae
and Freddie Mac. A jumbo mortgage will carry a higher interest rate
than a conventional mortgage

Lease-purchase A financing option that allows a potential
homebuyer to lease a property with the option to buy   Often
constructed so the monthly rent payment covers the owner's first
mortgage payment, plus an additional amount as a savings deposit to
accumulate cash for a down payment   A seller may agree to a lease-
purchase option if the housing market is saturated and the seller is
having a difficult time selling the property

Lien: A legal hold or claim from one person on the property of
another The lien placed by a first mortgage is special. It is called a
first lien and takes precedence over others

Lifetime Rate Cap: In an ARM, it limits the amount that the interest
rate can increase or decrease over the life of the loan. See also caps

Lis Pendens: A pending lawsuit; in real estate, the constructive notice
filed in public records that a legal dispute exists over a piece of
property

Livery of Seizen: Under common law, the process of transferring
title

Loan Origination: The process by which a mortgage lender obtains a
mortgage secured by real property An origination fee is charged by the
lender to process all forms involved in obtaining a mortgage

Loan-to-value (LTV) Ratio: The ratio of a mortgage loan amount to
the property's appraised value or selling price, whichever is less For

example, if a home is sold for $100,000 and the mortgage amount is $80,000 the LTV is 80%

Lock: Lender's guarantee that the mortgage rate quoted will be good for a specific amount of time. The homebuyer usually wants the lock to stay in effect until the date of the closing

Lock-and-Float: Rate programs offered by companies that allow borrowers to lock in the current interest rate on a mortgage for a specified period, while also letting them "float" the rate down if market conditions improve before closing

Low-down Mortgages: Mortgages with a low down payment, usually less than 10 percent. Frannie Mae and Freddie Mac design loan programs that spell out a set of standards for lenders. In recent years, these government-chartered agencies have made low-down mortgages more available

Margin: The number of percentage points added to the index on a one-year ARM

Maturity : The date on which the principal balance of a loan becomes due and payable

Mortgage: A legal document that uses property as collateral to secure payment of a debt

Mortgage Banker: The lender that originates a mortgage loan, the one making the loan directly, and closing the loan

Mortgage Broker: An individual or company that brings borrowers and lenders together for the purpose of loan origination Unlike a mortgage banker, brokers do not fund the loan but work on behalf of several lenders. Brokers typically require a fee or a commission for their service See broker premium

Mortgage Insurance: A policy that insures the lender against loss should the homeowner default on a mortgage. Depending on the loan, the insurance can be issued by government agencies such as the FHA or a private company. It is part of the monthly mortgage payment. (See also private mortgage insurance PMI)

Negative Amortization: A gradual increase in mortgage debt that happens when a monthly payment does not cover the entire principal and interest due The shortfall is added to the remaining balance to create "negative" amortization

No-doc or low-doc Loan: These no-documentation or low-documentation loans are designed for the entrepreneur or self-employed, for recent immigrants with money in foreign countries or for borrowers who cannot or choose not to reveal information about their incomes

Note: The document giving evidence of mortgage indebtedness, including the amount and terms of repayment

Origination Fee: A fee paid to the lender for processing a loan application

Owner financing A transaction in which the seller of a house provides all or part of the financing Sellers may provide financing because they need to sell the property right away or they are having difficulty selling the house and want to provide financing as an incentive to a buyer

Periodic rate cap: In an ARM, it limits how much an interest rate can increase or decrease during any one-adjustment period See also caps

PITI: Stands for principal, interest, taxes and insurance that are the usual components of a monthly mortgage payment

PITI Reserves: A cash amount that a homebuyer must have on hand after making a down payment and paying all closing costs. The reserves required by a lender must equal the amount a buyer would pay for PITI for a specific number of months

Plat: A map that shows a parcel of land and how it is subdivided into individual lots Plat maps also show the locations of streets and easements

PMI: See private mortgage insurance

Points: A point equals 1 percent of a mortgage loan. Lenders charge points as a way to make a profit. Borrowers may pay discount points to reduce the loan interest rate. Buyers are prohibited from paying points on HUD or VA guaranteed loans

Pre-approval: This process goes a step further than pre-qualification. It means the lender has contacted the borrower's employer, bank, and other places to verify all claims of earnings and assets. In return, the borrower receives a letter stating the lender is willing to grant a mortgage for a specific amount within a limited period with the stipulation that there are no material changes to the borrower's situation

Prepayment Penalty: A fee imposed by certain lenders if the first mortgage is paid off early

Prepayment Plan: Similar to biweekly mortgage, but operated by a third party In it, the borrower pays to the third party, half the monthly mortgage payment every two weeks At the end of the year, the plan operators typically take the extra money that results from the process and sends lump sum payment to the participants' lenders

Pre-qualification: An early evaluation by a lender of a potential homebuyer's credit report, plus earnings, savings, and debt information The homebuyer gets a non-binding estimate of the mortgage amount the borrower would qualify for, or how much house the borrower can afford. Buyers who pre-qualify can go a step further and seek a pre-approval

Rate Lock: A commitment issued by a lender to the homebuyer or the mortgage broker guaranteeing a specific interest rate for a specified amount of time See also lock

Real Estate Agent: A person licensed to negotiate and transact the sale of real estate on behalf of the property owner

RESPA: Real Estate Settlement Procedures Act A consumer protection law that requires lenders to give homebuyers advance notice of closing costs, which are payable at the closing or settlement meeting

Realtor: A real estate broker or an associate who holds an active membership in a local real estate board that is affiliated with the National Association of Realtors

Refinancing: Securing a new loan in order to pay off the existing mortgage or to gain access to the existing equity in the home

Roll-in Loan: A refinance loan that rolls any closing costs or fees into the loan. These programs best serve people who have a reasonable amount of equity, want to reduce their overall interest expense, and plan to stay in their homes

Rural Housing Service (RHS): The agency in the US Department of Agriculture providing financing to farmers and other qualified borrowers buying property in rural areas who are unable to obtain loans elsewhere. It offers low-interest-rate loans with no down payment to borrowers with low-to-moderate incomes who live in rural areas or small towns

Sales Agreement: A written contract signed by the buyer and the seller of a house stating the terms and conditions under which the property will be sold

Second Mortgage: A mortgage on the property that has a lien position behind the first mortgage

Servicer: An organization that collects monthly mortgage principal and interest payments from homeowners and manages escrow accounts for paying taxes and homeowners' insurance premiums The servicer often services mortgages that have been purchased by an investor in the secondary mortgage market

Settlement: See closing

Sub-prime Mortgage: A mortgage granted to a borrower considered sub-prime, that is, a person with a less-than perfect credit report. Sub-prime borrowers either have missed payments on a debt or have been late with payments. Lenders charge a higher interest rate to compensate for potential losses from customers who may run into trouble and default

Time is of the Essence: A phrase inserted in contracts to require a punctual performance

Title: A legal document proving a person's right to claim entitlement to a property, including the history of the property's ownership

Title Binder: Written evidence of temporary title insurance coverage

Title Company: A company that specializes in examining and insuring titles to real estate

Title insurance: Insurance that protects against loss from disputes over ownership of a property. A policy may protect the mortgage lender and/or the homebuyer

Title search: A check of title records to ensure that the seller is the legal owner of a property and that there are no liens or other claims against the property

Transfer Tax: State or local tax levied when title passes from one owner to another

Treasury Index: An index used to determine interest rate changes for certain ARM mortgages. It is based on the results of auctions that the US Treasury holds for its Treasury bills and securities or is derived from the US Treasury's daily yield curve, which is based on the closing market bid yields on actively traded Treasury securities in the over-the-counter market

Truth-in-Lending Act (TILA): A federal law that requires lenders to disclose, in writing, the terms and conditions of a mortgage, including the annual percentage rate APR and other charges

Underwriter: A company or person undertaking the responsibility for issuing a mortgage Underwriters analyze a borrower's credit worthiness and set the loan amount

VA Mortgage: A loan backed by the Veterans Administration. It requires very low or no down payments and has less stringent requirements for qualification. Members of the US armed forces are eligible for the loans under certain qualifying conditions

Wraparound Mortgage: A new mortgage that includes the remaining balance on the old mortgage plus a new amount

Appendix B
Expanded Course Guide

Introduction

Chapter 1

Chapter 2

Chapter 3

Chapter 4

Chapter 5

Chapter 6

Chapter 7

Chapter 8

Chapter 9

Chapter 10

Chapter 11

Chapter 12

Chapter 13

Chapter 14

Chapter 1 - Lending Process

1.   What are the two classifications within the mortgage market?

_____

_____

_____

_____

_____

2.   What is an investing pool?

_____

_____

_____

3.   What are the three most common employment opportunities for a loan officer?

_____

_____

_____

4.   What is the purpose of a mortgage brokerage?

_____

_____

_____

_____

5.   What are the most common entities within the secondary mortgage market/

_____

_____

_____

_____

6.   Which is not a common entity within the primary mortgage market?

    a.   Mortgage Brokerage Office
    b.   Mutual Savings Bank
    c.   Credit Union
    d.   Insurance Company

Chapter 2 - Ethics and Disclosure

1.   What is the purpose of the laws that govern the ethics and disclosures with which you handle loan processes?

_____

_____

_____

_____

2.   What is HMDA?

_____

_____

_____

_____

3.   What is the purpose of fair housing laws?

_____

_____

_____

_____

4.   What other act assists in the prevention of discrimination against applicants?

_____

_____

_____

_____

5.   What items are illegal for use in evaluating applicant's qualifications?

_____

_____

_____

_____

6.   What are the three common notices you might provide an applicant with regard to their credit application?

_____

_____

_____

_____

_____

7.   What is RESPA?

_____

_____

_____

_____

_____

8.   What is the disclosure notice requirement if a loan is transferred to a new servicer?

_____

_____

_____

_____

_____

9.   What is a settlement statement?

_____

_____

_____

_____

10.   What is TILA?

_____

_____

_____

_____

_____

11.   When must a right to cancel be provided?

_____

_____

_____

_____

12.   Explain the reason for HOEPA.

_____

_____

_____

_____

13.   When will PMI be automatically cancelled in a normal risk mortgage?

_____

_____

_____

_____

14.   When will PMI be automatically cancelled in a high-risk mortgage?

_____

_____

_____

_____

15.   What is HUD and what is their function?

_____

_____

_____

_____

16.   What is PMI?

_____

_____

_____

_____

_____

17.   What is the annual mortgage-insurance premium?

_____

_____

_____

_____

18   Why have ethics and disclosure laws been created?

        a.   To provide the lender with a series of practical directions
        b.   To protect the interest of the public
        c.   To make the obtainment of mortgage funds a fair practice
        d.   All of the above

19.   The Loan Officer must:

        a.   educate the consumer
        b.   act in an ethical manner
        c.   incorporate the required practices into their daily workload
        d.   all of the above

20.   Many states have created educational and licensure requirements for lending professionals.

        a.   True
        b.   False

21.   HMDA requires the reporting of

        a.   pipeline reports
        b.   loan origination referral data
        c.   public loan data
        d.   none of the above

22.   Information for the HMDA reports should be gathered:

        a.   at the closing table
        b.   at the time of pre-qualification
        c.   at the initial application
        d.   during post-close processes

23.   Fair housing laws are designed to prevent

        a.   discrimination in a credit related transaction
        b.   discrimination in the setting of application appointments
        c.   too many underprivileged loan disbursements
        d.   none of the above

24.   ECOA is

        a.   equal credit origination act
        b.   every credit opportunity agenda
        c.   equal credit opportunity act
        d.   none of the above

25.   ECOA addresses:

        a.   discriminatory actions
        b.   predatory lending tactics
        c.   required action disclosures
        d.   all of the above

26.   RESPA

        a.   Helps consumers shop for settlement services
        b.   Eliminates referral fees
        c.   Requires specific borrower disclosures
        d.   All of the above

27.   A point is .10 percent of the loan amount

        a.   True
        b.   False

28.   The borrower has the right to cancel any credit transaction involving their home within 3 days of the funding of the transaction.

        a.   True
        b.   False

29.   All borrowers must purchase flood insurance

    a.   True
    b.   False

30.   HUD is a direct lender

    a.   True
    b.   False

31.   The automatic insurance premium cancellation requires that the principal balance of the loan fall below:

    a.   78%
    b.   85%
    c.   80%
    d.   75%

Chapter 3 Borrower Pre-Qualification

1.   What is the primary reason that many loan Officers fail to obtain the information that will be needed for a pre-qualification?

_____

_____

_____

_____

_____

2.   What is the essential element to gaining the information you need from a borrower?

_____

_____

_____

_____

3.   Why is the initial contact with any potential borrower important?

_____

_____

_____

_____

4.   Why should you request referral information of each pre-qualification?

_____

_____

_____

_____

5.   Why do you ask if the applicant has chosen a home to purchase during the pre-qualification interview?

_____

_____

_____

_____

6.   What is your most important product?

_____

_____

_____

_____

7.   Most loan inquiries are taken

      a.   by the underwriter
      b.   by the loan Officer
      c.   over the telephone
      d.   both b & c

8.   Your most valuable tool in planning a loan strategy is

      a.   customer service skills
      b.   information
      c.   qualification skills
      d.   loan knowledge

9.   The pre-approval questionnaire contains

      a.   all of the information you will need from the borrower
      b.   most of the information you will need for the loan application
      c.   all of the information the underwriting team will require
      d.   most of the information necessary to close the loan

10.   The initial contact

      a.   sets the tone for your relationship with the borrower
      b.   is the most essential information-gathering period
      c.   sets the loan program you will use for the borrower
      d.   none of the above

11.   You will request a credit authorization verbally before pulling borrower credit.

      a.   True
      b.   False

12.   You may enter common nicknames for the borrower

      a.   True
      b.   False

13.   You must always have a co-borrower for the loan

        a.   True
        b.   False

14.   You should complete the pre-qualification questionnaire as soon as the borrower locates the home they wish to purchase

        a.   True
        b.   False

15.   The most important lending product is

        a.   low rate loans and fixed products
        b.   professionalism and responsiveness
        c.   varied products with low down payment
        d.   none of the above

16.   The pre-qualification questionnaire will provide you with

        a.   answers to every question on the questionnaire
        b.   information that will be noted in the explanation of credit section
        c.   all of the required documentation
        d.   none of the above

Chapter 4 Reading the Credit Report

1. What does a credit report show about a borrower?

    _____

    _____

    _____

    _____

    _____

2. What is your primary concern when reviewing a borrower's credit report?

    _____

    _____

    _____

    _____

    _____

3. What is the score range you can expect to see on a credit report?

    _____

    _____

    _____

    _____

    _____

4. What are the three credit bureaus you will encounter?

    _____

    _____

    _____

    _____

    _____

5. What is a FICO?

    _____

    _____

    _____

    _____

    _____

5. How is the FICO generated?

    _____

    _____

    _____

    _____

    _____

6. Fair, Isaac credit bureau scores do NOT use what as predictive characteristics:

    _____

    _____

    _____

    _____

    _____

8. What do credit bureau scores provide to a lender?

    _____

    _____

    _____

    _____

    _____

9. How can you gain information to assist you in understanding why a credit report scored   the way it did?

    _____

    _____

    _____

    _____

10. Credit Reports are:

    A. A great way to see how many things people buy
    B. A way to get to know a borrower's likes and dislikes
    C. An overview of a person's entire history of spending and payment
    D. None of the above

11 Credit reports are an overview of a person's entire history of spending and payment habits.

    A. True
    B. False

12.   A bankruptcy can remain on a credit report for

A.   3 years
B.   7 years
C.   10 years
D.   Life

13.   Accounts to medical services that a borrower has failed to pay as agreed are

A.   Often treated differently
B.   Never a concern
C.   An underwriting condition
D.   Always to be paid in full

14.   Repeatedly requesting a borrower's credit report may

A.   Adversely effect the credit score
B.   Show the borrower's can obtain further credit
C.   Cause an underwriting condition
D.   All of the above

15.   A late payment is any payment paid past the due date even when within the grace period

A.   True
B.   False

16.   Credit bureau scores are based upon

A.   Every action taken by a borrower with regard to debt
B.   The data contained within the credit bureau
C.   All information contained within the loan application
D.   None of the above

17   A credit bureau score will rank order potential borrowers based upon the number of good loans to bad loans.

A.   True
B.   False

Chapter 5 - Compensating Factors and DTI

1. What is a compensating factor?

2. Why do you use compensating factors?

3. Name three potential compensating factors:

4. What does a debt ratio tell you about a file?

5. What is a front-end ratio?

6. Which ratio is defined as the gross income divided by the new PITI mortgage payment and the minimum monthly payment from all other liabilities?

_____

_____

_____

_____

7. Name three items not commonly factored into the debt ratio:

_____

_____

_____

_____

8. What are three methods that you might employ to assist in adjusting debt ratios?

_____

_____

_____

_____

9. How many times do you factor each debt when calculating debt ratios?

_____

_____

_____

_____

10. Whose income and credit history do you use when calculating debt-to-income ratio for married applicants?

_____

_____

_____

_____

11. Explain the premise of debt-to-income ratios.

_____

_____

_____

_____

_____

12. Gross income is:

_____

_____

_____

_____

_____

13. Explain the formula for factoring a potential mortgage payment.

_____

_____

_____

_____

_____

14. What is a compensating factor and why is it important?

_____

_____

_____

_____

15. When a borrower falls just below or on the edge of a credit tier, you may

A. Bump them up to the next level
B. Request an exception
C. Submit every document possible
D. None of the above

16.   The debt ratio will determine

        A. What loan programs the borrower may obtain
        B. If the borrower has sufficient monthly income
        C. How much additional debt a borrower can afford
        D. All of the above

17.   Which monthly liability will not be used to calculate the debt ratio?

        A. Car Payment
        B. Child Support
        C. Utilities
        D. None of the above

18.   The Debt-to-Income Ratio can be adjusted if

        A. There are items that can be paid off
        B. The interest rate can be lowered
        C. There are items that will be paid in full within 4 months
        D. All of the above

19.   A compensating factor would be

        A. Larger than minimum down payment
        B. Credit scores within a few points of the next highest level
        C. Excellent savings history
        D. All of the above

20.   A compensating factor is used to

        A. Exceed normal guidelines
        B. Subvert normal guidelines
        C. Coerce the underwriter
        D. None of the above

21.   You will calculate the debt ratio using

        A. Gross Income
        B. Net Income
        C. Additional Income
        D. None of the above

22.   The ability to borrow more money is affected by

        A.   How much debt potential a borrower currently carries
        B.   How many things a borrower has in his house
        C.   How a borrower treats you and your company
        D.   All of the above

23.   Debt to Income is

        A.   The amount of debt a borrower carries
        B.   The amount of income a borrower brings home
        C.   The amount of income a borrower makes before taxes
        D.   None of the above

Chapter 6 - The Loan Application

1.   Why is it important to include the amortization method planned for a loan package on the initial application?

_____

_____

_____

_____

2.   What is the appropriate entry on the application if a borrower is applying for a pre-approval with no property in mind?

_____

_____

_____

_____

3.   Why is it important to enter information regarding the use the borrower plans to make of the property?

_____

_____

_____

_____

4.   What factors may alter the source of funds information entered as the loan process moves toward completion?

_____

_____

_____

_____

5.   What action should you take if you need additional space to reference residence history, employment history, debt information or other borrower specific information that needs to be included in the application?

_____

_____

_____

_____

6.   Why would you include borrower income that cannot be used for qualifying purposes on the application?

_____

_____

_____

_____

7.   What monthly payment amount will you enter for a revolving liability that currently has not balance?

_____

_____

_____

_____

8.   What is the premise behind requesting the highest loan amount that a borrower will be eligible to receive when submitting for a pre-approval that has no actual subject property?

_____

_____

_____

_____

9.   Why should you include any information you have regarding possible subordinate financing early in the approval process?

_____

_____

_____

_____

10.   If you do not use the space provided on the continuation sheet page what action   should you take?

_____

_____

_____

_____

11.   The method of amortization should be included on the loan application because

A. It dictates the monthly payment
B. It will affect the debt ratios
C. It affects the required disclosures
D. All of the above

12.   You must always have the subject property address prior to completing the loan application.

A. True
B. False

13.   Federal Housing Acts have differing guidelines for

A. Single Family Houses
B. Multiple unit property
C. Second Homes
D. All of the above

14.   Occupancy Status will effect

A. Approval Levels
B. Underwriting Schedule
C. Appraised Value
D. All of the above

15.   It is a portion of your job function to assist borrowers in determining the source of funds to be used in a transaction.

A. True
B. False

16.   Non-qualifying income should be disclosed

A. Always
B. Only in compensating factor requests
C. Only at the request of the borrower
D. Never

17.   Pre-paid items are dictated by

A. the sales agreement
B. underwriting guidelines
C. available funds
D. none of the above

18.   Seller concession toward closing costs must appear

        A. on the sales agreement
        B. within the loan application
        C. on the settlement statement
        D. all of the above

Chapter 8 Appraisals

1.	Why is an appraisal vital to the loan process?

2.	What is a red flag?

3.	What is URAR?

4.	What is your goal when reviewing an appraisal?

5.	What action should you take if you discover an error in a loan document?

6.   Why is it important to locate red flags early in the process?

_____

_____

_____

_____

7.   What alterations should you make to a completed appraisal if you discover an issue during your review?

_____

_____

_____

_____

8.   What does the sales comparison valuation approach consider?

_____

_____

_____

_____

9.   The property in a loan process is as important a factor as borrower history

    A. True
    B. False

10.   The appraisal will be used for

    A. Equity assessment
    B. Title insurance
    C. LTV Assessment
    D. All of the above

11.   URAR is an abbreviation for

    A. The Uniform Residential Appraisal Report
    B. The 1004
    C. The most common appraisal you will encounter
    D. All of the above

12.   The appraiser will note Red Flags during the appraisal process

A. True
B. False

13.   The appraiser will assess

A. The property
B. The neighborhood
C. Recently sold property
D. All of the above

14.   You should never read the appraisal before underwriting

A. True
B. False

15.   If you note a discrepancy, error or issue on the appraisal report you should

A. Notify underwriting
B. Influence the appraiser to alter the item
C. Notify the appraiser of the issue
D. Request a field review appraisal

16.   Property Valuation will be determined by

A. Comparison with other property
B. Sales price of other property
C. Proximity to recently sold property
D. All of the above

Chapter 9 - Guideline Matrix

1.   Why is it important to become familiar with the guidelines of the various loan products available through your branch?

_____

_____

_____

_____

_____

2.   What is a product matrix?

_____

_____

_____

_____

3.   What is the first step in grading a package for loan placement?

_____

_____

_____

_____

4.   What factor may alter the pricing you initially plan for a loan placement?

_____

_____

_____

_____

5.   What are some steps you might take if the new loan causes the borrower to exceed the ratio limitations set by the loan guidelines?

_____

_____

_____

_____

6.   You must place each loan carefully because there are a limited number of loan products to choose from

     A. True
     B. False

7.   A product matrix is

     A. The final underwriting guideline manual
     B. A snapshot of minimum requirements
     C. A snapshot of final requirements
     D None of the above

8.   A product matrix will allow you to assess a loans suitability for your borrower.

     A. True
     B. False

9.   You will begin grading using

     A. The loan application
     B. The pre-qualification questionnaire
     C. The credit-scoring key
     D The borrower history

10.   You will need to compare

     A. At least one decisioning factor
     B. All decisioning factors
     C. Specific decisioning factors
     D. None of the above

11.   You should begin grading

     A. At the lowest approval tier
     B. At the highest approval tier
     C. At the highest paying approval level
     D At the bottom of the matrix

12.   You may exceed an approval level by

     A. Changing the credit report
     B. Speaking to underwriting
     C. Supplying adequate compensating factors
     D. Never

13.   If the housing expense exceeds the loan criteria, you must

        A. Move on to the next loan matrix
        B. Suggest alternative options to the borrower
        C. Request underwriting change the matrix
        D None of the above

Chapter 10 - Pricing the Loan

1. What is a pricing restriction?

_____

_____

_____

_____

_____

2. What is the second step in loan pricing?

_____

_____

_____

_____

3. What three items must you determine prior to beginning the actual pricing?

_____

_____

_____

_____

4. Who is the best candidate for a fixed rate program?

_____

_____

_____

_____

5. What is a prepayment penalty?

_____

_____

_____

_____

6.   What common pre-pay terms do most lenders offer?

_____

_____

_____

_____

7.   What benefit does the pre-payment penalty offer to a lender?

_____

_____

_____

_____

8.   What is the primary benefit to the use of a pre-pay penalty for the borrower?

_____

_____

_____

_____

9.   What does it mean to price at PAR?

_____

_____

_____

_____

10.   When do you use the Margin?

_____

_____

_____

_____

11.   When pricing a loan you should use

A. The rate sheet that generates the most income for your branch
B. The most current rate sheet
C. The rate sheet provided by your branch manager
D. None of the above

12.   Pricing restrictions may occur as a result of

A. Internal requirements
B. Applicable laws
C. Pre-payment penalty
D. All of the above

13.   All rate sheets will include qualifying information for you to review

A. True
B. False

14.   You will determine the interest rate offered using

A. The loan term
B. The LTV
C. The branch income
D. All of the above

15.   The pre-payment requirements may

A. Impact the final rate
B. Generate additional branch income
C. Violate regulations

Chapter 12 – Documentation

1. Why is it important to document each loan package you submit?

_____

_____

_____

_____

2. Why should you note any missing information on the loan cover letter that you submit with the package?

_____

_____

_____

_____

3. Why should you include compensating factor information at the time of the initial submittal even when an exception request is not expected?

_____

_____

_____

_____

4. Why should you include information regarding the approval and transaction specifics you are requesting as part of your loan cover sheet?

_____

_____

_____

_____

5. What is the purpose of a stipulation list?

_____

_____

_____

_____

6.   What are the three common written decisions you will see from underwriting?

_____

_____

_____

_____

_____

7.   What is an affinity provider?

_____

_____

_____

_____

8.   Who is ultimately responsible for the smooth process and timely closing of the loan?

_____

_____

_____

_____

9.   How can you avoid loan process delays?

_____

_____

_____

_____

10.   How can you foster positive relationships with affinity service providers?

_____

_____

_____

_____

11.   Why must you request income documentation from each borrower?

_____

_____

_____

_____

12.   What does the mortgage or rental history tell the loan underwriter?

_____

_____

_____

_____

13.   What is a VOM?

_____

_____

_____

_____

14.   What is a CLTV?

_____

_____

_____

_____

15.   Explain the general rule regarding credit risk and borrower investment.

_____

_____

_____

_____

16.   Why should you request all borrower documentation at the beginning of the loan process?

_____

_____

_____

_____

17.   Overtime and bonus income may be used to qualify a borrower providing there is:

    a.   A one-year history
    b.   A three-year history
    c.   A two-year history
    d.   A verbal history

18.   What type of rental income is an acceptable source of income?

    a.   Income from roommates
    b.   Income from boarders
    c.   Rent received by parents
    d.   Income from an investment property received under a lease

19.   What percentage of business must a borrower own to be considered self-employed?

    a.   25%
    b.   75%
    c.   90%
    d.   85%

20.   A borrower may choose to use alimony, child support, or separate maintenance if they provide what documentation?

    a.   12 month payment history from the courts
    b.   Evidence that the payments will continue for at least three years
    c.   Court documents showing who was awarded the largest portion of the overall assets
    d.   Both A & B

21.   Mortgage or rental history is often used to project the probability of a borrower repaying their new mortgage in a timely manner.

    a.   True
    b.   False

22.   If the mortgage or rental history is not included in the credit report, which of the following is an acceptable replacement?

    a.   Verification forms sent to the mortgage holder or rental management company, if these are an entity not an individual to verify the history of the account

    b.   A letter from the landlord or mortgage holder saying the rent or mortgage payment was received in a timely manner

    c.   12 months cancelled rent checks showing a timely payment to an individual landlord or mortgage holder

    d.   Both A & C

23.   Bank statement as income documentation programs are typically not penalized with a higher interest or down payment requirement because the statements are considered full documentation.

    a.   True
    b.   False

24.   An outright gift of money toward a purchase of a home is typically acceptable if it is a gift from:

    a.   A charitable organization
    b.   A small loan
    c.   A credit card
    d.   None of the above

25.   The loan officer is the liaison between

    a.   the borrower and the loan funder
    b.   the borrower and underwriting
    c.   the broker and underwriting
    d.   the lender and the broker

26.   Each time you submit a stipulation the underwriter will

    a.   review the entire loan file
    b.   request additional documentation
    c.   complain about the documentation
    d.   request a different stipulation

27.   If you must repeatedly return to the borrower for additional documentation, you will gain

    a.   borrower loyalty
    b.   a poor reputation
    c.   underwriting approval
    d.   all of the above

28.   The underwriting summary is a form of

        a.   checklist of inclusions
        b.   guideline
        c.   application overview
        d.   none of the above

29.   When requesting an appraisal you should note

        a.   the borrowers approval rating
        b.   the method of billing and payment
        c.   the title company who will close the loan
        d.   the possibility of a field review

30.   The most important product a Loan Officer has available is

        a.   low interest rates
        b.   fast underwriting approvals
        c.   customer service skills
        d.   the ability to relate well to borrowers

31.   The first act you will take on a loan package is to

        a.   pull the credit report
        b.   review the application
        c.   complete the pre-qualification
        d.   send VOE/VOR/VOM forms

32.   You should revise the good faith estimate

        a.   frequently throughout the loan process
        b.   upon altering any borrower credit specifics
        c.   upon receipt of the sales agreement
        d.   upon receipt of the initial loan approval

33.   The borrower should be informed of the final loan specifics

        a.   before the closing
        b.   the day of closing
        c.   at the closing table
        d.   none of the above

34.   The loan officer should take gifts to the closing

        a.   True
        b.   False

35. The underwriter will review all aspects of the file including:

    a.   Source of down payment
    b.   The borrower's personal recommendations
    c.   The borrower's professional references
    d.   All of the above

36. The underwriter will review the file and issue an

    a.   approval
    b.   denial
    c.   conditional approval
    d.   Any of the above

37. Prior to closing documents must be provided to the underwriter before the loan documents can be requested.

    a.   True
    b.   False

38. The processing stage is a stage where

    a.   all information is verified and submitted
    b.   missing documentation is requested
    c.   data is transferred to the underwriter
    d.   all of the above

39. A verification of deposit is a form sent

    a.   To the closing or settlement agent to verify the funds to close
    b.   To the bank to verify the average bank account balance of the borrower
    c.   to the real estate agent to verify the earnest money deposit
    d.   none of the above

40. The funding is when

    a.   the underwriter completes a final loan review
    b.   the monies borrowed are wired or sent to the closing agent
    c.   the monies borrowed are disbursed to the proper individuals
    d.   none of the above

41.   Delays in the loan process can be avoided by

      a.   implementing a loan process follow-up and reminder system
      b.   creating strong relationships with affinity service providers
      c.   efficient pipeline management
      d.   all of the above

42.   Many loan officers forget to create

      a.   a good closing team
      b.   an adequate filing system
      c.   positive service relationships
      d.   borrower commitment

43.   An affinity service provider includes any individual who must accomplish tasks in a timely and professional manner in order for you to accomplish your goal of closed loans.

      a.   True
      b.   False

44.   You should treat your affinity service providers

      a.   Respectfully
      b.   Friendly
      c.   With Consideration
      d.   All of the above

KEY TERMS AND DEFINITIONS

Use the knowledge you have obtained from the text to provide the definition of the terms.

1.   Closing costs: _____

_____

_____

_____

2.   VA Mortgage: _____

_____

_____

_____

3.   Amortization Schedule: _____

_____

_____

_____

4.   Closing: _____

_____

_____

_____

5.   Title search: _____

_____

_____

_____

_____

6.   Disbursement: _____

_____

_____

_____

_____

7.   Credit report:

_____

_____

_____

_____

_____

8.   Acceleration Clause:

_____

_____

_____

_____

_____

9.   Loan-to-value (LTV) Ratio:

_____

_____

_____

_____

_____

10.   Housing Expense:

_____

_____

_____

_____

_____

11.   Pre-approval:

_____

_____

_____

_____

_____

12.   Good Faith Estimate:

_____

_____

_____

_____

_____

13.   Freddie Mac: _____

_____

_____

_____

_____

14.   Debt-to-Income Ratio: _____

_____

_____

_____

_____

15.   Comparables: _____

_____

_____

_____

_____

16.   RESPA: _____

_____

_____

_____

_____

17.   Pre-qualification: _____

_____

_____

_____

_____

18.   PITI Reserves: _____

_____

_____

_____

_____

19.   Loan Origination: _____

_____

_____

_____

_____

20.   Hazard Insurance: _____

_____

_____

_____

_____

21.   Ginnie Mae: _____

_____

_____

_____

_____

22.   Fair Credit Reporting Act: _____

_____

_____

_____

_____

23.   Fannie Mae: _____

_____

_____

_____

_____

Chapter 1 Lending Process

1.   Primary Mortgage Market   Secondary Mortgage Market

2.   A group of smaller investors seeking a low risk, long term investment and having capital available to purchase packaged loan products

3.   Bank   Brokerage Office   E Commute

4.   To act as a liaison between the borrowers seeking mortgage funds and multiple funding sources.

5.   Insurance Companies   Pension funds   Individual investors
Primary Lenders with excess deposits

6.   d.   Insurance Company

Chapter 2 Ethics and Disclosure

1.   To protect the interest of the public and make the obtainment of housing and home mortgage funds a fair practice for all applicants.

2.   The home mortgage disclosure act

3.   To prevent discrimination against any borrower in the sale, rental, financing, or other housing related transaction

4.   The equal credit opportunity act

5.   Race, color, religion, sex, national origin, marital status, age, source of income, handicap, and familial status

6.   Approval, counter-offer, or denial

7.   Real Estate Settlement Procedures Act, which helps consumers shop for settlement services and eliminates referral fees that increase the costs of certain settlement services

8.   15 days

9.   HUD 1 is the statement that itemizes all of the closing costs payable at the closing.

10.   The truth-in-lending act that is part of the consumer credit protection act. The act is meant to protect and inform the consumer by requiring specific disclosures regarding the loan terms and costs.

11.   Any credit transaction that involves a security interest in a borrower's primary residence must provide the borrower with the right to rescind.

12.   The homeowner's equity protection act is designed to protect a borrower against unfair and abusive lending tactics.

13.   When the borrower's equity position reaches 22% if the borrower is current on mortgage payments or when the borrower reaches a 22% or greater equity position and the borrower brings their mortgage obligations current.

14.   When the loan reaches a 77% LTV, or the loan reaches the half-life whichever occurs first in time.

15.   Department of Housing and Urban Development that is not a direct lender but rather maintains an ongoing program to monitor the quality of HUD originated loans.

16.   Private Mortgage Insurance – a policy that protects the lenders who make loans to individuals without obtaining a full 20% down payment.

17.   5% of the loan amount paid at a rate of 1/12 of the overall premium monthly

18.	D	19.	D	20	A	21.	C	22.	C	23.	A
24	C	25.	D	26.	D	27.	B	28.	B	29	B
30.	B	31.	A								

Chapter 3 Prequalification

1.   Because they are afraid to ask for information

2.   You must ask for the information

3.   The initial contact sets the tone for the entire relationship with that borrower. Most people will make decisions concerning your professionalism and character within the first 30 seconds of contact.

4.   To assist in tracking referral source information, assessing marketing and advertising effectiveness and to provide follow-up information regarding the applicant to the referral source

5.   This question enables you to assess the urgency of the query and determine if the borrower thus enabling you to prioritize the flow of work within your office.

        You will also be able to determine if the borrower is working with an agent thereby strengthening referral relationships.

        If the borrower has chosen a home, you will be able to use real purchase numbers to assess DTI and borrower expectations prior to the first face-to-face meeting.

6.   The professionalism, attentiveness, and responsiveness you provide to your borrowers.

7.   D   8.   B   9.   B   10.   A   11.   B   12.   B

13.   B   14.   B   15.   B   16.   B

Chapter 4 Reading the Credit Report

1.   Credit reports are an overview of a person's history of spending and payment habits.

2.   Any action that had a negative or derogatory impact on a borrower's credit history.

3.   450 to 850

4.   Beacon at Equifax   Empirica at Transunion   TRW/Fair Isaac at TRW

5.   The Fair, Isaac Credit Bureau Score

6.   The FICO is generated using a system of scorecards created by compiling the credit data from millions of consumers and then applying complex mathematical methods and extensive research to note credit patterns that predict probable credit performance.

7.   Race, color, religion, national origin, sex, marital status, age, occupation, length of time at present housing, or any information not contained within the credit file

8.   A means of rank ordering potential borrowers based on the likelihood that they would pay their obligations as agreed

9.   By reviewing the score factor reason codes included on the report

10.   C.   11   A   12.   B.   13.   A.   14.   A.   15.   B.

16.   B.   17.   A.

Chapter 5 Compensating Factors and DTI

1.   Any items that exist in the borrower's profile that may exceed the normal circumstances commonly encountered and reflect favorably on the borrower

2.   To provide underwriting with a solid reason to approve a borrower at a higher level when that borrower falls on the edge of a credit tier or approval level

3.   Less than 10% increase from the old rent/housing payments to the new housing expense.

        A decrease from the old rent/housing payments to the new housing expense

        A borrower's excellent savings ability (as shown by savings accounts, etc)

        Income that is not qualifying income

        Larger than minimum down payment

        Residual income (excess after expense) of $500 per adult and $250 per child

        Time at current residence exceeds 5 years.

Time at current employment exceeds 5 years.

Debt-to-income ratios below maximum guidelines as set forth for that approval level.

Credit scores fall within a few points of next highest level.

A perfect mortgage or rental history, as proven through the credit bureau

4.   How much loan borrowers can afford

5.   The gross income divided by the new PITI mortgage payment

6.   The back end ratio

7.   Utility Bills   Car Insurance   Health Insurance   Cell Phone Bills

8.   Pay off certain items
        Lower the interest rate of the new loan
        Lower the loan amount offered to the borrower

9.   One time, regardless of the number of times the debt appears in the report(s).

10.   Both parties' income and credit history is considered, but you factor each debt only once even if it appears on both credit reports.

11.   Debt-to-income ratio's are the amount of open debt a borrower carries weighed against the borrower's monthly income and in general, the higher the DTI the greater the potential risk of borrower default on a loan.

12.   Income before taxes

13.   Gross monthly income x 29% (max qualifying ratio) = Max Mortgage Payment

14.   A compensating factor is any item that exists in the borrower's profile that falls outside of the standard or norm and may reflect favorably on the borrower from the perspective of the underwriter.

        A compensating factor may be used to overcome any item that exists in the borrower's profile that falls outside or exceeds standard guideline criteria.

15   B   16.   C   17.   C   18.   D   19.   D   20.   A

21.   A   22.   A.   23.   D.

Chapter 6 - The Loan Application

1.   The amortization method dictates the monthly payment, debt load, and types of disclosures required on an application.

2.   To be decided

3.   Approval levels will vary depending on the occupancy status of the property.

4.   Subordinate finance negotiated   Seller assistance toward closing costs
        Sales price   Other possible factors not yet visible

5.   You should include additional information on the last page of the application.

6.   To bring this information to the attention of the underwriter early in the process in order to set the stage for compensating factors in the event an exception is required.

7.   A standard figure is $15.00 for each revolving line the applicant has available if the balance is zero but the specific underwriting guidelines for the loan program you are planning should be consulted.

8.   You can easily lower the loan amount later but an increase in the loan amount requested will require the underwriting department to recalculate all numbers and issue a new approval.

9.   Including the terms of a subordinate finance agreement early in the process allows the underwriter to approve or decline the terms of subordinate financing before the deal has progressed.

10.   If the space available for additional information is not used you should cross through the blank area. This crossing through assures the borrower that you will not alter or add any items to their application after their signature is affixed.

| 11. | D | 12. | B | 13. | D | 14. | A | 15. | A | 16. | C |
| 17. | B | 18. | D | | | | | | | | |

Chapter 8- Appraisals

1. A borrower is responsible for repaying the loan but the property acts as collateral in the event the borrower does not fulfill their obligations.

2. Any information that appears regarding issues that will stand in the way of the completion of the loan

3. Uniform Residential Appraisal Report

4. To scrutinize any item that appears to vary between documents in the file and the entries on the appraisal to determine which document contains the error and to note any item that is below the minimum requirements of the loan guideline, which you are planning for the loan file.

5. You should have the person responsible for the errors address them in writing.

6. Because it is sometimes more effective and a faster process to request the necessary correction items or additional information immediately rather than waiting for the underwriter to generate a stipulation regarding the matter.

7. You should only request alterations arising because of an error or omission not an alteration to the opinion or decision of the appraiser.

8. The sales comparison approach assesses the characteristics of the subject property as compared to other similar properties sold within a given time period.

| 9. | A | 10. | D | 11. | A | 12. | A | 13. | D | 14. | B |
| 15. | C | 16. | D | | | | | | | | |

Chapter 9 - Guideline Matrix

1. The more familiar with loan guidelines you become the more capable you will be at moving the loan package through the loan process and to a successful closing. Familiarity allows you to locate and address any red flag issues that may be apparent before an issue inhibits the closing of the loan.

2. A snapshot of the minimum requirements needed to place a loan in a particular program and approval level.

3. Rate the credit report scoring key elements against the product matrix levels.

4. The debt ratio may change after you price the loan because of interest rate and subsequent monthly payment. If this ratio becomes excessive, you may need to re-price the loan.

5. Obtain an exception to the ratio limitations with compensating factors.

   Reduce the maximum sales price/loan amount the borrower may obtain.

   Reduce the points wrapped in the interest rate and allow the borrower to make payment for the services of your office on the front end.

   Pay off consumer debt in an attempt to reduce overall debt load.

   Obtain seller assistance toward closing costs or additional borrower funds to buy down the interest rate to a level that generates a payment that fits within the borrower debt-ratio guidelines.

   Search for a different program that allows the borrower to approve at the levels needed to close the loan under the present circumstances.

| 6. | B | 7. | B | 8. | A | 9. | C. | 10. | B. | 11. | B. |
| 12. | C | 13. | B | | | | | | | | |

Chapter 10 - Pricing the Loan

1. An internal limitation or requirement and applicable laws regarding loan pricing.

2. Review the minimum qualifying guidelines included on the rate sheet to confirm that your borrower meets the current criteria.

3. Preferred loan terms   The LTV required   Pricing including office payment

4.   Perpetual high-risk borrower   Long-term purchaser   Cautious borrower

5.   A monetary penalty which is assessed for the early payoff of a loan containing a prepay clause.

6.   0, 2, 3, and 5-year penalties

7.   Security that the borrower will retain the loan for a certain period thereby securing the expected interest payments for the lender or that if the borrower pays the loan off early the interest loss to the lender will be offset by the penalty.

8.   Lenders will often offer a reduction of the initial interest rate in exchange for the pre-payment clause because of the added longevity of loans on the books.

9.   There are no points included in the interest rate and you must obtain payment for the branch as points charged on the good faith estimate and HUD Settlement Statement.

10.   When you use an ARM option in the loan, you will note the margin that refers to the rate of adjustment that may occur

11.   B   12.   D   13.   B   14.   D   15.   D.

Chapter 12 - File Documentation

1.   Without proper documentation, the underwriter cannot make a valid decision on the loan package and will request additional items or stipulations prior to issuing an approval or conditional approval.

2.   To assure the underwriter that you are aware of the lacking information and are working to obtain all necessary documentation

3.   To set a positive tone for the loan package

        To bring the compensating factors to the attention of the underwriter before they initially review the borrower profile

        To set the stage if something occurs later in the process that requires a positive decision or exception from the underwriter

4.   This inclusion allows the underwriter to review the material and is a courtesy action that will smooth the underwriter's workload.

5.   To allow the underwriter to request information required for loan decision, closing or secondary market sale and to provide clarification information regarding any file item that is unclear to the underwriter.

6.   Approved   Everything contained within the file meets the guidelines for final approval

        Conditional   Additional documentation will be needed to ensure final loan approval

        Denied   Aspects of the file do not conform to the guidelines

7.   Any individual who must complete their tasks in a timely, professional manner in order for you to accomplish your goal of closing the loan

8.   The loan officer

9.   By maintaining an organized flow process, using an adequate loan process follow-up and affinity service provider reminder-system.

10.   By treating these providers in a respectful, friendly, and considerate manner to foster positive relationships, build rapport and create an overall good relationship.

11.   All lenders require that a borrower have sufficient and adequate income to cover the repayment of the mortgage. The stability and probability of continuance must be established.

12.   The probability that the borrower will repay their new mortgage in a timely manner

13.   Verification of Mortgage

14.   Combined Loan to Value

15.   Generally, the higher the credit risks the higher percentage of funds the borrower must invest.

16.   To ensure you are able to verify information, structure the loan package correctly, and request supporting information in an efficient manner.

17.   A two-year history

18.	D	19.	A	20.	D	21.	A	22.	D	23.	B
24.	A	25.	B	26.	A	27.	B	28.	A	29.	B
30.	C	31.	C	32.	C	33.	A	34.	B	35.	D
36.	D	37.	B	38.	D	39.	B	40.	B	41.	D
42.	C	43.	A	44.	D								

Appendix D
Creative Loan Structure

There will be many times when your strength at creatively structuring a loan package will gain you closings your competition cannot achieve. This method of creative loan structuring is what sets a well-trained and certified Loan Officer well above the basic marketing originator or the paper-pushing officer.

Creative structuring begins when you determine your borrower's exact financial situation and compare it to their exact wants and needs.

A borrower with no cash and a Credit Level D approval rating who wishes to purchase a $100,000 home will create one type of structure difficulty. A borrower who owns a $100,000 home and has a DTI of 55% before you begin the process and an excellent credit history creates another type of difficulty.

You will note that as you move you through the loan structure it is often necessary to work backwards. Taking the dollar value needs and filling in the sources of funding, concession, required property value, etc. to suit that particular package rather than following an in the box style scenario.

To rise to the top of your new profession you must maintain a flexible approach and an open mind when reviewing each loan package that crosses your desk. The key point in creatively structuring is to keep all the options of funds to close a package available in your head. Relying only on the borrowers own funds and the loan amount to close loans simply will not work. The loan amount, subordinate financing, seller concession toward closing costs, gift funds, sale of personal property, increased appraised value, even gifts of equity between family members are all source of funds options. Keep an open mind and make sure you ask your borrower questions and creative structuring will come easily.

Below is a breakdown of funds to close a purchase mortgage. Each package you look at must balance financially before it can be considered a "real deal".

#1 REFINANCE

Borrowers who own their home but need to refinance to do some repairs and to pay off existing debt loan qualify for a LTV of 80%.

Appraised Value	$75,000
X LTV %	x 80%
= Loan Amount	$60,000
Loan Amount	$60,000
- Existing Mortgage Pay off	-$37,753
= Available Cash	$22,247
Less any Debt to Pay Off	-$ 5,487 Cash Needed for Repairs
	-$ 1,742 Collection Debt
	-$ 9,487 Credit Cards/Personal Loans
Cash Available for Closing Costs	$ 5,531

Note that you are building this in order. You are taking the appraised value and structuring the loan package around that figure. You may also structure the package backwards. You may wish to do this when a borrower first interviews with you to get an estimate of the loan amount and appraised value needed for the package. To structure in a reverse order you simply take all the figures in reverse.

Closing Costs	$ 5,531
+ Cash Needed for Repairs	$ 5,487
+ Funds to pay off Collection/Debt	$ 1,742
+ Funds to pay off Consumer Debt	$ 9,487
+ Existing Mortgage Pay Off	$37,753
Total Funds Needed	$60,000
Divided by LTV Approval	.80%
Appraised Value Needed	$75,000

#2 PURCHASE

Borrowers with A- Credit want to purchase a home listed for $92,000.

The credit scenario does not qualify them for a Government Loan.

They have $4,800 of their own funds available toward the purchase.

The current debt loan is 21% and with the house, the debt load is 40.67%.

The maximum DTI allowed under their program guideline is 55%.

The loan approval is for a 90% LTV with a 95% CLTV maximum.

Seller Concession is limited to 6%.

Structure

The first item to determine is the amount of cash needed to close the loan. This figure will include the sales price of the property plus all closing costs.

Sales Price	$92,000
+ Closing Costs	$ 4,279
= Cash needed	$96,279

The second item to determine is the loan amount. That is the sales price multiplied by the LTV approval.

Sales Price	$92,000
X LTV	.90%
Loan Amount	$82,800

Now you need to determine the source of all funds to close the loan. Begin by taking the total for all cash needed for closing the loan and deducting the amounts you have available. The result is the amount of funds you are short for closing.

Cash Needed	$96,279
-Loan Amount	$82,800
-Borrowers Funds	$ 4,800
Additional Funds	$ 8,679 You must find these funds in order for the loan to close.

The first option to look at is typically – will the sellers pay a portion of the closing costs from the loan proceeds. At times, the sellers will agree to this added request if the borrowers are willing to raise the purchase price. This option is typically easier to negotiate if the Sales Agreement has not yet been finalized. If the sales agreement has been finalized, Underwriting will not usually allow a "bump" or increase in the sales price. Check the loan guidelines to determine the maximum amount of seller concession allowed under the borrower's loan program. Remember – you work for the borrower in this transaction! In this scenario, you are allowed up to 6% of the sales price to be contributed by the seller towards the borrower's non-recurring closing costs. 6% of the sales price is $5,520. The closing costs in this scenario only total $4279. Although the maximum allowed is $5,520, the sellers will not be able to contribute the maximum amount but only the amount of actual costs. If you have not disclosed closing costs, this is an excellent opportunity to add more fees for you into the overall closing figures.

The second option to look at is do the borrowers have any additional funds available. Some borrowers may have a retirement or investment account that may be cashed out from which funds may be borrowed. If borrowers, keep in mind that the re-payment figure must meet DTI guidelines. Some borrowers may have personal property available for sale. If personal property is sold, you must properly document the sale of the property including proving ownership of the property in the first place and fair market value of the property. Gift funds from a family member, agency designed for the purpose of helping people purchase homes or the borrowers employer may also be used providing a letter is signed stating that the funds will not be repaid.

The last option available is secondary financing. In this case, the borrowers are allowed up to 5% of the sales price in the form of a loan. Secondary financing may come from the seller. This financing must be negotiated on the Sales Agreement and must be secured against the property being purchased in the form of a second mortgage. Secondary financing may also be secured through another financing company. Any secondary financing must be by contract and the monthly repayment must meet the borrowers DTI Ratio guidelines.

In this scenario, we will use a combination of those items:

$ 8,679	Additional Funds Needed to Close
-$ 4,279	Seller Concession toward Non-Recurring Closing Costs
-$ 1,200	Sale of borrower property sourced with Bill of Sale
-$ 3,200	Second Mortgage held by Seller with 0% interest and monthly payment of $55.00 per month for 57 months with one payment of $65.00
$ 0	Funds unaccounted for toward cost of property.

The ability to creatively source funds to close will allow you a greater ability to close loans than your less creative counterparts. Many Originators quit after the initial inquiry upon discovering the limited resources of cash on hand available to the borrower. The act of digging deeper and using your creativity allows you to present options that your borrowers may not have considered toward sourcing funds.

Appendix E
Lending Mathematics

DEBT-TO-INCOME RATIO EXCERCISES

To calculate a borrower's debt to income take the total monthly debt load and divide it by the total monthly income. For example:

A borrower who earns $2800.00 monthly and has installment debt of $750.00 monthly has a debt-to-income ratio of 26.78%.

D   I   R
750 / 2800 = 26.78%

1.   Income $6200
      Debt $1900

      Ratio   %

2.   Income $3000
      Debt $1350

      Ratio   %

3.   Income $3750
      Debt $ 970

      Ratio   %

4.   Income $1600
      Debt $ 340

      Ratio   %

5.   Income $2000
      Debt $ 420

      Ratio   %

6.   Income $2480
      Debt $ 920

      Ratio   %

7.   Income $4200
      Debt $1850

      Ratio   %

8.   Income $4800
      Debt $2175

      Ratio   %

9.   Income $5100
      Debt $1950

      Ratio   %

10.   Income $5500
      Debt $1775

      Ratio   %

11.   Income $5750
      Debt $1900

      Ratio   %

12.   Income $3425
      Debt $1350

      Ratio   %

13.   Income $4387
      Debt $1218
      Ratio   %

14.   Income $2330
      Debt $ 961
      Ratio   %

CALCULATING LOAN-TO-VALUE

When calculating loan to value, assuming the Value and the LTV Percentage are given the formula is Value multiplied by percentage.

Assume a house with a value (sales price) of $112,000 with a LTV of 95% would have a loan amount of $106,400.

Sales Price	**x LTV Percentage**	**= Loan Amount**
$112,000	**x .95**	**= $106,400**

1. Sales Price $99,000
   LTV   85%
   _____
   Loan $

2. Sales Price $110,000
   LTV   90%
   _____
   Loan $

3. Sales Price $144,900
   LTV   95%
   _____
   Loan $

4. Sales Price $75,000
   LTV   80%
   _____
   Loan $

5. Sales Price $69,900
   LTV   70%
   _____
   Loan $

6. Sales Price $104,900
   LTV   75%
   _____
   Loan $

CALCULATING COMBINED LOAN TO VALUE

When a Combined Loan-to-Value is offered, you will calculate the secondary financing figure using the same formula above.

Sales Price   x CLTV Percentage = Subordinate/Secondary Financing Loan Amount
$112,000   x .05   = $5600 maximum second mortgage

1.   Sales Price $99,000

     LTV 85% CLTV 95%

     _____

     Loan $

2.   Sales Price $110,000

     LTV 90%   CLTV 95%

     _____

     Loan $

3.   Sales Price $144,900
     LTV 90% CLTV 95%

     _____

     Loan $

4.   Sales Price $75,000
     LTV 80%   CLTV 90%

     _____

     Loan $

5.   Sales Price $69,900
     LTV 70% CLTV 80%

     _____

     Loan $

6.   Sales Price $104,900
     LTV 75% CLTV 85%

     _____

     Loan $

Any funds toward the purchase price not included in LTV or CLTV will be required as cash invested on the part of the borrower. Funds for closing costs may be acquired through other means.

SELLER CONCESSION

When calculating seller concession toward borrower's non-recurring closing costs you will want to use the SALES PRICE of the property as your base number. The seller concession figure is negotiated in the sales agreement and can be a fixed dollar amount or it may be a percentage. For these exercises, assume the seller is willing to grant 6% of the sales price toward borrower's non-recurring closing costs.

Sales Price **x Concession Percentage**   **= Dollar Concession Amount**
$112,000   **x 6%**   **= $6720**

1.   Sales Price $99,000   2.   Sales Price $110,000

3.   Sales Price $144,900   4.   Sales Price $75,000

5.   Sales Price $69,900   6.   Sales Price $104,900

7.   Sales Price $49,500   8.   Sales Price $219,900

9.   Sales Price $53,350   10.   Sales Price $189,000

SELLER CONCESSION

For additional exercise in calculating maximum seller concession, you can calculate using a maximum seller concession toward buyer's non-recurring closing costs of 3% of the sales price. (6% and 3% are the most commonly allowed maximum seller concessions under most underwriting guidelines.)

Sales Price	**x Concession Percentage**	**= Dollar Concession Amount**
$112,000	**x 3%**	**= $3360**

1.   Sales Price $99,000

2.   Sales Price $110,000

3.   Sales Price $144,900

4.   Sales Price $75,000

5.   Sales Price $69,900

6.   Sales Price $104,900

7.   Sales Price $49,500

8.   Sales Price $219,900

9.   Sales Price $53,350

10.   Sales Price $189,000

MAXIMUM HOUSING EXPENSE (PITI)

It is important to be able to calculate the maximum monthly housing expense (PITI – Principal, Interest, Taxes, and Insurance) your borrower could afford under any loan program approval. This allows you to set borrowers and Agents expectations as to the cost range of properties that the borrowers should be shopping.

Begin with the maximum DTI as per the approval level. Subtract the borrowers current DTI (excluding any housing expense from the ratio). The total is the percentage of income available to spend on PITI. This percentage should be multiplied by the borrower's total monthly income to achieve a maximum dollar amount that may be spent toward PITI.

The formula for calculating Maximum PITI payments is as follows:

Maximum DTI %	**– Current DTI %**	**= % Income Available for Housing Costs**
41%	- 22%	= 19%

Monthly Income	**X % of Income Available for PITI**	**= Maximum Mthly PITI**
$3200	X 19%	= $608 maximum PITI

For the following problems, assume a maximum DTI of 45%

1. Current DTI   29%
   Income $3750

2. Current DTI 18%
   Income $2100

3. Current DTI   22%
   Income $2880

4. Current DTI 31%
   Income $4195

5. Current DTI   24%
   Income $2655

6. Current DTI 12%
   Income $3875

7. Current DTI   19%
   Income $3150

8. Current DTI 26%
   Income $1775

9. Current DTI   14%
   Income $1980

10. Current DTI 36%
    Income $3650

LENDING MATH ANSWER KEY

DTI RATIOS
1. 31%
2. 45%
3. 26%
4. 21%
5. 21%
6. 37%
7. 44%
8. 45%
9. 38%
10. 32%
11. 33%
12. 39%

SELLER CONCESSION 3%
1. $2,970.00
2. $3,300.00
3. $4,347.00
4. $2,250.00
5. $2,097.00
6. $3,147.00
7. $1,485.00
8. $6,597.00
9. $1,600.50
10. $5,670.00

MAXIMUM MONTHLY PITI PAYMENT

LTV
1. $ 84,150
2. $ 99,000
3. $137,655
4. $ 60,000
5. $ 48,930
6. $ 78,675

CLTV
1. $ 9,900
2. $ 5,500
3. $ 7,245
4. $ 7,500
5. $ 6,990
6. $10,490

SELLER CONCESSION 6%
1. $ 5,940
2. $ 6,600
3. $ 8,694
4. $ 4,500
5. $ 4,194
6. $ 6,294
7. $ 2,970
8. $13,194
9. $ 3,201
10. $11,340

Ratio for PITI		$ Value for PITI
1.	12%	$ 450.00
2.	23%	$ 483.00
3.	19%	$ 547.20
4.	10%	$ 419.50
5.	17%	$ 451.35
6.	29%	$1123.75
7.	22%	$ 693.00
8.	15%	$ 266.25
9.	27%	$ 534.60
10.	5%	$ 182.50

www.ingramcontent.com/pod-product-compliance
Lightning Source LLC
Chambersburg PA
CBHW080244030426
42334CB00023BA/2690